ENEMIES AND PASSING FRIENDS

ENEMIES AND PASSING FRIENDS

Settler Ideologies in Twentieth Century Ulster

Pamela Clayton

Pluto Press

LONDON • EAST HAVEN, CT

First published 1996 by Pluto Press
345 Archway Road, London N6 5AA
and 140 Commerce Street, East Haven, CT 06512, USA

British Library Cataloguing in Publication Data
A catalogue record for this book is available from the British Library

ISBN 0 7453 1011 7 hbk

Library of Congress Cataloging in Publication Data
A catalog record for this book is available from the Library of Congress

Designed, typeset and produced for Pluto Press by
Chase Production Services, Chipping Norton, OX7 5QR
Printed in the EC by T J Press, Padstow, England

I dedicate this to
my children, Sarah-Jane and Alexander Clow,
for their forbearance,
to David Clow for his support,
and to my uncle, Geoffrey Palmer,
for being my role model since my childhood.

Contents

Abbreviations

APNI   Alliance Party of Northern Ireland. Formed out of the New Ulster Movement of the early 1970s, it contains equal numbers of Protestants and Catholics.

BBC   British Broadcasting Corporation.

BO   *Ballymena Observer*. A unionist weekly newspaper, founded in 1855 and owned by Belfast Telegraph Newspapers Ltd, serving Mid-Antrim. It was merged in 1985 with the *Ballymena Times* (see BTimes) but was taken over by the Morton Group in 1986. It has reverted to being a separate newspaper once more.

BT   *Belfast Telegraph*. A daily newspaper serving the North of Ireland. See Kennedy (1988) for its history.

BTimes   *Ballymena Times*. See BO.

CDS   *County Down Spectator*. A conservative weekly newspaper founded in 1904 by D E Alexander and still owned by the Alexander family. It serves Bangor, Holywood and North Down.

CT   *Craigavon Times*. The *Portadown Times*'s name was changed to this from March 1975 to October 1977, when it was merged with the *Portadown News* to form the *Portadown News and Craigavon Times*. See PDN and PDT.

DUP   Democratic Unionist Party. Led by Ian Paisley, it is a successor to the series of parties he formed from the late 1960s. The DUP was the first of his parties to take a substantial proportion of the Unionist Party vote.

EEC   European Economic Community, disliked by ultras because of its Catholic members. Nevertheless Paisley, the DUP leader, is a Euro-MP. The EEC is now called the European Union.

INLA   Irish National Liberation Army. An offshoot, after a dispute, of the IRA, with a reputation for indiscriminate violence, claimed by the IRA to be merely a terrorist group recruiting among psychopaths and the intrinsically violent, it has lately concentrated on internal feuding but in the past claimed responsibility for major acts of terrorism such as the death of Airey Neave, the Droppin Well bombing and, under the name 'Catholic Reaction Force', the Darkley Pentecostal murders. It is proscribed. Its political wing is the Irish Republican Socialist Party, which attracts very few votes.

IR   *Impartial Reporter*. A weekly unionist newspaper, founded in 1825 by William Trimble and still owned by the Trimble family. It serves County Fermanagh, South Tyrone, Cavan and Monaghan.

Abbreviations

IRA   Irish Republican Army. Originally formed to fight the British state in Ireland, it has been re-formed at various times as an illegal terrorist group to fight the settler state in Northern Ireland as well as the British state. After internal disputes in the early 1970s the movement split into three groups, the INLA (qv), the 'official' IRA (which renounced the use of violence and turned to socialism) and the 'provisional' IRA which continued the campaign of violence. Originally right-wing, the 'provisional' IRA has since adopted socialism as well. The 'official' IRA's violent activities have been confined for most of the period to feuding with the 'provisional' IRA. As far as most Protestants are concerned there is no valid distinction between the two IRAs, and the term IRA will be used throughout this study irrespective of origin. The IRA, which regards itself as a guerrilla army rather than a terrorist group, has been responsible for the majority of deaths and injuries caused by republicans. It was the first paramilitary group to declare a ceasefire in 1994.

ITV   Independent Television.

LOL   Loyal Orange Lodge of the Orange Order, an exclusively Protestant organisation dedicated to preserving the British connection. Each Lodge, or local branch, has a number and letter-writers sometimes use this as an address.

LS   *Londonderry Sentinel*. A unionist newspaper, formerly thrice-weekly but now weekly, founded in 1829 by the Colhoun family and now part of the Morton Group. It serves the City of Derry and Counties Londonderry, Tyrone, Antrim and Donegal.

NICRA   Northern Ireland Civil Rights Association. Founded in 1967, with mainly Catholic but some Protestant members, it was the first civil rights movement to seize the attention of the world media by a series of marches and protests. One of its leaders, John Hume, became a co-founder of the SDLP (qv).

NILP   Northern Ireland Labour Party. A non-sectarian working-class party founded in 1924, it has never had the electoral success of its British counterpart though its existence persuaded the Unionist Party to take its working-class members seriously. Attempts to revive it have not been successful.

NIO   Northern Ireland Office.

NL   *News Letter*. A daily newspaper serving the North of Ireland. See Kennedy (1988) for its history.

NUM   New Ulster Movement. Precursor of the APNI (qv).

NUPRG   New Ulster Political Research Group. UDA 'think tank' 1978 to 1981.

OS   *Orange Standard*. Monthly newspaper of the Orange Order, founded in 1974.

OUP   Official Unionist Party. See UUP.

PAF   Protestant Action Force. Illegal Protestant terrorist group, and part of the UVF (qv), operating in south-east Antrim and mid-Ulster, and during UVF 'ceasefires'.

PD   People's Democracy. A movement active during the civil rights agitations of the late 1960s and early 1970s, it attracted some Protestants as well as Catholics and was particularly active in Queen's University. It no longer has a separate existence though some of its members are still active in politics and academia.

PDN   *Portadown News.* Local weekly newspaper, founded in 1859 by J Young, serving Counties Armagh and Down. It was edited by Douglas Sloan, an ultra, from the 1940s until 1973 when it was taken over by the Morton Group and a new editor, David Armstrong, put in place. The tone changes from this time. In October 1977 it merged with the *Craigavon Times* (see CT) to form the *Portadown News and Craigavon Times.* In December 1982, on the wishes of the staff, who disliked being connected with the views expressed by the old *Portadown News,* its name was changed to the *Portadown Times and Portadown Express.*

PDT   *Portadown Times.* Local weekly newspaper, founded in 1922 by William Henry Wolsey, serving Counties Armagh and Down. It was taken over by the Morton Group in 1956. After the *Portadown News* (see PDN) was added to the Morton stable, the *Portadown Times* continued until October 1977 when its name was changed to the *Craigavon Times* (see CT). It re-emerged in December 1982 as the *Portadown Times and Portadown Express.* For an explanation of the complicated history of the Portadown papers I am indebted to David Armstrong.

PR   Proportional representation system of voting, abandoned by the Unionist government soon after partition and restored for local elections by the British government in the 1973 crisis.

PT   *Protestant Telegraph.* Newspaper founded, edited and largely written by Ian Paisley from the late 1960s to the mid-1970s.

PTA   Prevention of Terrorism Act.

RIC   Royal Irish Constabulary, the all-Ireland police force up to 1921.

RTE   Radio Telefis Eireann.

RUC   Royal Ulster Constabulary. Formed on the foundation of Northern Ireland from the mainly Catholic Royal Irish Constabulary (RIC), the armed RUC, despite places reserved for Catholics, became a largely Protestant police force. There was also an Ulster Special Constabulary with three branches, of which the armed part-time 'B' Special force was the most active and long-lived. It was an all-Protestant force. This latter was abolished on the recommendation of the 1969 Hunt Report but many of its members finally joined the UDR (qv). The RUC was temporarily disarmed following the Hunt Report but has been an armed force for almost the whole period since partition.

SDLP   Social Democratic and Labour Party. A constitutional nationalist party which renounces the use of violence, it was formed in 1970 by Gerry Fitt, John Hume and others and replaced the old Nationalist Party. For some Protestants it is indistinguishable from its main nationalist electoral rival, Sinn Féin. The latter was originally the name of a party resisting British rule in Ireland. It is now the political wing of the 'provisional' IRA and the main rival of the

SDLP for Catholic votes. Its past refusal to renounce IRA violence makes Sinn Féin for most unionists indistinguishable from the IRA.

SOS   Secretary-of-State for Northern Ireland.

UDA   Ulster Defence Association. Formed in 1971 out of a number of Protestant vigilante groups, it is the largest paramilitary organisation, proscribed only in 1993 though individual members have been convicted of murder and racketeering. It is thought to carry out terrorist activities under the rubric of the UFF (qv) but the leadership denies this.

UDI   Unilateral Declaration of Independence.

UDR   Ulster Defence Regiment. Formed on the recommendation of the 1969 Hunt Report as a section of the British Army, it operated specifically in Northern Ireland during the period of this study. Resisted initially by loyalists who distrusted the encouragement given to Catholics to join, it is now seen by republicans as a successor to the 'B' Specials (see RUC), and is largely a Protestant force. It has now been fully incorporated into the British Army as the Royal Irish Regiment.

UFF   Ulster Freedom Fighters. A proscribed terrorist group, it is widely believed to be a sub-group of the UDA and first used this name in 1973.

UK   The United Kingdom of Great Britain and Northern Ireland, formerly the United Kingdom of Great Britain and Ireland. Northern Ireland is part of the UK but not of Great Britain (which is normally referred to as Britain).

UPNI   Unionist Party of Northern Ireland. Formed in 1974 by Brian Faulkner, chief executive of the power-sharing government of 1973–7. The UPNI was committed to retain power-sharing in the face of opposition from the UUUC (qv) but it won no seats in the 1974 general election for Westminster and only 5 of the 78 seats in the 1975 Convention election in Northern Ireland.

UPV   Ulster Protestant Volunteers, a paisleyite organisation responsible for bomb attacks on public utilities in 1969, including the Silent Valley reservoir.

USC   Ulster Special Constabulary (see RUC).

UTV   Ulster Television.

UUP   Ulster Unionist Party. In 1904 the Ulster Unionist Council was formed to coordinate all local Unionist Associations in Ulster, and on gaining the exclusion from Home Rule of the six counties known as Northern Ireland, the Unionist Party formed the government in the Stormont years. It was renamed the Official Unionist Party to distinguish it from the newly-formed Democratic Unionist Party and other unionist rivals but later became the Ulster Unionist Party. Still the biggest unionist party in Northern Ireland, it has spent the last few years in uneasy and unstable partnership with its erstwhile challenger, the DUP (qv).

UUUC United Ulster Unionist Council. A coalition of the DUP, Vanguard and Harry West's Official Unionist Party, formed in 1973 to oppose the power-sharing Executive.

UVF   Ulster Volunteer Force. Originally formed in 1912 to defy a British government bent on giving Ireland Home Rule, many of its members volunteered for army service in the First World War, forming the 36th (Ulster) Division which suffered heavy casualties in the Battle of the Somme (1916). There were moves to re-form it on the foundation of Northern Ireland but the establishment of the RUC (qv) and the Special Constabulary satisfied Protestant aspirations in the policing of the new entity. Today the name is used by a Protestant terrorist group formed in 1966, proscribed for most of its history though briefly legalised in the mid-1970s, and responsible for a significant number of murders.

WP   Workers' Party. The latest name of what was Sinn Féin the Workers' Party, then Republican Clubs the Workers' Party, this political wing of the 'official' IRA (qv) is a non-sectarian socialist working-class party hoping for the non-violent reunification of Ireland but content to work within existing structures. It attracts few votes. It has recently become a unionist party.

Preface

THE CURRENT SITUATION in Northern Ireland has attracted academics and journalists from many countries to offer analyses and solutions. Yet the impression gained from reading much of this work is a troubling one. Although much of the writing on Northern Ireland puts it into a comparative framework of one sort or another, it often seems curiously inward-looking. Above all, the conflict is often portrayed by the media as an incomprehensible and anachronistic sectarian squabble, or as a cynical and self-interested manipulation of a minority of psychopaths or wrong-headed young idealists by 'hard men'.

Placed in a wider historical and comparative context, however, the picture looks more familiar. Northern Ireland consists of six counties out of the thirty-two that made up England's first colony. The six counties were deliberately chosen, moreover, to shelter most of the descendants of Protestant and British settlers in a Catholic and Irish land whose earlier inhabitants see themselves as 'natives'. 'Settlers' are defined not merely as migrants but as groups of people who establish hegemony over already-occupied territories, set up societies based on the model of their 'mother country' or original homeland, and attempt to maintain domination over the 'natives'. Not all colonies with large white populations are settler colonies: two essential features are the existence of a class structure among the settlers similar to that of the metropolis, and a measure of economic and political autonomy from the metropolis (Good 1976:597, 599). 'Natives' are the peoples whose territory is usurped by settlers and who are forced into a subordinate role. They may or may not have been the first peoples living in the territory: what matters is not the distant origins of either group but the form of social relations established between settlers and the existing population.

I am conceptualising Ulster, therefore, as the remnants of a settler colony, unusual only in that most of its settler minority has escaped some of the effects of decolonisation, namely dispossession and exile. What they have not escaped, however, is armed conflict. All settler societies established in territory which was already occupied by societies with some degree of political organisation have seen conflict, in which the power of the dominant (though numerically inferior) settler group has been challenged. It is, of course, true that not all societies in conflict are settler societies; but given the history of Ulster it seems curious to overlook this factor.

No one would wish the deadlock in Northern Ireland, and the constant threat of renewed violence, to continue for ever. It is likely to do so, however, without a fresh approach, based on a recognition of history and an acknowledgement of the many characteristics which the region shares with settler colonies. Although the conflict has led to Northern Ireland being one of the most extensively re-searched areas in the world, in many ways it is one of the least understood. Ulster's history of settler colonialism is not the only explanation for the conflict, but to ignore it, as largely happens, is unwise and unhelpful.

Another example of historical myopia is the 'discovery' of 'Protestant alienation', allegedly a modern phenomenon arising from dissatisfaction with British policy in Northern Ireland since 1969. What has largely escaped notice is, first, that British policy has been perceived as unsatisfactory at least since the beginning of the twentieth century and, second, that a central feature of settler societies is the ambivalence of settlers towards their metropolis. Just as many Protestants today complain that the British do not know how to deal with rebel Catholics, so have settlers always objected to 'native policy' as proposed by the imperial government.

This work highlights the settler colonial dimension to the current situation in Northern Ireland by examining salient aspects of Protestant ideologies during the three periods of the current century which had the greatest potential for conflict between Protestants and the British state over the question of the distribution of political power within Ireland: 1912–21, from the third Home Rule crisis to the foundation of Northern Ireland; 1939–49, from the 1939–45 war to the Ireland Act of 1949; and 1968 to the present. Above all, what is important is the triangular relationship between Protestants, their 'enemies', Irish Catholics, and their 'passing friends', the unreliable untrustworthy British. Part of this triangle was summed up by a loyalist prisoner:

> The truth of the matter is that the British Government has today placed us in the ironic position, where, tragically, it is easier to believe our enemies, those who murder and bomb us, than those who supposedly govern us (Geoffrey Edwards, letter to *Combat*, June 1994).

Few labels are viewed as neutral in Northern Ireland and a major problem is deciding what to call the main actors. To choose sectarian labels might imply that the conflict is 'religious', to choose political labels suggests that denomination plays no part. Whyte (1990:20), facing the same dilemma, chose 'Protestants' and 'Catholics' on the grounds that these terms are common currency both in Northern Ireland and among those writing about it, and I have chosen the same terms. Protestant settlement, which began in the sixteenth century, has been an ongoing process and some of the most militant defenders of Northern Ireland as a political entity (as well as some of its critics) arrived in this century. Whatever the length of residence in the North of Ireland, in structural terms Protestants represent the 'settler' group and Catholics the 'native' group.

The word 'settler' is not necessarily pejorative. Not all settlers have been determined to retain power over the 'natives'. Such societies have always included moderates, who prefer accommodation with the 'natives', and dissidents who seek to surrender power to them. Ireland is no exception. Ulster Presbyterians led the United Irish rebellion of 1798 which aimed to establish an Irish Republic separate from Britain. There were Protestants throughout the nineteenth century who campaigned for the relief of Catholic disabilities and there were Protestant Home Rulers. In the 1939–49 period some Protestants were involved in an interdenominational labour movement which had some electoral success and was seen as a threat by the Unionist Party. It is in the modern period, however, that the greatest range of Protestant positions is apparent. Of these I have chosen to focus on two Protestant groups: first, 'ultras', a term borrowed from Richard Rose (1971:33), who are arguably a majority, and who are prepared to defy the metropolis to retain not only the Union but also the predominant political position of Protestants in Northern Ireland; and second, 'moderates', who favour retaining the Union of Northern Ireland with Great Britain but wish to incorporate Catholics fully into the state and society along the lines preferred by the British government, and thus favour power-sharing. 'Dissidents', who appear to favour a united Ireland, are so small in number that I have omitted them here, along with anarchists, 'greens' and other minority groups.

This is not the first work to conceptualise Northern Ireland as a settler society. Several years ago a book called *The Children of Wrath* (MacDonald 1986) appeared, was dismissed for lack of evidence from primary sources, and has been largely (and unjustifiably) ignored since. This study, by contrast, is very firmly based on primary sources (for full references see Clayton 1993). These consist of all editorials and letters in a range of local newspapers in the three periods chosen, a total of nearly 50 years, and the editorials of two provincial newspapers during particularly fraught periods. Newspapers may today be distrusted as a source of news, but these sections of the paper, which specifically and usually consciously aim to make converts or to reinforce existing views, are important documentary sources for the study of ideology. As Scott (1990:8) points out, lack of credibility concerning factual information is unproblematic when it is genuine opinions that are being put forward and that are the object of study.

In general, with the replacement of personal by corporate ownership of newspapers and the modern dominance of commercial interests, notably the need to attract advertising and sell copies, the influence of the editor and the importance of the editorial have declined since the late nineteenth century. Hence the editorial has become less important and less (overtly, that is) an attempt to influence views. Nevertheless, whereas in the past the editor's views pervaded the whole newspaper, the editorial column of today (where one exists) is the surest place to find the personal views and political opinions of the editor who, whatever success s/he has, uses this column to try to influence events or to speak for his/her readership.

Letters to the editor, on the other hand, are given much more prominence today than in the early part of the century. Svirsky (1947:147) calls them 'the people's editorials' and cites surveys showing that more people read the letters than read the editorials. People 'talk back' to the media and, very often, to fellow-citizens through the medium of the newspaper. The observation that it is mainly the powerful who have access to the media (Glasgow University Media Group 1982:113) is qualified by the existence of the letters column. Although candidates for political office have been known to organise campaigns to have letters written to the editor (Janowitz 1967:xv) and many letters are clearly from Roper's group of 'participating citizens' who are better educated, more articulate and take more interest in current affairs than most (Katz & Lazarsfeld 1955:xvi), it is clear from a perusal of local newspapers in particular that many correspondents are 'ordinary' people rather than acknowledged opinion-leaders or powerseekers.

A number of sociologists have noted the importance of the local press. Although bound as much as the national press by commercial considerations, the local press, with its ties to a community which often has a sentimental attachment to its locality, must sympathetically reflect local social structure, sense of pride and identity and area traditions. In addition it is held to act as a mechanism for maintaining local consensus and limiting controversy. Another important function is ascribed to the local press: as the only institution with a long-term general interest in the community, it largely sets the local civic agenda even though it has no governing role. The editor will have personal relationships with community leaders and with at least some of his/her readers. Those who write letters to the editor also have personal relationships with or are known by repute to other readers of the newspaper. In contrast with national newspapers, the local press is expected to be accurate in its reporting and even trivial errors concerning local matters are frequently spotted and challenged by readers. The local press thus operates midway between the mass media and informal communication (Janowitz 1967:145).

Local newspapers have played an important role in Ulster since the late eighteenth century and, in addition to the local papers, the northern province supported three important Belfast-based unionist dailies, the *News Letter*, the *Belfast Telegraph* and the *Northern Whig*. These were sustained by a highly literate population: by 1911 at least 95 per cent of Protestants over the age of nine were literate (Kennedy 1988:7). For most people newspapers were the only source of information until 1928 when the first daily radio news bulletins from Belfast began. During the Second World War newspapers grew in significance again when regional broadcasting was virtually suspended. Editors, staff and proprietors were closely involved in the community, from membership of church committees, the Orange Order, the Unionist Party and the Masonic Order to close relations with, or even membership of, the government. Although the importance of local newspapers has been diminished by the advent of radio and television, and the influence of their personnel reduced since the advent of direct rule in 1972, they still attract a lively correspondence and are widely read, as is shown by the circulation figures (see Willing's Press Guides) and by the fact that letters (infrequent in the early part of this century but now an important part of some of the newspapers) are frequently prompted by items in the newspapers.

Operating a provincial or local newspaper in a divided society such as Northern Ireland does pose special problems. Even what appear to be minor parochial concerns may agitate religious or political sensibilities and editorial attempts to forge a consensus inevitably fail. It is not surprising then that most editors today either take a partisan line on major issues or simply do not have an editorial column. One editor, who does write an editorial column and lives in the local area, told me that there were times when he feared physical attack. Only one newspaper in this study, the *Impartial Reporter*, claims to be, and indeed attempts to be, 'impartial' and by implication neutral. Furthermore, the presence of a powerful countervailing nationalist ideology means that unionist assumptions are constantly under attack and therefore cannot be taken for granted: they are therefore openly and often asserted and defended. Nevertheless, unionist editorials (whether in papers calling themselves Unionist or in ones calling themselves Conservative or Independent but which are of unionist tendency) are predictable only on one topic: the need to maintain the Border and the constitutional connection with Great Britain. As long as they remain 'sound' on that issue, they may retain their Protestant readership, however widely their views on other topics vary from those of many of their readers. This situation has changed somewhat since the earlier part of the century, when after partition Armour, the editor of the *Northern Whig*, commented that 'the only thing which a prudent editor actually can safely comment upon and remain "loyal" is the unhappy plight of the Irish Free State' (Kennedy 1988:20). This change no doubt arises from the reduced importance of the editorial, which allows the editor more freedom of opinion.

In line with national trends most local newspapers have now fallen into corporate hands. This applies to the following papers used in this study: the *Belfast Telegraph*, the *News Letter*, the *Londonderry Sentinel*, the *Portadown News*, the *Portadown Times*, the *Craigavon Times* and the *Ballymena Observer*. It should be noted that the *Portadown News* underwent a change of ownership and of editorship in 1972, turning it from an ultra to a moderate paper. Two of the papers were founded in the modern period, the *Protestant Telegraph*, largely written by Ian Paisley, and the *Orange Standard*, an organ of the Orange Order. The other two papers, the *County Down Spectator* and the *Impartial Reporter* of Fermanagh, remain in the ownership of the original founding family and have retained a remarkably consistent editorial policy and outlook in some respects from 1912 to the present. The bulk of the modern data comes from the period up to December 1989, but a perusal of the newspapers since then reveals few changes. The *Belfast Telegraph* has become less moderate since the Anglo–Irish Agreement, the *News Letter* has changed ownership and become a tabloid with far fewer editorials, and the *Impartial Reporter*, which had its front page entirely covered with classified advertisements in emulation of the *London Times*, ceased this practice in 1987 when there was a change of editorship.

The local newspapers were selected primarily to represent a range of areas. Craigavon, Derry and Fermanagh represent border areas. North Down is close to the city of Belfast and Ballymena is in the heart of County Antrim. Fermanagh is essentially rural, and Ballymena and to a lesser extent North Down are towns with rural hinterlands. Craigavon is a new town based on Portadown and Derry is Northern Ireland's second city. North Down is the most prosperous area, followed by Ballymena. The areas had differing proportions of Catholics to Protestants at the start of the modern period. Estimated percentages of Catholics in the district council areas in 1971 ranged from 11.4 per cent in North Down and 17.7 per cent in Ballymena, through 38.7 per cent in Craigavon, to 52.5 per cent in Fermanagh and 64.5 per cent in Derry. The proportion of Catholics had risen by 1991 in line with the general rise in Northern Ireland (from 36.8 per cent in 1971 to 43.1 per cent in 1991) in all these areas except North Down, where it fell slightly. They still form a majority only in Derry and Fermanagh, but have risen to form 44.5 per cent of the Craigavon population (Cormack et al. 1993:14).

By and large unionist papers in general, wherever they are published attitudes held to varying degrees by nineteenth-century unionists were:

> fear and distrust of Catholicism, a conviction that the economic welfare of Ireland depended on legislative union with Britain, a rejection of, or an indifference to, any romantic concept of a Gaelic Irish nation, and a converse belief in the supreme virtues and importance of the British Empire (Anderson 1988:2).

These attitudes have been maintained, with necessary modifications, by most unionist papers and their correspondents to this day.

IT WOULD HAVE been impossible to carry out this research without help and support. Libraries and their personnel have been indispensable and I thank them, together with the newspaper editors who kindly gave me information on editorial policy and the Reverend Martin Smyth, MP, for his courtesy in permitting me to quote his Oxford Union speech in full. Important too have been the support of friends, in particular Dr Mohan Nair for his invaluable help with my computing queries, and the understanding of my family, who encouraged me in my work and forgave my neglect of them. Finally I gratefully acknowledge Dr Liam O'Dowd, Reader in Sociology, the Queen's University of Belfast, for his advice, support and interest throughout what turned out to be a very long, but rewarding, travail.

A Brief Chronology of Events

1910–1921

1910 Two UK general elections. Liberal Party takes office with support of Irish Nationalists and Labour.

1911 Parliament Act restricts House of Lords to delaying powers only. William Craig and Edward Carson propose Protestants declare Provisional Government and take over Ulster. Bonar Law becomes leader of Conservative Party.

1912 Winston Churchill visits Belfast. Third Home Rule for Ireland Bill introduced. Ulster's Solemn League and Covenant.

1913 Home Rule Bill passed by Commons but rejected by Lords. Ulster Volunteer Force (UVF) formed. Provisional Government set up in Ulster. Irish Citizen Army formed. Irish Volunteers formed.

1914 Government proposes county opt-out of Home rule. Prepares to prevent UVF and Ulster Unionist Council from seizing Ulster. Curragh mutiny. UVF smuggles guns into Ulster. War with Germany is declared. 36th (Ulster) division formed. Home Rule Bill becomes law but is not to be implemented until after the war and special provision for Ulster is promised.

1916 Easter Rising in Dublin. Leaders executed without trial. Six counties of Ulster to be excluded from Home Rule. Battle of the Somme.

1917 Sinn Féin revived.

1918 Sinn Féin under Eamon de Valera fights Nationalists in by-elections. Armistice. General Election. Sinn Féin wins majority of seats in Ireland.

1919 Dáil Eireann makes Declaration of Irish Independence. Appeals to Paris Peace Conference for the right to self-determination. Irish Volunteers now named Irish Republican Army (IRA). Lloyd George declares Dáil illegal. War in Ireland begins.

1920 Nationalists win control of Derry Corporation in local government elections. Catholics driven out of Belfast shipyards. UVF revived. Ulster Special Constabulary (USC) established. Bill for the Better Government of Ireland partitions the island.

1921 Northern Ireland comes into being. Ulster Unionists win

Northern Ireland elections. Craig becomes prime minister. Truce between IRA and British government. Anglo–Irish Treaty establishes the Irish Free State within the empire on the promise of a boundary commission.

1937–1949

1937 Irish state adopts a new constitution.

1938 Anglo–Eire Agreement and return of British-held ports.

1939 IRA bombing campaign in England. War with Germany. The Irish state declares its neutrality.

1940 De Valera rejects British offer of Irish unity in return for the use of Irish ports.

1941 German air raids on Northern Ireland.

1942 US forces land in Northern Ireland. New IRA campaign. Belfast Corporation suspended for gross corruption.

1945 German surrender. Labour Party wins power in Britain. Irish Anti-Partition League formed.

1948 Dáil passes Republic of Ireland Act.

1949 Westminster passes Ireland Act.

1964–1995

1964 Terence O'Neill becomes Northern Ireland prime minister and starts limited reforms.

1965 Nationalist Party becomes official opposition in Stormont.

1966 Modern UVF formed.

1967 Northern Ireland Civil Rights Association (NICRA) formed.

1968 Derry Civil Rights march. People's Democracy (PD) formed. Harold Wilson summons Unionist leaders and insists on reforms.

1969 PD march attacked at Burntollet. Loyalists bomb water pipelines. O'Neill resigns. Battle of the Bogside. Battles in Belfast. British Army leaves barracks. Cameron Report. Hunt Report. 'Provisional' IRA splits from 'Official' IRA.

1970 Alliance Party of Northern Ireland (APNI) formed. Social Democratic and Liberal Party (SDLP) formed.

1971 Internment. Democratic Unionist Party (DUP) formed.

1972 Bloody Sunday. Bombs in Belfast. Unionist cabinet resigns. Stormont suspended. Assassination campaigns. Bloody Friday. Bombs in Dublin.

1973 First Loyalists interned. Northern Ireland Constitution Act. Power-sharing Executive formed. Council of Ireland proposed.

1974 Strike ends power-sharing.

1975 Elections for Constitutional Convention.

1977 Paisley calls strike.

1980 Thatcher–Haughey meetings.
1981 Maze hunger strike. Sands elected MP. Sinn Féin enters electoral process.
1982 War with Argentina. Assembly elections.
1983 New Ireland Forum. Maze break-out.
1985 Anglo–Irish Agreement.
1986 Unionists announce civil disobedience plan.
1991 Brooke talks begin.
1993 Downing Street Declaration.
1994 IRA ceasefire. Loyalist ceasefire.
1995 Framework Document.

1 Imperialism and Colonialism

MANY WHO SEE the Northern Ireland problem as the result of imperialism frequently overlook the fact that, although the territory was indeed originally part of the British expropriation of Ireland, it has remained under British jurisdiction largely because of the size and determined resistance of its settler population. Imperialism and settler colonialism in general are not identical; and in respect to the 'native' peoples, the imperial ideology of the metropolis has differed in important ways from the colonial ideology of settlers. The British and French empires have been the most extensively studied in this context, both being particularly relevant because they included two important settler colonies which fiercely resisted majority rule, namely Southern Rhodesia and Algeria. Works on the Spanish, Portuguese, Dutch, German and Belgian empires, however, draw very similar conclusions to those on the British and French (Alatas 1978:7).

THE TERM 'IMPERIALISM', which was coined in 1858 to mean 'despotism', changed in 1881 to take on the meaning 'principle or spirit of empire; advocacy of imperial interests' (Shorter Oxford English Dictionary 1959). To this could be added Lord Rosebery's definition, 'greater pride in Empire' (Eldridge 1978:3). It is probably misleading to apply the term indiscriminately to the whole of the 400 or so years of modern European expansionism. This ranged from the plunder empires of the sixteenth through the settlement colonies of the seventeenth and eighteenth to the tropical empires of the nineteenth century. The 'spirit of empire' of the latter, with its certainty, conceit and confidence, was very different from the critical self-evaluation and humbling cultural comparison of the previous two centuries when confronted with much older civilisations such as India, and from the self-doubt of the twentieth century (Faber 1966:45; Betts 1976:150).

The form of empire also changed. By the eighteenth century both British and French empires had evolved into a system based on the political ascendancy of the metropolis with its dependent white settler colonies, first in North America and later in Australia and New Zealand. These existed for the economic well-being of the 'mother coun-

1

try', and consisted of a large settler population and a small 'native' population, considered unimportant, especially when nomadic and marginalised by extermination or by herding on to reserves. The late nineteenth century, however, saw European nations adding to their previous conquests in the East almost the whole of Africa, where populous and settled societies had long existed.

Whether the primary motive for empire was strategic or economic is still debated; but whatever the motivation, imperialism in practical terms was still the exercise of power, economic and political. It was, however, only from the nineteenth century onwards that naked power was dressed up in the 'respectable' garb of European responsibility for the progress of backward peoples. An age which had seen the American and French Revolutions based on principles of liberty and equality needed to justify its seizure of land and mastery of areas which were already inhabited by large numbers of indigenes (Thornton 1965:11). The principle of 'trusteeship' served to justify the European hold on power over subject peoples, and side-stepped that fact that these, in the vast majority of cases, had neither invited nor showed much sign of appreciating this European interest in their well-being.

The keyword in this self-justification was civilisation: the 'civilising' mission was the duty of European nations to share their advances with the backward and barbarian parts of the world. Civilisation, of course, meant European languages, religion, and politico-legal systems. Above all European technological superiority was taken as proof of cultural superiority, although the extent of the technological gap was greatly exaggerated. In reality, this gap had opened for many peoples only in the eighteenth century (Alatas 1978:216). Nevertheless, since no reasonable person could reject the 'gift' Europeans brought, this reinterpretation of imperial power made it possible to regard dissent as no more than the work of 'agitators' (Worsley 1967:68).

Interpretations of European superiority ranged from humanitarian to racist. The existence of these competing doctrines of imperialism documented by Thornton (1965) can be seen in the shifts back and forth in the dominant ideology of empire during the nineteenth and twentieth centuries. The universalistic and liberal ideas which saw all people as equal in the earlier part of the nineteenth century gave way gradually to racism in thought and practice. Feelings of British racial uniqueness, imaginatively traced back to fifth-century Anglo-Saxon society, led to assumptions of racial and national moral superiority. These both helped to inspire the imposition of imperial rule over 'inferior' peoples and to serve as justification for it. Such notions took a different form under French rule. It was French 'culture' rather than the French 'race' which was held superior; but the belief that France was the true guardian of civilisation, the

2

resulting contempt for the indigenous cultures under their rule and their actual practice of imperial rule had a similar end-result to the avowedly racist British imperialist ideology.

So in both empires, the notion evolved that European languages and culture were the only vehicles for progress. A series of insurrections such as the Indian rebellion of 1857 emphasised the need for order and at the same time 'proved' that indigenous society was unfit for self-rule. Earlier notions of strictly limited liability for the imperial power were dropped – 'natives' had a right (however theoretical) to law, to protection, to a measure of education – but not to self-determination.

ANOTHER DIFFERENCE between the nineteenth and earlier centuries was that white settlements in Africa formed 'mixed' colonies, with minority populations of settlers and adventurers setting up colonies of white domination over the existing inhabitants, who were numerically superior but whose weapons were no match for the Maxim gun. In this situation, the settlers attempted to create societies similar to that of the metropolis (Fieldhouse 1966:11). This became a logical impossibility, for by the late nineteenth century the franchise was beginning to be extended in the European metropoles (which in any case did not consist of a small recognisably foreign elite subordinating a large 'native' majority). The contradiction did not have to be addressed, however, as long as the 'native' majority acquiesced in their subordination.

Metropolitan British and French attitudes to these mixed colonies show some ambivalence. In principle, they were treated in the same way as other colonies, but the presence of settlers certainly made a difference. Although French colonial possessions were generally subordinated to the metropolis politically, according to Fanon (1965:180), it was the rapacity and racism of the French settlers which increased the impact of French imperialism. Even non-settler British possessions were administered in a much more decentralised way, following the principles of the 1839 Durham Report, which pronounced that people in the colonies were the best fitted to run them. The 'people in the colonies', however, were the white settlers and imperial representatives, not the 'natives', and in practice, the system of 'collaboration' between settlers and their metropolis was even looser than imperial control over other dependencies (Denoon 1983:66). Furthermore, the British were less 'liberal' about social relationships with colonised peoples. French settlers and officials were far less racially exclusive and much more indulgent to sexual relations between Europeans and 'natives'.

Although France shared with other European nations the quest for new markets, it had a declining birth-rate and no need to shed surplus labour. Hence Algeria was the only important settlement colony, and although there was very substantial state involvement in its conquest, this was prompted chiefly by economic pressure from settlers. The nineteenth-century British government did not set out to create mixed settlement colonies, although it ended up with some, founded by individuals or groups seeking their own advantage. Yet settlement colonies had their uses for the metropolis. For example, some British imperialists argued that exporting some of the glut of labourers and malcontents would preserve social stability, and that new markets and raw materials generated by settler enterprise would relieve domestic unemployment. In 1833 Edward Gibbon Wakefield pointed out that overseas colonies might also serve to:

> turn the tide of Irish emigration from England to her colonies; not to mention that the owners of land in Ireland, most of them being foreigners by religion, might thus be taken out of the dilemma in which they are now placed: that of a choice between legally giving up a great part of their rental to the hungry people, and yielding to the people's violence the land which was taken by violence from their fathers (cited in Winks 1969:47–8).

Settlers were also built into the British ideological model of empire and the true character of the British 'race'. An image was painted of the ennobling effects of living in open space far from the metropolis, allowing 'dynamic action and personal fulfilment'. The colonial personality was free, noble and energetic, moulded according to Curzon 'in the furnace of responsibility and on the anvil of self-reliance' (Betts 1976:15, 16). There was a strong feeling that life in Europe had become too materialistic: colonial life had an elevating moral purpose which would improve the national character (Ridley 1983:59–60, 103). Migration would also establish enduring sentimental ties within the empire. For Seeley this empire was an enlargement of England that made her a leading state instead of the small nation she would otherwise be, so the white settlements (and India, for other reasons) had to be retained (Faber 1966:59, 65).

The establishment of mixed colonies also contained the seeds of future metropolitan unease, and some imperialists were more wary of settlers. Merivale was wholeheartedly devoted to the notion of British settlers maintaining British supremacy throughout the globe, but he was unimpressed with the new colonies. In a lecture published in 1861 he scolded them for living in the past, in the society which they had left, and in the future, the society they dreamt of, and therefore not giving much thought to forming carefully thought-out and permanent institutions in the present. Instead, he complained, they let institutions grow up carelessly and framed laws merely for actual emergencies (Winks 1969:86). It has been argued more recently that metropolitan governments were obliged to take under their flags many of the territories carved out by settlers, in order to 'direct this world revolution along orderly paths and to control the boundless, irresponsible, freebooting and destructive enterprises of pioneers and adventurers' (Lüthy 1964:32–3).

Certainly the 'national interest' of the metropolis was not necessarily the same as the more immediate and personal interests of the colonial adventurers; and what happened in the colonies was often beyond imperial control, including the unauthorised take-over of territory. The settlement of Southern Rhodesia is an example of this. Rhodes in an election speech in South Africa in 1898 summed up his view of the imperial government's role:

> We are not going to be governed from home ... we do everything. We pass a Bill and the Queen just puts her name to it ... what she does for us, and without our paying for it, is this: she protects us with her fleet, and when I take a new country for you she protects me from the German and the Frenchman ... Whenever I took a country I simply said to the Queen: 'I have taken that: you must put your flag over it' (cited in Huttenback 1975:109).

This view was substantially accurate. However, although the creation of Southern Rhodesia is commonly attributed to the arch-imperialist Rhodes and his British South Africa Company, it is clear from the contemporary literature that it was the settlers who took the major part in determining the course of Rhodesian history (see, for example, Hone 1909; Hole 1928; Hickman 1960; Olivier 1975). It was they, not Rhodes, who shared their living space with the indigenous population and it was in the settlers' own interests to gain as much economic and political power for themselves as they could. Rhodes' ideology, especially in his later years, was that of the imperialist rather than of the settler, though like other imperialists, he found it impossible to control 'his' settlers in their conflict with the Matabele (Huttenback 1975:108), however much settler behaviour contravened the imperial ideal of the civilising mission.

Settlers had their merits and settler colonies their usefulness, especially in helping to paint the globe red; but imperial statesmen generally had a lofty attitude towards them: 'They constituted a lesser rank in society' (Thornton 1965:41).

Equally, settlers had an ambivalent attitude towards the 'mother country'. They gloried in its achievements and claimed to be the only local representatives of its culture, civilisation and values; but they were as wary of the imperial government as it was of them. Settler views of the metropolis were coloured by perceptions of metropolitan greed, incompetence or arrogance, and by the awareness that their own interests were diverging from those of the mother country. Attempts at direct imperial control aroused violent settler reaction. Memmi in *The Coloniser and the Colonised* (1974:65) sums up the ambiguity of relations with the mother country: 'These exaltation–resentment dialectics uniting the colonialist to his homeland give a peculiar shade to the nature of his love for it.'

Kipling's work exemplifies some of these feelings. He seems to have loved the empire but not England, and in 'The Native-Born' (1894) he despairs of 'our English brother (But he does not understand)' (in Winks 1969:14). The English attitude to the empire was unenlightened in comparison to that of men of the frontier like himself; and in *Puck of Pook's Hill*, where the Roman empire is an emblem for the British, it is the stern men of the frontier who defend the boundaries against barbarian attack. The troops from Rome are effeminate and decadent, and there is growing social crisis in the capital. These views were echoed by many other colonial writers from France and Germany as well as Britain. The contradiction between the notion of 'civilisation' and the 'decadence' of the metropolis which was its fount rarely, however, led settlers or colonial writers to question the value of imperialism. Outside his fiction Kipling campaigned for a strong army and told soldiers that their duty was not to any politician or party but to the empire and the white race. Yet at the same time, though the imperial frontiers might form his noblest subject-matter, the best place for a writer to live was England, with its intellectual tradition, the company of fellow-writers and large numbers of readers. These were luxuries not commonly found in the settlement colonies, where the ethos of 'action' was allied with contempt for intellectualism.

Generally, however, it was only when settler colony and metropolis clashed on specific points that the relationship became overtly strained; and even then settler demands for independence were very much a last resort. In the twentieth century, such problems were often solved by alternatives such as Dominion status or legal incorporation into the metropolis. It was quite possible for settlers to grow attached to their new land while remaining within the empire, and 'though habitually disobedient, European settlers were also instinctively loyal' (Fieldhouse 1966:396). There was, however, one feature which distinguished the new British Dominions from other settler colonies: in the latter, settlers remained small if dominant minorities and hence Dominion status was barred to them.

Despite this disappointment, settlers both in Kenya and Rhodesia, as remarked by Michael Blundell, himself a Kenyan settler, when 'about to indulge in some desperate action to demonstrate their contempt for Colonial Office rule, ... invariably prefaced it by singing God Save the Queen at the same time to show their loyalty' (cited in Thornton 1978:283). White settlers saw themselves as more loyal than the inhabitants of the metropolis. Only they faced directly the threat from the 'natives'. British troops were welcome when they were sent to protect settlers against the 'natives' but when they tried to protect 'natives' the metropolis and its troops were regarded as 'a tyrannical imposition' (Baker 1983:54). Thus settler loyalty was conditional on being allowed to deal with 'native affairs' themselves. It is hardly surprising then that the occasions when settler–metropolitan conflict could not be resolved peacefully arose over the issue of the transfer of political power to the hitherto powerless 'natives'. It was in such circumstances that loyalty became such an issue that 'overt attention must to paid to invoking [it]' (Field 1982:239). Settler loyalty, however, was essentially to the late nineteenth-century metropolis, not to that of the 1950s and 1960s: in other words, it was loyalty to a nation still largely committed to the maintenance of empire – a nation which no longer existed.

Settlers also tended to claim that the majority in the colony was 'disloyal'. The British minority in Lower Canada did this *vis-à-vis* the French (Boyce 1970:101), and in other British colonies 'natives' rebelling against being dispossessed of their own lands were often accused of disloyalty to the imperial power. Such claims were heightened when there was a settler minority whose dominance was threatened by the metropolis itself. Claims of 'loyalty' to something higher than the government or parliament of the metropolis became a justification for the pursuit of aims which contravened both those of the metropolis and of the 'natives'. For all these reasons, a stress on loyalty is generally characteristic of settlers.

Identity is another issue in settler societies. Louis Hartz, in his seminal work, *The Founding of New Societies* (1964:11–13, 53–4), observed that identity formation by European settlers in a new land is a complex process. Changes in Europe and the presence of 'native' peoples in the new land make it difficult to maintain identification with the old country. The 'racial element' becomes an integral part of settler consciousness and national identity in a way that does not occur in Europe. The settlers in Hartz's study, however, eventually won political independence from the motherland; colonists in North Africa did not, and 'conceding no merits to the colonial community, recognising neither its traditions, nor its laws, nor its ways, he cannot acknowledge belonging to it himself ... The result is that the colonialist is unsure of his true nationality' (Memmi 1974:68). Religion was, however, another kind of identity available. Although here the reference is to the colonised, it is equally applicable to some settler groups:

> With its institutional network, its collective and periodic holidays, religion constitutes another refuge value, both for the individual and for the group. For the individual it is one of the rare paths of retreat; for the group it is one of the rare manifestations which can protect its original existence ... Formalism, of which religious

formality is only one aspect, is the cyst into which colonial society shuts itself and hardens, degrading its own life in order to save it. It is a spontaneous action of self-defence, a means of safe-guarding the collective consciousness without which a people quickly cease to exist (Memmi 1974:101–2).

However it is formed, the concept of identity has been seen as one which has peculiar relevance where groups are in competition:

> Group consciousness or identity occurs when a group recognises itself as possessing unique attributes that distinguish it from others ... It assumes greater saliency when groups compete for scarce resources, power or other desired goods, but group awareness also emerges when groups perceive their valued attributes (for example culture, religion, language, identity) threatened by the actions of others, be that threat real or imagined (Baker 1983:10–11).

Since settler loyalty depends on retaining control of 'native' policy, any divergence between settlers and the metropolis on this issue leads to major strains in the relationship; and one of the most significant divergences between colonial and imperial ideology arose precisely from conflicting attitudes towards 'native' peoples.

Imperial and colonial ideology had always diverged to some extent, owing to the conflicting economic and strategic interests of the metropolis and the settlement, leading to conflicts such as the American War of Independence. 'Native policy', usually involving their subordination and control, was sometimes in the interests of both metropolis and settlers, and not therefore a common source of conflict. Even so, as early as the eighteenth century, the British government had attempted to protect Amerinds and French settlers against the British colonists (Faber 1966:49).

From the nineteenth century onwards, however, the very 'civilising mission' which legitimated imperial conquest and control brought to the fore the issue of 'native policy'. The 'white man's burden' meant that, in imperialist theory and to some extent in practice, 'native policy' involved the role of the Colonial Office as guardian of 'racial' minorities and 'backward' peoples. In the mixed colonies, however, it continued to mean principally the legalised theft of 'native' land and the use of 'natives' as a source of cheap labour. Settler societies were therefore quick to seek political autonomy in order to deal with the 'natives' in their own way and acquire what territory they wanted. Hence the nineteenth century saw a further divergence between colonial and imperial ideology. Two contradictory sets of principles were on a collision course within the settlements: the concept of trusteeship within the

8

imperial philosophy of a non-racial empire, and the settlers' deter-mination to create a 'White Man's Country' (Huttenback 1976:21). Some in the metropolis appreciated these conflicting aims. Philan-thropic and religious groups lobbied the British government to curtail settler aggression; and the case of New Zealand shows that the im-perial government was aware of the dangers (already proved in Tas-mania and Australia) of white settler power. Until 1849 the British government tried to stop large-scale settlement in New Zealand because there would inevitably be clashes with non-Europeans. The new Governor in 1856, believing that the Maoris should not be left to the mercy of the settlers, reserved the conduct of Maori affairs to the Crown. In 1865 the Imperial Parliament passed the Colonial Laws Validity Act to prevent settlement colonies enacting legislation that went against British common law, and in 1870 British troops were withdrawn from New Zealand, no doubt partly to save money but also in order to make the New Zealand government face up to the conse-quences of antagonising the Maoris by confiscating their lands while failing to raise their own military force against the warfare that their policy made inevitable. In the event the settlers were unable to defeat the Maoris, who were perhaps for this reason able to attain more rights than the 'natives' in any other settler state (Huttenback 1975:96).

The New Zealand case was, however, exceptional. Metropolitan withdrawal usually left indigenes at the mercy of settlers. The pro-claimed British intention of protecting 'native' people was under-mined partly by the practical difficulties for an over-stretched empire of controlling distant settler colonies; but there were also contradic-tions at the heart of British imperial policy. British settlement areas were regarded as individual societies with their own destinies though bound, in the case of settlers only, to the imperial family by ties of blood; so there was an underlying feeling that they should have a fair degree of autonomy. In addition, by the 1850s demands for economy in imperial government expenditure led to the grant of responsible government to a number of settler states, despite the presence of unrepresented 'native' peoples. Thus there was an early contradiction between imperial rhetoric and imperial action.

The British failure to protect 'native' interests against settlers was most apparent in settler-farmer societies, and here the colonial situa-tion was at its most explosive: 'The confrontation is not only total, it is also peculiarly direct, and the antagonisms fall along the same line of division in every sphere of relationship between White and colo-nised' (Worsley 1967:49). The greater the land hunger the greater the drive to repel or crush the resident population, using the traditional settlers' claim that they would make more efficient use of the land for the benefit of all, a claim made with particular force when the in-digenes were nomadic pastoralists (Fieldhouse 1981:74). Land was described as 'waste land' when it was 'not yet the property of individuals, but liable to become so through the intervention of government' (Wakefield 1833, cited in Winks 1969:39). Imperial intervention on behalf of the 'natives' was then most urgently needed in land-intensive economies; yet where such colonies were distant from the metropolis, colonial policy was formed in favour of settler concerns, not of imperial interests or policy. The imperial authorities knew about settler atrocities in Basutoland in 1881 and in Southern Rhodesia in 1896–9 but did nothing. They did attempt to protect 'native' interests in South Africa, Rhodesia and Kenya, but not with notable success: 'native reserves' were created, supervised by British or colonial officials on tiny budgets, unable to become self-sufficient political or economic units; and in South Africa the reserves were the root of the later apartheid policy of the Union government. The legacy of this half-hearted British attempt to protect 'native' interests came in the twentieth century. It was the land issue that sparked off the Rhodesian crisis in 1960, when African land grievances swelled into nationalism and the white government therefore proposed to abolish the Land Apportionment Act. The Rhodesian Front won power because it opposed any changes in the Act.

In the nineteenth and early twentieth century, then, it was frequently the settlers whose interests triumphed, with their 'frontier mentality of cultural arrogance, brutal force, rough-hewn individualism and disdain for the humanitarianism which at times permeated imperial policy' (Betts 1976:220). Even in the more centralised French empire the debate over whether to achieve development in Algeria by working through indigenous institutions (*association*) or by imposing French civilisation (*assimilation*) was coloured by the presence of large numbers of French civilians and military. These repudiated any idea of eventual equality with the 'natives' and it was partly the presence of white *colons* which prevented the majority of the colonised from 'becoming French' as the assimilationists had proposed (Ross 1982:4).

It would perpetrate too rosy a view of the metropolis to suggest that it was only white settlers who exploited and repressed the local population. Whether as settlers or as colonial administrators, Europeans were generally masters of the colonial situation. Even though administrators attained high professional standards and often were genuinely interested in defending 'native' interests, they sometimes acted for specifically European interests and were far too prone to treat their subjects like children (Fieldhouse 1966:376). Many imperialists were racist in their thinking about the very 'natives' they were attempting to defend against white settlers; and despite differences in official 'native policy' it made little overall difference whether these Europeans were British or French (or any other kind of European). The major empires imposed intensive control, adopted the concept of trusteeship for 'backward races' and assumed their empires would last for ever. Hence the virtual autonomy of settler regimes was aided by the growth of racist ideas in the metropolis itself. For both the imperial power and settlers, a racist ideology served to justify capitalist exploitation and the destruction of indigenous economies and cultures; and when indigenous movements began to claim the right to self-determination, both imperialists and settlers denied the legitimacy of this claim: the colonised had no history; they owed 'loyalty' to those who had taken power over them; and their pretended 'nationalism' when it arose in the twentieth century was 'irrational' or the work of agitators.

The contradiction between metropolitan stated principles and actual failure to protect 'native peoples' against white settlers can be partly explained by something other than 'ties of blood': what they also had in common was that they were capitalist societies. Debates about whether capitalist societies were of necessity also racist and imperialist occupy much of the literature on imperialism; but it is clear that the great European empires were formed at a time when capitalism was rapidly becoming the dominant mode of production in Europe. The new emphasis on the creation of material wealth both inspired and financed colonial ventures as well as other foreign investment. The establishment of the principle of private ownership of property, including land, clashed with the widespread system of communal tenure in the lands seized by the European powers and by settlers (Lemon & Pollock 1980:85). Colonial conflict involved a clash between contradictory values, for in a capitalist system power comes from wealth (rather than, for example, wisdom or physical strength) and so it is the rich who exploit the poor; competition and individualism replace cooperative venture and the bonds of family, clan and community; and the emphasis is on money, personal gain and self-help (Gladwin 1980:25–6).

Britain's economic, strategic and foreign policy interests ultimately remained paramount above those of both 'natives' and settlers; but where there were no immediate conflicts of interest, the imperial government made no attempt fully to govern such colonies, at least up to the 1920s and in some cases beyond. Despite the principle of 'trusteeship', 'native policy' in the mixed colonies was largely dominated by settler interests. There were signs in the earlier part of the twentieth century that this situation might not last. Between the two world wars much parliamentary time was spent at Westminster on colonial issues, and this focused above all on the conflicting interests of settlers and 'natives' in British colonies. Churchill caused great resentment among Kenyan settlers by ruling in 1921 that forced labour could be employed only by permission of the Secretary-of-State; and white Rhodesian attempts to gain Dominion status for their colony failed to win acceptance. Despite imperial reservations, however, all the settlement colonies were eventually granted representative (that is, effectively settler) government, which usually meant a minimum of metropolitan interference. Thus from 1923 until 1953 the government of Southern Rhodesia remained firmly in the hands of the settlers, and their openly discriminatory 'native policies' were never challenged in Whitehall. The French case was rather different. Colonies were overseas territories of France, representation was in Paris, and the local body in Algeria gave settlers no legal control over any aspect of government; but settlers did influence French policy.

By and large, then, metropolitan interference with settler domination was, despite pious affirmations of the principle of trusteeship, minimal or non-existent until the 1920s and beyond. Imperial policy was racist in practice and largely indifferent to the well-being of its imperial subjects. It was accompanied by an ideology which attempted to legitimate the seizure of other people's lands and labour on the grounds of European superiority, notions of 'trusteeship' and a 'civilising mission'. So racism and pretensions to legitimacy were not confined to settler societies. It can, however, be demonstrated that in such societies they took – and still take – a particularly vehement form.

Good (1976:603) claims that initial settler violence towards the 'natives' sprang not out of racism or sadism but from the need to control their land and labour. Nevertheless, settlers developed a racist ideology which was different from metropolitan racism. Since any change in the balance of power in the colony would be against settler interests, the alleged inferiority of the 'natives' as a group was held to be either unchangeable or unlikely to be remedied in the foreseeable future. These notions of the immutability and universality of 'native' inferiority make it appropriate to speak of racism rather than ethnocentricity (Fanon 1967b:40). What is really noteworthy is that settler racism, in the form of structures, personal attitudes and behaviour, is similar everywhere, irrespective of the settlement's origins.

Settler racism differs from metropolitan racism because settlers are in actual contact with the 'inferior' peoples, in a colonial situation involving the subjection of a majority by a minority. This situation favours the settlers, and it is in their interests to maintain it. Its basis is coercion, or the threat of coercion, which is necessary to forestall any 'native' attempts at throwing off colonial domination. The peculiar nature of settler racism, therefore, arises out of fear.

However varied the group of settlers, they are united in the matter of the 'natives'. They are determined to retain their dominance, and individual settlers who have contrary views are often branded 'traitors' by their own community (Hartz 1964:22). Memmi too has noted the difficulties for settlers who recognise the injustice of the situation: they have only two real choices, to emigrate or to stay and join a group seeking 'native' emancipation. The latter course is the more difficult: not only will they face hostility from their fellows, there are problems assimilating with the 'natives', whose culture may be very different. It is also difficult to avoid a trace of racism 'in a country where everyone is tainted by it' (Memmi 1974:23). The difficulties are compounded for left-wingers, because of their 'very intense doubts and real uneasiness in the face of the nationalistic form of ... attempts at liberation' (Memmi 1974:28), by the left-wing tradition which abhors the use of violence for political ends and by the conservative social order that is often the aim of liberation movements. Racism in varying degrees, then, is endemic in the colonial situation; but it is generally the less-privileged settlers who are the most overtly racist, and these have a powerful voice in those settler societies which claim to subscribe to democratic (or, at least, populist) values. Their concept of democracy does not, however, extend to incorporation of the 'natives' (Kuper 1972:402–5).

Various ways are used to enforce settler domination. Coercion is the commonest way to establish a colony, but once set up there are always special laws intended to deter 'rebellion', and relations between settlers and 'natives' are based essentially on force. This was most apparent in Algeria where settlers were reinforced by the French Army. Coercive domination alone, however, is not enough if society is to function with some degree of normality. Hence 'structural' and 'psychosocial' domination also develop (Baker 1983:30).

Structural domination takes a variety of forms. Systems might be openly discriminatory, such as South African apartheid, or superficially 'non-racial' with all subject to the same laws, as in Rhodesia, where local authorities were left to decide the extent and type of segregation, absolving central government from any blame. The essence of structural domination, however, is that settlers have greater access to economic and political sources of power. At the same time, being wealthier and more powerful than the majority allows settlers to claim – and even to believe – that this is proof of their innate worth. This makes them more determined to keep a gap between themselves and the 'natives' as continued evidence of their right to dominance (Thornton 1965:188–9).

This gives rise to psychosocial domination – essentially, the process by which a powerful group convinces both itself and the subordinate group that its superior character and worth gives them a right to power. It takes the form of setting up a mythical portrait of the 'natives'. This picture is usually shared by the metropolis to some extent but it takes a particularly vehement form in the settler colony. Groups like the Masai, when they were no longer a threat because their numbers were declining, were romanticised as 'noble savages' (Hughes 1963:104); but in general the portrait is insulting and contemptuous. It is often the character of the 'natives' which is allegedly inferior – or in some cases even non-human, as when

Afrikaners referred to Africans as baboons (Lemon & Pollock 1980:84). At the same time settlers set up a mythical portrait of themselves as custodians of civilised values and hence worthy of their privilege. The 'primitive Manichaeism of the settler' (Fanon 1967b:115) divides colonial society into two groups, the settlers representing good and the 'natives' evil. Real or imaginary differences are stressed, to the detriment of the 'natives'. Significantly, there is a large degree of similarity between the mythical portraits of different sets of 'native peoples'. The commonest slur is laziness, supplemented by inefficiency, lack of ambition, ingratitude, deviousness, childishness, moral laxity, emotionality and superstition. They are easily manipulated by their traditional culture or leaders, and are prone to violence.

Not only does this portrait excuse settlers' usurpation of land and domination but in particular the accusation of laziness has been used to justify forced labour (Alatas 1978:2). Memmi (1974:79–82) uses several examples to illustrate this self-justification. The 'laziness' of the 'natives' contrasted with the 'industriousness' of the settlers justifies the latter's privileged position and the former's poverty; their 'weakness' justifies the establishment of a protectorate over them; their 'wickedness' justifies the police force and legitimates the severity of the system; since the 'natives' seem not to worry about their poverty, the settlers are absolved from making it their concern, especially as any attempts to help on the part of the settlers are likely to result only in 'ingratitude'.

The portrait is never totally without foundation, for if it were its falsity could soon be demonstrated; but whatever the 'natives' might have been before the settlement, the colonial situation itself encourages a lack of interest in the type of work available. Allport (Sunar 1978:517) claimed that dishonesty and deviousness are typical traits of the victim; and the colonial situation inevitably creates violence, among the 'natives' as well as against the settlers (Austin 1983:94–5). Nevertheless, whatever grain of truth there may be in the mythical portrait of the 'natives', it is still essentially mythical – the embodiment of popular ideas rather than an objective description.

'Native' culture, language, religious beliefs and practices, law and customs are similarly denigrated (Fanon 1967a:14), and attempts have been made to destroy it. Arabic was deemed a foreign language in Algeria and not taught in schools until 1947 (Guérin 1973:275). More frequently, however, the local culture has affected settlers, and settler societies develop a hybrid culture, different from that of the metropolis but not thoroughly assimilated into the 'native culture' (Lemon & Pollock 1980:81). On the whole, however, the gap between settlers and 'natives' is conveniently maintained by the cultural gap. Cultural denigration necessarily varies in its content according to the nature of the 'native society'. Raffles claimed that Malay society was backward and Malays were intellectually inferior on the grounds that they had no well-defined system of law, they were Muslims, they had previously been under Hindu influence and they tolerated the vices of their rulers (Alatas 1978:39).

A typical portrait of a 'native culture' is presented by a Rhodesian settler at the time of the Unilateral Declaration of Independence (UDI). It is no longer respectable to argue for biological inferiority (Fanon 1967b:31–2), and Peck (1966:7, 52–3, 59–63, 163) claims that culture, not skin colour, divides 'natives' from settlers. He describes the indigenous population at the time of early European settlement as illiterate, technologically two thousand years out of date, dirty, ignorant of money and all but rudimentary medicine, confirmed believers in witchcraft, lacking in common competence and uncivilised. It is clear that Peck thought little had changed or was likely to do so for a very long time.

One aspect of cultural denigration is the negation or rewriting of the colony's history before its conquest: only settlers make history (Fanon 1967c:39–40). One historical fact, however, that was hard to deny was the conquest of territory that 'began' the history of the colony. This was a clear act of usurpation which colonisers needed to transform into legitimacy. For Memmi (1974:52) this creates a problem of conscience for settlers, evidenced by their 'strenuous insistence, strange for a victor, on apparently futile matters. He endeavours to falsify history, he rewrites laws, he would extinguish memories – anything to succeed in transforming his usurpation into legitimacy'. This unacknowledged and never-resolved guilt explains for Memmi and other observers the peculiarly vicious and enduring form of racism in a colony, and the rage with which the settlers attack the 'natives', verbally if not physically.

The greatest source of stress is fear of the 'natives'. That a group so despised should be so feared is one of the contradictory features of the mythical portrait of the 'natives'. This fear has a variety of roots. Settlers fear their culture being 'swamped' by 'native' culture, and this fear usually heightens group solidarity, as do threats of economic competition. Settlers rightly assume that the 'natives' want to take their place; and, despite stereotypes of the 'lazy native', this threat can be real. The efficiency of African farmers in South Africa posed a threat which was banished only by discriminatory legislation (Baker 1983:82–3). Another fear is of 'native' sexuality and dilution of the 'superior' race through 'interbreeding' (Ridley 1983:74–90). Fear arises above all, however, from the possibility of the 'natives' attaining any degree of power and, in the twentieth century, of decolonisation and subsequent exile. Hence the greatest fear is of 'native aggression' leading to loss of power and of the stolen lands. So the stereotype of the 'native's' passionate, even violent, nature adds fear and distrust to contempt, and when the 'natives' strike back this is merely proof of their savage nature. They cannot insult and intimidate the settlers in return for racism as an institution depends on an unequal distribution of power. Not all of the 'natives' are considered rebellious or ungrateful, but agitators serving their own ends are claimed to have malign influence on 'natives' who would otherwise behave themselves (Porter 1975:181).

The subconscious knowledge that force alone would be insufficient if there were a 'native revolt' makes psychosocial and structural domination all the more important: hence the alarm, anger and panic which greets any attempt at 'native' emancipation (Mannoni 1964:87). It is not surprising that this fear is the most likely to enhance group solidarity and generate a 'siege mentality'. Whether it is their culture or their persons that settlers believe are under threat, they take extreme measures to ensure their survival when the threat reaches a climax (Baker 1983:115–6). Until then the siege mentality may be manifested in a physical sense such as the Boer *laager* or psychologically by imposing social and political barriers against the 'natives'. In most settler societies these threats from the 'natives' have indeed materialised, and have been publicised by the world media; and the conflict has been the more bitter because the settlers' behaviour is 'a composite of fear and rage' (Thornton 1978:303). As a result, events crystallise race prejudice so that most settlers are paralysed into an inability to think intellectually, consider change or admit past mistakes (Fanon 1965:167–8).

It is true that some individuals may cross the barriers and become assimilated into the settler group, but it is impossible for the whole group to rise, for this would end the colonial situation. It may even be of advantage to allow some 'natives' to attain greater status. They may be needed for the lower ranks of administration, policing and so on, or this may allow the settlers to deny charges of discrimination. They can point out that merit is rewarded in their society and claim that those who do not succeed are lazy or unambitious. The rise of some individuals (and indeed the kindness and concern of some settlers) does not, however, change the overall picture: 'a collective drama will never be settled through individual solutions' (Memmi 1974:126). Furthermore, even where the 'natives' have formal equality they may be informally excluded from full participation: 'The boundaries may shift but must always be retained, or the colonial situation loses its meaning and ceases to exist' (Mirande 1978:297).

MILITARY PHILOSOPHY applied to 'native revolts' in imperialist thinking holds that leniency is interpreted as timidity and the swiftest and most decisive way of putting down such revolts is 'the knock-out blow'. The laws of war among civilised nations do not apply to warfare against 'native peoples'. The British metropolis, however, which needed no standing army to guard its frontiers, could afford to be more 'liberal' in outlook, and used force less than other empires (Kiernan 1982:111), but for settlers in mixed colonies, ethics were a luxury, and even non-hostile 'natives' could not be conceded the same rights as settlers nor their lives the same value. Instead, the thoughts and actions of settlers and their descendants were conditioned by the necessity to ensure the success and continuing stability of the colony, and their main aim to keep what they had inherited, together with whatever their own efforts had added (Thornton 1965:188). Settlers knew that without their own efforts, however brutal they might be, the 'natives' might be able to take over power – and they would exercise it in their own interests. There was then a divergence of attitude between those living in the safety of the metropolis and those living in a 'perpetual state of emergency', whether actual or potential, and several writers have commented on the continuation and prevalence of violence in colonial situations after the initial, usually violent, expropriation of land from the 'natives'.

For settlers the violence of the 'natives' was inherent in their nature, and violence was not a result of colonisation but a valid reason for seizing the territory in the first place. The only defence against 'native' violence was more violence. Power could not be shared with the colonised since they could not be trusted; so it must be monopolised and defended by force if necessary. Frequently the mere possession by settlers of superior force was sufficient to deter revolt (Memmi 1974:93), but when they did attack, 'natives' were accused of cowardice, because the most appropriate form of attack, given their inferior resources, was guerrilla warfare involving hit-and-run tactics and often civilian targets. This kind of violence was denied legitimacy whereas the violence carried out by the state and bolstered by imperial law was seen as legitimate defence.

Another settler claim was that troublemakers formed only a minority of a generally contented 'native population' – so the solution was simply to eradicate the troublemakers. The often-quiescent behaviour of most 'natives' and their conformity, which is easily understood in the context of their powerlessness, was taken for acceptance (Berreman 1972:407). A contradictory settler perception, however, was that any form of protest, however mild, was ultimately aimed at destroying settler power; hence all popular movements were aborted and where possible destroyed.

The great majority of writers on settler societies are critical of them. Such societies contain distortions, even pathologies. Not only does simple justice demand the end of the colonial system, but the contradictions within the system and the subconscious and destructive guilt of the settlers make colonised societies, which are symbolised by racism, diseased and incapable of reform. Such a society is doomed to 'slowly drift away as a closed system, toward a condition of total meaninglessness' (Lanternari 1980:60). Hartz (1964:21–2), however, more optimistically believes that modern communications are such that societies of this type can no longer remain closed and will perforce change.

THE SETTLER REBELLIONS in Algeria and Rhodesia were among the major problems that settlers created for the metropolis. Both were exacerbated by the notion of 'kinship' between settlers and their metropolis (although it should be noted that in each case large numbers of the settlers had their origins outside the nominal 'mother country'). Emmanuel (1972:40) argues that the greatest problems for the British imperial power from the nineteenth century were its struggles with settlers and not with the 'natives', but this view devalues the resistance to imperial rule, from Ireland to India. Indeed, it was the successful resistance to French rule in Indochina that made the French army determined to hold Algeria. In the event, the settlers' dream of autonomy was, for most of those in countries where they formed a visible minority, eventually to end. The latest example is South Africa.

Metropolitan enthusiasm for empire was never universal, and it waxed and waned in Britain from the mid-nineteenth century onwards. There was even more antagonism to empire in France, though in the end empire was seen as a counterbalance to German might (Nadel & Curtis 1964:17–18). In both cases imperial rhetoric was not matched by actual expenditure on improving the lives of colonial subjects nor by giving them real liberty and equality. In Britain and France, most people were ignorant both of imperial policies and of the conditions in the imperial possessions. Only slavery aroused real public interest, and empire aroused real emotion only when imperialism was popularised among the British masses, above all by the cheap newspapers catering for the newly-literate towards the end of the nineteenth century. After the 'scramble for Africa' of the 1880s, there was a brief age of self-conscious imperialism when the British empire was vaunted as the strongest, largest and most benign the world had ever seen, and flags and banners became sacred symbols of the nation which now seemed to dominate the world (Thornton 1965:85).

Much of this was already illusion. Britain's economy was falling back in the world, her army was inadequate to defend such a huge empire and she was diplomatically isolated (Porter 1975:124). The greatest rhetorical excesses of imperialism occurred only shortly before the shaming outcome of the Boer War. Recruitment had revealed the poor physical quality of the British and the near-defeat by people regarded as nothing more than farmers exposed fundamental weakness in imperial might. Those who had dreamed of a liberal and humanitarian empire were disillusioned too, by the abandonment of South Africa to its white settlers (Huttenback 1975:96). By the 1930s, after the 1914–18 war and the economic miseries which followed, there had been a resurgence of ideas about the equality of all peoples (Fieldhouse 1966:378). This ideological change in the metropolis was not mirrored by change in the settler colonies, and the strains in the settler–metropolis relationship became worse in the twentieth century:

As the nineteenth century developed, this world of high policy grew ever more sophisticated and even more impatient with the obscurantism of primitives, whether white colonials or savages, who did not because they could not keep pace with its own kind of progress ... The improvements in world communications served only to emphasise this time lag in ideas, attitudes and practices between the metropolis and the colonial outpost (Thornton 1965:60).

A number of studies has observed the resistance to change in settler societies compared with the metropolis. Memmi (1974:98–9) describes the life of the colony as 'frozen ... its structure is both corseted and hardened ... a mask under which it slowly smothers and dies ... unable to be transformed'. Hartz (1964:6–7) explains this rigidity as the result of the hardening of early values to form a national value-system to which later immigrants conformed. Mannoni (1964:128) complains of a lack of originality and creativity, which Thornton (1965:43) explains by the small size and close-knit relationships of settler societies, such that anyone who aired radical or even innovative views might be thought disloyal and excluded from social life. Above all, continuance of the settlement depended precisely on the absence of change, both in the colony and in the metropolis which sustained it.

Dislike of change has been associated with higher than usual degrees of suspicion, rigidity, compulsiveness and anxiety (Austin 1977:31). A situation which breeds uncertainty, as the settler–'native' relationship does, is likely to produce individuals given to conservatism, reaction or even fascism, as they can support only governments that maintain the status quo, or in other words the framework of oppression (Memmi 1974:55–6). However, the root of settler conservatism and dislike of left-wing metropolitan governments can most plausibly be linked to a fear of political change that threatens settler interests. This fear is rational, for the greatest threat to settlers has been metropolitan acquiescence in independence under majority, that is, 'native', rule, though right-wing as well as left-wing imperial governments have 'betrayed' their settlers.

Decolonisation started between the world wars, when most of Ireland, excepting the majority of its settler community, broke away in a welter of violence while the white settler colonies of Canada, Australia, New Zealand and South Africa, which had loyally supported Britain in the war, were peacefully translated by the 1931 Statute of Westminster into Dominions with the power to make their own laws. There were serious disturbances in 1919–20 in Egypt, the Punjab and Iraq by nationalists for whom the First World War had revealed the weakness at the heart of empire. They, however, were not strong enough to exploit the situation, despite the revival of liberal anti-imperialism in Britain; and immediately before the Second World War, despite the gathering force of resistance movements, particularly in India, neither Paris nor London thought self-determination for other imperial possessions was inevitable or imminent.

The 1939–45 war, however, inevitably changed things, even if some were slow to realise this: Leo Amery complained in 1944 that the BBC overseas services were creating the impression that Congress was entitled to speak for all India; and the British post-war government devised a scheme, to run for forty-four years, to settle ex-soldiers in Kenya. Yet in 1947 India, Britain's largest and most prestigious colony, became the first of many independent members of the newly created British Commonwealth. This new phase of decolonisation was, however, a reaction to uncontrollable events rather than a policy, however much the British might claim that the transformation of empire into Commonwealth had always been its intention (Thornton 1978:280).

One of these uncontrollable factors was the further tarnishing of the image of imperialism in the eyes of colonial subjects. The savagery of the war on both sides sat uneasily with the notion of the civilising mission, and any kind of imperialism was a negation of the freedom for which the war had ostensibly been fought. Africans were not slow to see the implications of their own role in the war, when they had been taught to kill white men (Kiernan 1982:189). Most important perhaps was the fact that Britain no longer had either the military capacity, the economic strength nor the prestige to hold its reluctant empire, especially in the face of American and United Nations political opposition. There had long been guilt in liberal quarters at the disparity between domestic principles of liberty and the right of nations to self-determination; and the British Labour Party, steadily increasing its influence, had always taken an anti-imperialist line, even if it became more cautious about the timing of decolonisation as its accession to power became more likely (Robinson 1965:59). There was relatively little difficulty, then, in imperial ideology adapting to changed circumstances, especially with the invention of the Commonwealth.

The idea of empire was not given up immediately. The creation of two federations in Africa and one in southern Arabia was intended to retain British power there for a period at least. In Africa each federation consisted of one white settler state and two with little white settlement, which would gradually move towards some kind of independence guaranteeing whites an assured future. Gradualism was, however, unacceptable to nationalists. The Suez adventure of 1956, one of the last stands of imperialism, ended in ignominious retreat for the British and French forces in the face of furious opposition not only from the USA but from India and Canada; and in the end Macmillan's 1959 government resolved to depart as advantageously as possible from Africa, without overmuch concern whether indigenous political elites would be able to run the new states with the inadequate resources bequeathed them (Thornton 1978:283). The strategic motive for empire, however, was still important and the Aden revolt in 1964 was treated with severity against both militants and the civilian population (Kiernan 1982:211).

The French did not give up easily either. The war had split metropolitan France, which had effectively lost control over French North Africa, Syria and the Lebanon to the Anglo-American command. French pride, severely dented by the Vichy years, required the maintenance of empire. Coercion was the rule, and in 1945 40,000 Arabs were massacred in an 'Arab hunt' (Fanon 1965:176). The creation of the French Union, consisting of all its possessions united into the French Republic, was an attempt to avert the end of empire. All of the Union's residents became French citizens, and the protectorates of Tunisia and the Union of Indochina also had full autonomy except in foreign policy. The new citizens, however, were not convinced that anything had really changed. The regular army, which had carved out France's African empire, committing atrocities from the first against the ever-present 'native' resistance in Algeria, was still imbued with Vichy ideology and anxious to avenge its wartime humiliation. The professional army, which opposed decolonisation to the last, carried out a massacre in Madagascar and waged vicious colonial wars in Indochina and Algeria, giving substance to the fears of the colonial 'citizens'. Then in 1958 de Gaulle transformed the Union into the Community, and within a few years all but a few of the smaller possessions were politically independent.

WE CANNOT SPEAK of a straightforward dichotomy between settlers resisting and metropolis insisting on decolonisation. Even in the 1920s, those who sought to prevent white settler self-government in Kenya included 'mavericks among the white settler pack, who provided a steady stream of informed and lethal ammunition in books and articles and pamphlets' (Porter 1975:274). After the 1939–45 war there were those in white settlement colonies who welcomed or accepted decolonisation and the loss of white power (Hancock 1984:*passim*). Metropolitan reactions to settler opposition were

21

mixed and certainly some in the metropolis opposed decolonisation. It is fair to say, however, that, setting aside the special case of the French army, the bitterest opposition to decolonisation came from settlers threatened by it. Now the enemy consisted not only of the 'natives' but also the metropolis.

The metropolis certainly bore much responsibility for the situation in the mixed colonies. It was the artificial conditions of the empire that had allowed settler communities to take strong root and retain their dominance. Protected by the authority of the metropolis, they had no need to assimilate to the host community as minorities are usually constrained to do; but there was always indigenous opposition, and it was no accident that three of the world's main trouble spots in the 1970s, Northern Ireland, Israel and Rhodesia, could be directly attributed to the British empire's original interference with smaller and weaker communities than itself and the incursion of settlers (Porter 1975:348).

The resulting troubles were hardly new, however: settlers had always tended to defy metropolitan demands for reform. The Spanish colonists decided to sever their ties with Spain in the nineteenth century when ideas of progress for all led to a demand for drastic reforms in the colonies, in a very similar way to Rhodesia's UDI much later in 1965 (Gladwin 1980:8). The situation was further exacerbated when the mother country or powerful groups within it supported their colonists, as in both the Algerian and Rhodesian cases. These mixed messages from the metropolis gave settlers some grounds for hope that they might be allowed to keep their gains. French colonialism in particular was based on the assumption that it would last for ever and the British seemed unable to hold a consistent line on, for example, the future of Kenya. Despite the Devonshire Commission's proclamation in 1923 that Kenya was an African territory, Kenyatta was not allowed to testify before the Hilton Young Commission in 1929, which returned to the principle of trusteeship. The long history of unrest from this time, culminating in the emergency in 1952, did not prevent the settlers in a handbook of 1949 from portraying Kenya as an ideal settlement area (Winks 1969:125–6). Clearly they did not believe that the British would cease to support them, and the behaviour of the police during the 1952 uprising, which has been compared with that of Nazi Germany or Japan, seemed to confirm their hopes (Kiernan 1982:221). In the event the white community was too small to survive alone, and concern at the repression, in Britain as well as other Commonwealth countries such as India, led to Kenyan independence under majority rule being granted in 1963, despite bitter settler opposition.

The Southern Rhodesians, however, formed a larger and more powerful group, and even though their daily lives were shadowed by guerrilla warfare, their independence survived as long as South Africa underwrote it. Despite these factors, metropolitan ambivalence about decolonisation is thrown into relief by reactions to the Rhodesian settlers' defiance. A Labour government was in power, but few, even among the most anti-imperialist, advocated the use of force against settlers, and this fact was noted by Africans who remembered that Britain had shown less hesitation when Africans or Asians rebelled. Conservative opposition to force was predictable. The recent release of official documents has revealed that the Labour government was advised by 'experts' that force would fail, and since 1912 in Ulster the obedience of the officer corps of the British army could not be relied on. Similar trends had been apparent in the Algerian crisis. The French attempts at repression, on a bloodier scale by far than most British equivalents, continued throughout socialist as well as right-wing governments, and they culminated in the revolt of part of the army in favour of the settlers.

Despite this ambivalence, it is clear that formal empires are no longer fashionable and whatever lingering nostalgia for empire on the part of the British or French still exists, the open retention of colonial possessions without economic or strategic significance is no longer on the political agenda.

2 Can Ulster Protestants be Conceptualised as Settlers?

THE LITERATURE ON imperialism is huge and there is a number of studies of settler societies. Yet reading this literature induces a growing sense of puzzlement and unease. For Ireland, Britain's oldest and longest-held colony, is ignored by the majority of imperial theorists. Where they do refer to Ireland, they largely ignore the presence of a large settler minority. In studies of the effects of colonisation on 'native peoples', the Catholic Irish are rarely mentioned. The problems of settler–metropolis relations are occasionally included in accounts of empire, but the first major crisis that these invoked, the Irish Protestant resistance to Home Rule, is rarely mentioned. Yet at many points in the general surveys of the British and French empires, for example, comparisons with the Irish case come spontaneously to mind.

There are exceptions to this apparent conspiracy of silence in the general literature. Wallerstein (1974:88, 233, 261, 281), for example, defines Ireland not only as a colony but as an overseas possession whose colonisation was moreover a blueprint for that of North America and partly carried out by the same people – Gilbert, Raleigh and Grenville. It underwent typical colonial exploitation in England's mercantilist period of around 1650–1750; and its colonial status was confirmed by the Treaty of Limerick. A few other historians make passing references to Ireland's status as a settler colony, but on the whole a reading of the literature would suggest that Ireland has no place in the debate on imperialism or settler colonialism.

It is understandable that Ulster Protestants themselves should be uneasy at being categorised as settlers, given the current unpopularity of such a status in liberal thinking. Many Irish nationalists too have defined their problem as emanating directly from the imperial power rather than from that 'third factor that intervenes between imperialist capitalism and the peoples of the exploited countries' (Emmanuel 1972:36), that is, the settlers. The puzzle is why, although in recent years a small body of literature has appeared focusing specifically on Northern Ireland's origins as a settler colony, Ireland is so widely ignored in the general literature. Robinson (1965:4) points out that it was the British writers who paid little attention to Ireland. It is a matter for conjecture whether this is from shame; from the well-known British ignorance and apathy concerning Ireland; or perhaps from unease at categorising white European Irish Catholics in the same way as Africans and Asians. Whatever the reasons, a history of imperialism and settler colonialism without Ireland is like a play whose central character is missing from the stage – a 'Waiting for Godot'.

It would be an extraordinary perversion to deny that Ireland's history has been colonial at least since the time of Elizabeth I. The attempted twelfth-century conquest by the Normans was only partial and they retreated to the area known as the Pale and to various strongholds in eastern Ulster, where the Norman colonisers settled down to become members of the Catholic Anglo-Irish aristocracy. However a new stage in the relationship between Ireland and England arose from England's transformation into a Protestant state, completed under Elizabeth I, which also involved conflicts with Catholic European states. The renewed interest in Ireland therefore was not only economic but also strategic, as the security of Protestant England was threatened by the landing of Catholic French and Spanish expeditionary forces in Catholic Ireland.

A reliable garrison was needed to safeguard English interests, and this took the form of the Plantation, the expropriation and settling of large tracts of land, notably in the northern province of Ulster but also in Munster, by English and Scottish Protestants. The methods adopted for the Plantation in Ulster were brutal, according to an account by Lord Deputy Chichester: 'We killed man, woman and child, horse, beast and whatsoever we could find' (cited in Mansergh 1936:80). To establish legal title to the lands was hardly an obstacle since England had, by its own definition, established title to most of Ireland through the Norman incursions. The removal of the 'native' Irish from these lands, however, to make way for colonists did present a legal problem, and so the slaughters that occurred in both Ulster and Munster needed to be justified.

One line of justification was to consider the Irish as pagans. It was argued that the Irish must be heathen by choice since their system of government was antithetical to Christianity, and therefore the first step towards bringing the Irish into the Christian fold was not conversion but a change of government and the ousting of Gaelic law. Well-behaved 'natives' were to be treated as subjects under English law. Smith and Essex however soon found an opportunity to molest the Irish population and deprive them of the protection of this law. Ireland's cultural inferiority was advanced as the reason for this change of mind and since Gaelic law was 'opposed to all civility' the Irish had to be subjected by force (Canny 1973:592).

Since there continued to be a majority of 'native' inhabitants, Ireland qualified as a 'mixed colony', and so 'native trouble' was always a possibility. A major manifestation of this problem occurred with the 1641 rising. There had been no attempt on the whole by the colonists to assimilate. Catholicism, the religion of the Irish, had been proclaimed as damnable, and the Irish were despised as culturally inferior. Already uneasy at the uncertainties of life in a strange land, and inflamed by rumour and by greatly exaggerated reports of the numbers of settlers killed in the rising (Lecky 1916:69), Protestant fear and hatred of the Irish Catholics among whom they lived reached a height that lives on in Protestant folk memory. English retribution under Cromwell was swift and terrible, resulting in many more deaths among the Irish than had been perpetrated by them and a further loss of land throughout Ireland. This kind of 'overkill' was replicated in the late eighteenth century when the murder of a few Protestant gentry was avenged by the killing of hundreds of Catholic peasants in the 'Wexford massacres' (Goldring 1991:23).

There were further generalised conflicts between settlers and 'natives', the two best known arising in the wider European context. The first of these, the attempt by the Catholic James II to keep the English throne awarded by parliament to the Protestant prince William of Orange, brought Ireland into prominence in the late seventeenth century as the site of four major battles and the siege of the garrison town of Derry by James's troops. Notwithstanding Protestant historiography this was not a straightforward fight between the Protestant and Catholic denominations, but part of a wider European political struggle in which the Pope favoured the Protestant William and Irish Catholics were to be found in both the opposing armies. Nevertheless the Treaty of Limerick which ended the war asserted that the Crown's authority was the same over Ireland as it was over the colonies and Catholics were subjected to severe disabilities (Wallerstein 1980:265).

The second, the rising of 1798, which was an attempt to throw off British rule in Ireland, is similarly less straightforward than popular history would suggest and a good example of the difficulty the metropolis faced in dealing with settlers. It also involved European enmities, in this case between England and post-revolutionary France, and the rising was buoyed by the expectation of large-scale French military assistance, though this did not materialise. This was no uni-denominational affair either, as some Presbyterians, previously subject to certain of the same Penal Laws as Catholics had been in the eighteenth century, played a leading role in the United Irishmen movement which planned the rising. Other Protestants, including those in the Orange Order (which had originated in sectarian feuding between Catholics and Episcopalian Protestants in County Armagh), supported the British government. The end result of the rising, which was easily put down, was the abolition of the largely Protestant parliament which had sat in Dublin in the late eighteenth century.

This too, however, needs to be set into a wider context. In the time of the early British empire, England, Wales, and, after 1707, Scotland constituted the 'realm'. Ireland, the Channel Islands and the Isle of Man were 'dominions', and, although they were dependencies of the Crown, they had their own political institutions. However, Westminster could legislate for them, even though they were not represented in it. It was only in the economic sphere that British policy was clear-cut: the interests of the metropolis prevailed in trade and to some extent industry, to the grave detriment of the Irish economy (Wallerstein 1980:265–6). The British empire of the late eighteenth and early nineteenth centuries, on the other hand, operated on the principle that colonies should be under effective metropolitan control (Fieldhouse 1966:70). It was against this background, therefore, as well as against the background of the American and French Revolutions and the enmity of Catholic France and Spain, that Ireland was integrated into the realm of the United Kingdom.

The nineteenth century saw the spread of industrialisation; but in Ireland most industrial development was concentrated in Ulster, particularly in and around Belfast, which grew rapidly as a result of migration from other parts of Ulster. The linen industry paralleled the Lancashire cotton industry in giving birth to the new order and the proletarianisation of the Ulster peasantry. Engineering and shipbuilding industries followed, along with less tangible companions of industrialisation, notably a police force, which was established in 1839. In Ireland particularly this was a political police and an instrument of government policy, keeping watch on political associations that might threaten the state as well as keeping the peace in the normal sense (Boyce 1979:40). Irish Catholics had originally been forced to live outside the city walls, and the few who entered had been excluded from Protestant areas. Now they poured from rural areas into Belfast, constituting 34 per cent of the population by the 1850s, and Catholic–Protestant riots were frequent. In Derry too, which was already becoming a Catholic city, sectarian rioting accompanied the annual loyalist demonstrations, and throughout the nineteenth century the British government sought to ban these. Both cities were typified by residential segregation along sectarian lines. While North-East Ulster prospered, however, much of the rest of Ireland was devastated by a series of famines which brought slow reactions from the British government and even disbelief that there was any famine – and if there was it was due to 'Irish incapacity' (Field 1982:192). Famine and general poverty led to mass emigration, partly to Great Britain, but mainly to North America.

The nineteenth century also saw Catholic emancipation. This was followed by successive extensions of the franchise from 1832 onwards, which gave votes to Irish Catholics as well as to Irish Protestants. This gave constitutional nationalism a voice in the British parliament. At the same time there was agrarian violence in the

27

poverty-stricken areas of Ireland outside the relatively prosperous province of Ulster. All reforms which benefited Catholics were bitterly opposed by the Irish aristocracy and the Orange Lodges, and movements as mild as O'Connell's 1834 civil rights programme were greeted by a 'no popery' campaign in Dublin and much of Ulster, aimed at keeping Catholics powerless. This was to be the pattern with all attempts to accord Catholics equal treatment or to give them any degree of power. Gladstone's attempt to give Ireland Home Rule, which meant limited self-government, met virulent Protestant opposition. The Irish Unionist Party was born of this first Home Rule crisis. Many in Great Britain, however, also opposed liberalisation. Some opposed it on the grounds that England's security took priority over Irish aspirations. Others believed that the removal of grievances would be enough to kill 'the dream of a separate nationality which had no historical existence' (Thornton 1978:45). Nevertheless, during the period of 'constructive unionism' (1890–1905), some of Ulster's Protestants, and particularly the Orange lodges, were the fiercest opponents of attempted reforms (Gailey 1987:123–4).

The second Home Rule Bill was easily defeated but the third inspired military preparation as well as political action on the part of unionists. The constitutional changes promised in the Liberal election campaign meant that the monarch no longer had a veto and the House of Lords had only delaying powers. The Liberal Party under Asquith entered into an agreement with the Irish Nationalist Party. This formed an effective coalition with a substantial majority in the House of Commons. There was also a growing Labour Party which was unsympathetic to Irish unionism. So the passing of the Home Rule Bill was inevitable without resort to extra-constitutional means of resistance. It was clear that at least some Conservatives were prepared to act illegally or even treasonably, but the heartland of this resistance was Ulster where the majority of Protestant unionists were concentrated, and they chose as leader a Dublin barrister and member of parliament, Edward Carson. The 1912–14 crisis thus became the 'Ulster crisis'. As well as engaging in intensive political activity both in Ireland and in Britain, Irish unionists, in defiance of a government decree banning the import of weapons into Ireland, formed an Ulster Volunteer Force (UVF), armed themselves in preparation for civil war with England and selected a provisional government (Stewart 1967). They also exploited factors such as divisions within the Westminster parliament, the government's doubts about the officer class of the British army and the mood of the New Imperialism. All the major Protestant churches declared their opposition to Home Rule and, after a campaign involving every part of Ulster, a Solemn Oath and Covenant was signed by such huge numbers that there could be no doubt of the united resistance of the Ulster Protestants.

In the event, the bulk of the UVF volunteered for service in the 1914–18 war. Despite this the Home Rule Bill became law for the whole of Ireland in 1914 but was not implemented. The already existing sympathy for the cause of the Irish Protestants in some quarters in Britain was enhanced when the news finally broke of the tragedy of the Somme when the 36th (Ulster) Division (along with the predominantly Catholic 16th Division, as it happened) suffered spectacularly heavy losses; conversely, the 1916 Easter Rising in Dublin alienated some British sympathy, as did nationalists' refusal to accept conscription for Ireland.

The Dominions had responsible government and the trust of the metropolis: Ireland, like India, had neither, and the Irish had long been a security risk. Separation would therefore be dangerous; yet the very nearness that made Ireland a risk to England's security also meant that it could not easily be treated like a distant recalcitrant colony, and subjected to punitive measures whose extent would be unknown to and condoned by the public in the metropolis (Thornton 1978:135). In fact a dual policy was pursued, similar to that in India: concessions to moderates who wanted less than complete independence and fierce repression of 'sedition'. The latter included the punitive executions carried out after the Easter Rising and the actions of the 'Black and Tans' in 1920–21. In India this policy succeeded for a while but in Ireland nationalists refused either to be compromised with or suppressed. Guerrilla warfare made conventional British military victory impossible and the will to win was undermined by liberal and clerical criticism in Britain of the atrocities regularly reported in the press. The twenty years more of coercion desired by Lord Birkenhead in 1920 were supported neither by resources nor public opinion. In 1921 Lloyd George concluded a treaty with those he had previously branded 'a small nest of assassins' (Porter 1975:255) and in 1922 he handed most of Ireland over to Sinn Féin.

Irish unionists in the North had become Ulster unionists by 1912 and were forced to resign themselves to the new situation. Some had recognised that a war fought for the right of small nations to determine their own future had implications for Ireland too. British unionists had ceased to be reliable allies and Irish unionists resigned themselves to a compromise solution: the partition of Ireland. The struggle to prevent home rule for all of Ireland was abandoned, along with Protestants in the other three provinces. Three Ulster counties and their Protestant inhabitants were also sacrificed, because Unionists had only a small majority in the whole of Ulster. This left a British remnant to be known as Northern Ireland, containing an overall Protestant unionist majority of two to one over Catholic nationalists, although they held a clear majority in only three counties. Northern Ireland was to remain an integral part of the United Kingdom but with its own parliament at Stormont in Belfast. There was to be a Boundary Commission after six years which might exclude further land from this rump, but the Unionist government of Northern Ireland ensured that this proved a dead letter. Northern Ireland continued to be represented at Westminster but with larger constituencies than in England, Scotland or Wales.

Unionists quickly and, at first, illegally reassembled their own forces, numbering 20–30,000 men, almost all Protestants. From mid-1920 the Irish Republican Army (IRA) began to include the North in its attacks. The British Army was deployed, at first concentrating its forces against Derry Catholics but shooting civilians on both sides during sectarian rioting in Belfast. In order to give the Northern Ireland government virtual freedom from the necessity of appealing for help from the British government, official approval for transforming the illegal Protestant forces into a 'special constabulary' was soon sought and given, and special security legislation, the Civil Authorities (Special Powers) Act, was put in place. The target of these moves is clear from a 1920 memo:

> No rebel who wishes to set up a republic can be regarded merely as a 'political opponent', but must be repressed ... all officials who hold republican views ... should either be dismissed or given the opportunity of resigning or transfer ... This view should be firmly impressed on the military and constabulary authorities, who hitherto have considered that their responsibility is to act as mediators between those holding 'loyal' views and those desirous of establishing a republic (cited in Farrell 1983:41).

Only by the middle of 1922 (by which time 544 people had died in the North in two years) was Northern Ireland 'freed from what its Unionist population had seen as a combined military, economic and diplomatic assault on its very existence' (Kennedy 1988:8). In May 1922 Lloyd George acknowledged to the Cabinet that considerably more Catholics than Protestants had been killed in the North and that 'we had armed 48,000 Protestants' (cited in Farrell 1983:136). Thousands of Catholics had also been expelled from their homes and jobs. Nevertheless, and despite the fact that Britain was paying for Northern Ireland's local security forces, the convention was established by the 1922 Conservative government that Northern Ireland's domestic affairs could not be discussed at Westminster. British troops were from time to time deployed at the request of the Stormont government, but it was only with the arrival at Westminster of large numbers of Labour MPs that the draconian nature of the security legislation began to be questioned.

The rest of Ireland, although economically weak, posed a threat to Northern Ireland in laying claim to its territory and providing an 'ideological homeland' for Northern Catholics. This problem came to a head in the 1939–49 period, when southerners were granted residence permits for war work in Northern Ireland. This created fears in some quarters that Protestants would eventually be outnumbered and voted out of the United Kingdom. A big anti-partition campaign was launched to persuade the Labour government, long thought by Protestants to be over-sympathetic to Irish Catholics, to abolish the border and create an independent united Ireland. It became apparent that Northern Ireland's position was not secure: it was a detachable part of the United Kingdom. This led to a campaign to obtain Dominion status in order to secure Northern Ireland's future, but this was officially rejected by the Unionist Party. In the event the Ireland Act of 1949 not only freed the Irish state from membership of the British Commonwealth of Nations, as the empire came to be called, but promised Northern Ireland its continuation in the United Kingdom as long as its parliament so desired.

In 1963, in the light of accelerated economic decline, Prime Minister Brookeborough was replaced by Terence O'Neill, whose stated aims included building bridges 'between the two traditions within our community' (quoted in Bardon 1992:622). His efforts at reform, however, although very limited, increasingly alienated ultras, and the relative calm of the 1949–68 period ended with the rise to prominence of fundamentalist Protestant movements, the formation of the Northern Ireland Civil Rights Association (NICRA) and People's Democracy (PD), and the resurgence of the IRA and other republican military groups. Westminster not only sent troops but also took over the decision-making in security policy. Ultimately it suspended the fifty-year-old Northern parliament. Attempts to persuade Protestants to share power with Catholics foundered on ultra resistance, most notably in 1974, and direct or colonial rule was re-imposed while a quest for compromise continued. As in 1912–14 there was mass protest, including extra-legal activities and physical attacks on the Royal Ulster Constabulary (RUC). In addition Protestant military groups were formed with the stated aim of defending 'Ulster'.

There are obvious differences between the colonial history of Ireland and that of the nineteenth-century mixed colonies. Like Africans and other indigenes, Catholics were dispossessed of their lands, and their legal status was inferior to that of Protestants. This is no longer the case, and Catholics in Northern Ireland have equal rights in law with Protestants. More important is the fact that, in contrast with the settlement history of the nineteenth-century overseas colonies, it was an English government decision to settle Ulster. Moreover, in contrast with the virtually non-existent metropolitan interference in the overseas settler colonies, British intervention in Ireland has always been more direct, culminating in the current 'direct rule' of Northern Ireland from Westminster.

Nevertheless, what is remarkable about Irish colonial history is the extent to which it was a rehearsal for the acquisition, justification, maintenance and eventual loss of the wider British empire, with parallel problems elsewhere where settlers existed in significant numbers. Certainly nationalists in other subject nations of the British empire such as in India noted the similarities; and in particular took note of the fact that Britain could not even hold her 'Other Island'. This makes it all the more strange that this colonial history is ignored by many interpretations of the current conflict in Northern Ireland.

Of particular interest here are the similarities between twentieth-century Ulster Protestants and white settlers. For example, both claim that the 'natives' had no history until the settlement, and for Ulster Protestants history 'began' with the Plantation. Both see insurrections, such as the Indian Rebellion or the Easter Rising, as proof both that maintaining order is the prime need and that the 'natives' are unfit for self-rule. These attitudes have been apparent in Ulster Protestant thinking throughout the twentieth century. Such insurrections in Ireland have had similar effects to those observed in settler societies such as Algeria's – rather than consider change or admit past mistakes, ultras appear intellectually paralysed, unable to go beyond the old slogans of 'No surrender!' and 'Not an inch', and despite folk memories of the post-war Stormont years when Catholics and Protestants were allegedly good neighbours, unable to change the old ways of thinking of Catholics as different and dangerous.

UNIONISTS TODAY then can be expected to dislike implications that they are settlers for, as Whyte (1990:178) points out, to label a situation 'colonial' is to imply that it is both illegitimate and unlikely to last. The proud celebrations of that descent found among popular unionist historians earlier in the century (Jackson 1989:63) have therefore died, along with the British empire and the domination of white settlers in its African colonies.

Even when settler history was still regarded with pride, however, the threat of Irish nationalism provoked the defensive argument (which is still used) that there was no pre-Plantation Irish state and Ireland was never a nation: therefore the settlement was not a moral issue and Irish nationalism has no basis. In fact, there was no pre-existing state in many of the inhabited areas settled by Europeans, a factor which made settlement easier than if there had been, but no more ethical; and the concept of nationalism is in any case a modern one. In many cases it arises precisely out of the experience of conquest and/or subordination. Hence a claim to nationhood is no less valid an expression of common ethnic and cultural origins simply because it is relatively new. Nevertheless, behind such disingenuous arguments lie very real concerns.

A specific issue, rarely raised in public at any time this century and yet particularly important in the Irish context, is the former seizure of land from the Irish. In the early days of the Plantation Irish farmers were disadvantaged, not by being given poorer quality land than the undertakers, but by the proportion of land they were allotted, namely only 15 per cent in the Plantation counties outside Londonderry, where they had none. It was only as Protestant settlement spread that they were relegated to the poorer hilly districts (Robinson 1982:21). This pattern is still discernible today, and it is clear that a redistribution of land to its original inhabitants, were such a thing to be practical, would almost eradicate Protestant farmers, a fact of which they are aware. It is no wonder then that such large-scale expropriation of land is not a common feature of Protestant historiography; and it provides a particularly potent reason for playing down settler origins.

Republicans, nationalists and Marxists are on the face of it more likely to acknowledge the effects of the Plantation, but they have traditionally focused on British imperialism without differentiating it from settler colonialism. In this schema, Protestants were merely the agents and perhaps the victims of imperialism, and the existence of Northern Ireland is due to the British attempt to hold on to at least part of Ireland; if the 'imperial garrison' remained separate and evolved its own communal myths, this was either because it remained external to Ireland, or because of false consciousness. Certainly nationalists who propound the 'one nation' theory, which attempts to incorporate Protestants into an all-Ireland state, have an understandable motivation for their interpretation.

Modern unionist academics, especially those in Northern Ireland, tend to be as squeamish as 'ordinary' unionists about conceptualising Ulster Protestants as the descendants of settlers. Until recently most writers have simply remained silent on this aspect, effectively denying the present significance of Irish political history by focusing on other factors, such as the current sectarian divide. Since the current phase of the conflict began, however, there have been a few works asserting the primacy of Protestant settler origins. These use the comparative approach, in which the history and social structure of various groups is theorised as similar in essentials and the protagonists are labelled 'settlers' irrespective of their own views and desires on the matter, thus avoiding what in another context has been called 'the tyranny of popular conceptualisations for analytic purposes' (Mason 1985:420). The major comparisons are with Algeria, Rhodesia, South Africa and Kenya (see particularly Lustick 1985; Crotty 1986; MacDonald 1986; Weitzer 1990).

In response, a few unionist academics have been stung into attempting to refute the settler thesis or to deny that the Plantation has any relevance today. Their efforts, however, owe more to their politics than to intellectual rigour. One counter-argument is that the Plantation was a long time ago and no longer relevant (Walker 1990:37); another is that it consisted of little more than a continuation of millennia of migration in both directions across the Channel between Scotland and Ireland (Canavan 1988:207). These arguments use the terms 'migrant' and 'settler' as if they were interchangeable. Hence they rest on a definition of 'settler' that takes no account of the disproportionate amount of social, economic and political power involved in such a status. On the contrary, however, as long as settlers constitute a group which is seen to be distinct and which maintains status closure and a relatively powerful position *vis-à-vis* indigenes who present at least a latent threat to this supremacy, the settler society remains in place, however old the settlement is.

Status closure in Ireland was reinforced by endogamy, which was made practicable by the large number of settlers in Ulster (in contrast to the position of Protestants left outside the post-partition six counties). There is no doubt that conversions and inter-marriage took place; but flows over ethnic boundaries do not change the situation. Barth's (1969:9) observation is pertinent here: 'discrete categories are maintained despite changing participation and membership in the course of individual life histories'.

Furthermore, although it would be unrealistic to ignore the religious divide, it is impossible to disentangle it from the political one. Northern Ireland, although not the only place with a religious or sectarian divide, is a rare example of a region where religion is the best predictor of voting behaviour (Whyte 1990:72). Since every election since 1921 has been treated as a border poll, with nearly all Protestants and only a minority of Catholics voting to stay in the secular UK, it seems clear that more than doctrinal differences are involved.

The unionist academic stance is not, however, confined to academics from the North of Ireland; and O'Dowd (1990:55) observes that many intellectuals refuse the 'colonial' label 'not least on the grounds that it simply exacerbates the violence'. One could add that such a label legitimates republican violence and decriminalises its perpetrators, and hence is also unpopular with politicians from both Westminster and Dáil Eireann.

Of those works comparing Northern Ireland with other settler societies, the only sustained exercises in highlighting the main subject of this book, the triangular relationship between Protestants, Catholics and the metropolis, are Lustick (1985), whose work is on Ireland as a whole and substantially ends with the nineteenth century, and Weitzer (1985, 1990), whose focus is security policy in Northern Ireland, first under the Stormont government and then under the British government. My study is in some ways a continuation of Lustick's, carried over into the twentieth century and confined to the North of Ireland; and it covers roughly the same time-span as Weitzer's but is both broader, in looking beyond the security question, and at a different level, in focusing on the settler mentality rather than settler institutions. In contrast to the comparative literature, however, the approach here is phenomenological, in drawing on the expressed views of the people directly concerned.

The local newspapers and their correspondents are much less reticent than unionist academics or 'respectable' politicians, and some emphasise their settler origins in most definite terms, while others demonstrate a suggestive affinity with settler societies. Certainly as the twentieth century advances, direct references to settler origins become rarer as settler societies fall to decolonisation, illustrating Lustick's (1985:82) point that settlers' maintenance of 'a steadfastly instrumentalist view of the linkage between the peripheral territory and the metropole ... springing from settler interests in protecting their privileges, provided the political and psychological basis for expedient adaptation to changing circumstances'. Hence some take 1921 (or even 1972) as a historical starting-point, as indeed do some unionist academics (see, *inter alia*, Roberts 1986; Aughey 1990). This implies that imperial or settler interpretations of Northern Ireland are now redundant because of partition and the decline of empire. But such transitions do not occur simply through treaties. The British situation has certainly changed, from empire to nation-state to member of the European Community; the settler mentality on the other hand shows greater durability, as the following demonstrates.

IN THE 1912–21 PERIOD there are examples from three local newspapers of outright assertion of the settler origins of Ulster Protestants or the need for protection against the 'natives'. The *Londonderry Sentinel* (LS 2.1.13) feared they would be 'deserted by those whose forefathers planted them in the province under the guarantee of Imperial protection' and claimed that 'the people of Great Britain are responsible for the presence in Ireland of the Protestant minority' (LS 12.6.13). The danger of 'the two races mentioned by Macauley coming into collision', no matter whether one of them was now swayed more by Hibernianism than by Roman Catholicism, necessitates the continuation of Imperial control (LS 3.9.12). Similarly the *Portadown News* (PDN 25.5.12) sees the situation in settler–'native' terms:

> Should the British Crown place in jeopardy the property and the lives of the loyal subjects of the North of Ireland, history could record no baser betrayal. From time to time within the last 300 years, our forefathers came to this country on the invitation and under the guaranteed protection of the British Government. Some of these came from England; most from Scotland. Planters they

were called, and inducements were held out to them very similar to those that are being offered at the present time to the surplus population of this country to go out to our Colonies, where, as they are reminded, they will still be under the protection of the Army and Navy of the United Kingdom. The lapse of time has brought no fusion of races in Ireland. Between Saxon and Celt there is at best only an approach to friendship. The minority still requires protection, the only change in the situation being that if outside protection is withdrawn, they can and will protect themselves.

Furthermore the settlers had, according to a Presbyterian speaker, Montgomery, come to Ulster with a civilising mission:

> their forefathers had been brought to this land at the bidding of the Government of the day for the purpose of introducing useful industries, and setting before the inhabitants a better standard of duty and life than then obtained in Ulster ... habits of self-reliance, industry and perseverance ... Their sons and daughters had in turn gone out to colonise other parts of the Empire (PDN 8.6.12).

Thus the least the country that had 'sent their forebears pioneers in the dark days to a wild and perilous land' should do in gratitude was to thwart the Home Rule attempt (PDN 13.9.13).

The *Impartial Reporter* was also unequivocal on Protestant origins, describing the province as 'the Ulster of the Plantation' or similar (IR 9.5.12). The settlement (in some undefined way) made Ulster into 'the unconquered colony' (IR 1.5.13, 10.2.21), presumably because 'Ulster' is identified with Protestant settler interests and there had been no conflict between the metropolis and settler Ulster. One main concern of this paper, however (a Presbyterian-owned paper in a mainly Church of Ireland county), was the value of the Scottish as opposed to the English settlers and the kinship of modern Protestants with their Scottish ancestors:

> The average Ulsterman possesses the tough and indomitable stubbornness of his Scotch ancestors, combined with the enthusiasm of the Irish nature ... The opposition that would effectually stop the Celt has no terrors for him. The Ulster-Scot may be dogged in his views, perverse, if you like, in holding them, but hold them he will. The English settler in Ireland often fell into Irish ways or became absorbed; the Scotch remained distinct, and their stronghold is in the province which they have made what it is (IR 29.8.12).

Both English and Scottish were, however, differentiated from the 'native' Irish: 'The Ulsterman (two-thirds Scotch and one-third of him English) is altogether a different man from the Irish Celt' (IR 15.3.17).

The *County Down Spectator* and the *Ballymena Observer* were more cautious in their approach to Protestant origins. The former merely commented that 'we have been accustomed under the Imperial Parliament to rule in our own Province' (CDS 30.11.18). The *Ballymena Observer* from the start preferred the term 'loyal Protestants of Ireland' (BO 23.2.12). The vital matter of metropolitan protection for the loyalists, however, is unequivocal: without English law and 'the flag which has prospered them, and whose folds have ever been ready to shelter them in time of trouble' (BO 25.7.13) the very existence of Ulster (i.e. loyal Protestant Ulster) is in doubt (BO 12.4.12). The *Londonderry Sentinel* too became more cautious: it is clear that the Plantation had been used by enemies as an argument against Ulster Protestants and from 1918 the paper stressed their 'loyalty', opposed to Catholic 'hatred of England', rather than their origins (LS 25.4.18).

The *Portadown News* and the *Impartial Reporter* were not to change their basic approach, but both opined that the origins of the settlement were no longer relevant as the Protestant Ascendancy had died, deservedly in the opinion of the *Impartial Reporter* (IR 22.2.12). The *Portadown News* therefore found another explanation for Catholic discontent:

> at this day there is not a single advantage, religious or political, enjoyed by an Irish Protestant that is not possessed, if anything in fuller measure, by an Irish Roman Catholic. The way to wealth is open alike to all ... The lack of harmony between two peoples living in the same country, where they might be expected to work together for the common good, is of course greatly to be deplored. While each side blames the other, blame must be really laid at the door of British Statesmen who, instead of governing the country resolutely and justly, have pandered to the forces of sedition, and sacrificed its best interests to Parliamentary manoeuvres (PDN 25.5.12).

This dual recognition of settler origins and denial of their present relevance survives in the editorials of the *Impartial Reporter* in the 1939–49 period and beyond, even though Northern Ireland by 1939 had had its own government for eighteen years and references to settler origins were now rarer. The contribution of 'the "Planters" who came over to Ulster and made Ulster what she is to-day, in the same way as the white man made the United States' (IR 28.2.46), and the kinship with Great Britain (IR 2.1.47) were, however, less important than the fact that Irish or Catholic grievances, which the paper admitted to have had substance at one time, have been valid only in the distant past: 'Let the past bury the dead. Every nation has suffered in the past, but the leaders of the Irish nation alone keep harping on what happened 200 or 300 years ago' (IR 24.5.45). A more ingenious response (and a device typically used by certain writers to avoid answering criticism) is this excuse for the Plantation and its effects: 'one of our Republican friends, who is still moaning and groaning about the Irish who had to flee from Ireland a few hundred years ago, forgetting of course to relate how the Huguenots were turned out of France at the same time!!' (I L Montgomery IR 27.4.44).

A few referred to 'the spirit of the Planter stock' (LS 13.7.39) and to Ulster Loyalists as Britain's garrison in Ireland (LS 14.12.39), but more often the terms 'Mother Country' and 'Motherland' reveal self-perceived origins (LS 18.4.39; PDN 31.3.45), as do references to the British as kith and kin, the same blood and the same race, as opposed to Irish Catholics (LS 16.12.48). Only the *Portadown News* editor, however, went so far as to call Northern Ireland 'this western outpost of Empire' (PDN 19.4.47).

The self-appellation of settler survives among both ultras and moderates into the period from 1968, although with modifications and with differences between the two groups. Much of the material is inferential rather than explicit but there are some direct references. One of the few ultras who acknowledged settler origins admitted some reservations about them, but the end justified the means:

> I admit some horrible atrocities were perpetrated; families being slaughtered to make room for settlers is indefensible. However, I sincerely believe that the Plantation brought industries to Ulster which we might not have had otherwise (John S Davidson CDS 13.6.69).

In addition, it was the English who had terrorised Ireland whereas the Scots had brought the industrial spirit; and after the suspension of Stormont he suggested that the anniversary of the Plantation by Scots should be celebrated (John S Davidson CDS 27.6.69, 4.8.72).

Another claim that takes any odium out of the Plantation is that it is Catholics who are the outsiders:

> Can Britain now desert her friends and allow an alien population to determine the fate of Britishers who have lived here generation after generation and who by their skill and enterprise made this country to 'blossom as the rose'? (OS June 1984).

It can be conjectured that it was partly settler rebellions such as those in Algeria and Rhodesia which brought some odium on the concept of settler colonisation and hence a need among some of Ulster's Protestants to modify or deny such origins. One way of doing this was to point out that modern Ulstermen are a racial mixture ('British and Irish' PDN 14.3.69; I L Montgomery IR 10.6.71); more popular, however, is the adoption of Adamson's (1974, 1982) ideas to claim that the 'so called Planters ... were the descendants of the original inhabitants of the country' ('Observer' IR 7.9.72). This does not, however, preclude pride in the Plantation. Douglas Sloan managed to combine a denial of Planter origins with pride in them. In an editorial headlined 'Who are the Planters?' he wrote:

> if there is anything likely to raise the hackles of any Ulster Protestant it is the suggestion that he is not an Irishman. He may describe himself as British but certainly not as 'planter'. Of Planter stock he may be, but then so also are many of the so-called 'native' Irish. Some of the 'native' Irish are people who came via the Armada, and some who came from other European countries ... How many people who would today call themselves Irish are, in fact, the direct descendants of the Normans? ... Here in Northern Ireland we have families who have lived in Ulster for centuries ... there also arrived on our shores people from Scotland (the original Irish) who with their families even today must bear the stigma of 'planters'. They, with the English, took over desert land and made it blossom as the rose ... Berkeley, Swift, Goldsmith, Sheridan, Yeats, Lady Gregory ... would come under the term 'planter stock' (PDN 10.10.69).

Similarly Protestants have a stronger and prior claim on Ireland than anyone else, by their race (as the Plantation Scots were simply returning to their original homeland), by their religion (the independent British Church dates back to the first century) and, the eternal settlers' claim, by the fact that 'the Protestants also have a better claim to the land in respect to what they have made of it' (Jerry Hardy PDT 5.5.72).

There is even more indirect evidence. First there is the self-identification with the Scots and the Scottish origin of many Protestants, noted for the earlier period of this study and expressed by many modern letter-writers (see for example John S Davidson CDS 26.7.68 and 'Scotland the Brave' BO 1.3.79). Rather fewer express kinship with the people of Great Britain in general. Then there are expressions of the links with other settler societies.

The bicentenary of the American Revolution plus a later proposal to twin with a US town were reminders of the part played by Ulster-Scots, when they fought in Washington's armies ('Interested Loyalist' CT 11.8.76). More common, however, are comparisons with small threatened settlements such as Gibraltar and the Falklands. An early article claimed that 'the British Parliament is preparing to write-off the Province of Ulster, just as it is plotting to write-off Gibraltar and the Falkland Islands' (PT 8.3.69). Such parallels became more striking on the Argentinian invasion. The *News Letter* (which carried far more editorials on the Falklands crisis than the *Belfast Telegraph*) darkly hinted at the possibility of a similar Irish invasion encouraged by the 'appeasement policies' of the Foreign Office (NL 3.4.82); but the vigour of Britain's response and the hostile attitude of the Irish prime minister temporarily revived the editor's hopes that the re-discovery of Northern Ireland's strategic position as 'the nation's vital Atlantic lifeline' might save it from Irish unity (NL 7.4.82) and that the 'renunciation of flabby and appeasing policy' spelled hope for Gibraltar and Belize as well as for Ulster (NL 10.4.82). The paper rejected Prior's claim that the Falklands and Northern Ireland could not be compared (NL 19.4.82); but it was the *Impartial Reporter* (IR 22.4.82) which most clearly spelled out the comparison:

> The people of Ulster are watching with particular interest how the British Government handles the Falklands crisis for they see in it many parallels with the situation in Ulster. It involves in each case a people in the land of their birth who wish to remain under the Union Jack despite the attempted encroachments by larger neighbouring countries ... There is the inevitable choice: backing down in face of a dictator's invasion of an island whose people depended on Britain for their protection, or entering into armed conflict. Ulster and the world are watching.

Some moderates then, like ultras, see parallels between Northern Ireland and the Falklands. Reports that the British government was planning to hand over their sovereignty, 'although the 1,800 inhabitants of British descent want to preserve their present relationship with the UK' show that 'the situation has many parallels with Ulster' (IR 11.12.80); and when the argument developed into war those self-styled moderates who advocated a military solution for their own conflict (see chapter 8) hoped that similarly strong action would be taken in Northern Ireland (PDN 28.5.82; IR 17.6.82). The *Belfast Telegraph*, however, sees few parallels (BT 26.7.82). Hopes raised during the crisis soon gave way first to the suspicion and then to the conviction that Northern Ireland, on the government's past showing, might not receive the same determined aid as the Falklands ('Antrim Loyalist' BO 30.9.82). It is clear, therefore, that Ulster Protestants' interpretation of the problem differed from that of the British government.

There are also expressions of solidarity with white settler colonies in Africa, of British but not of French origin. The most popular were Rhodesia and South Africa. By the start of the modern period the Kenya settlers had long lost their struggle for independence under white rule, and the only parallel drawn between Northern Ireland and Kenya came after the 1983 IRA break-out from the Maze prison, when Professor Kennedy Lindsay (LS 1.2.84) compared the 'Mau Mau' with the Provisional IRA and Sinn Féin, and claimed that a terrorist break-out had similarly been connived at by the British authorities in order to prevent an electoral slide to the 'Mau Mau' (despite the writer's claim that the black majority in Kenya were 'law-abiding' and so presumably would not have voted for the 'Mau Mau'). This was followed by a reign of terror intended both to reassert the authority of Mau Mau leaders and to 'bring the demoralised and near-defeated members into a frame of mind where they could believe that the terms of the agreement were being extorted unwillingly from the authorities and were worth accepting'. This reign of terror was also useful to the 'Whitehall officials' as they could conceal the 'prison origins of the agreement and .. play upon the heightened fears of the law-abiding majority population when it baulked at the terms'. Lindsay's 'disquiet' at the parallels with the IRA escape is 'not lessened by the knowledge that various senior officials who formulate Northern Ireland policies served in Kenya during its emergency'.

South Africa received a number of sympathetic references. Two articles by local residents who had visited southern Africa (Col R L Carew CDS 19.4.68; Philip W Beach CDS 19.7.68) expressed admiration, the first of them claiming that apartheid is 'far from being oppressive' and is what Southern USA blacks were asking for; the same articles also praised Rhodesia and supported its rebellion. It is South Africa's great wealth that makes 'the Soviets want to kick out the Christian white man who governs this land' (PT 13.4.68). The *Orange Standard* gave addresses to write to for information on the two states (OS May 1976), and affinities with South Africa were also expressed by 'Another WASP' (OS Mar 1980) complaining about 'those despicable thugs who had the nerve to protest about our fellow brothers from South Africa over here while playing rugby'. Other examples are the bracketing of 'South Africa, Rhodesia and Ulster [as] invaluable allies to England in two world wars' (BO 2.7.81) and the information that 'Northern Ireland has very few friends around the world but one true friend is the *South African Patriot* (SAP) the magazine of the Herstigte Nasionale Party (HNP)' (OS April 1984).

Far closer to some hearts than South Africa, however, was Rhodesia. The Smith government's unilateral declaration of independence for 'loyal Rhodesia' (PT 7.1.67) led the *Protestant Telegraph* to devote much of its 13.4.68 issue to the support of Rhodesia, stressing its Christianity, civilisation, peace and prosperity, good treatment of Africans who nevertheless deserve segregation, self-sufficiency and record of volunteering in the last war. In similar terms to excuses for Protestant rebellion made in the third Home Rule crisis (see chapter 6), UDI is Prime Minister Wilson's fault rather than that of its perpetrators (Henry Clark BO 23.5.68). Once the Rhodesian war began in earnest, Beryl Holland (CDS 11.2.72) sighed for a security policy in Northern Ireland like that in Rhodesia. The suspension of Stormont, however, and Westminster's refusal to reinstate rule by simple majority while insisting on it in Rhodesia gave a different slant to the Rhodesian affair and created something of a dilemma. How could Protestants advocate majority rule for the province while denying it for Rhodesia?

One way was to stress the rights of settlers over backward peoples. Praise of Rhodesia's enlightened African education policy gave way to accusations that majority rule was being offered to uneducated coloured people (Beryl Holland CDS 6.7.73), 'bush natives' and savages at whose mercy the British government is prepared to leave the British communities of both Northern Ireland and Rhodesia (J W Stanfield CDS 12.3.76). The settler view is expressed in the claim that the British colonisation of Rhodesia has 'made it the prosperous country it is today' (Beryl Holland CDS 7.1.77). When majority rule was seen to be inevitable, one paper recognised the illegality and oppressiveness of the Rhodesian regime but nevertheless castigated the Zimbabwe Patriotic Front, and cautioned 'out of our Northern Ireland experience' that there should be no settlement involving terrorists (OS Sep 1978). That Britain has not been forgiven for handing over the settlers to the mercy of the said 'terrorists' is shown by an editorial at the time of the Falklands affair, speculating sympathetically that 'in Rhodesia ... the rapidly contracting white population ... will sigh that [Lord Carrington's] departure did not come years ago' (NL 10.4.82). Indeed, a strain running through ultra writings was distrust and dislike of 'the fatal Foreign Office attitude that has caused the loss of British possessions in various parts of the world' (NL 5.4.82) and dictated 'softly, softly' policies in its desire to 'placate international opinion, particularly in the United States' (NL 19.2.94). A final parallel was drawn as the Anglo–Irish talks progressed:

> Westminster stabbed the White Rhodesians in the back to give majority rule to the blacks; the result was catastrophe, the tribes fighting against each other. Does Mrs Thatcher want the same catastrophe in Northern Ireland, by also stabbing her loyal friends in the back? (Beryl Holland CDS 22.8.85).

Rhodesia was a problem, as it was for ultras, for those moderates who see a parallel with Northern Ireland. For example, for a Unionist Party of Northern Ireland (UPNI) member, identifying both Northern Ireland and Rhodesia as undemocratic dictatorships since power could not change hands, majority rule could be advocated for neither country (David Humphries CDS 25.2.77). The *Belfast Telegraph*, however, rejected the comparison with modern Ulster: 'Ulster is not Rhodesia ... there is no future for a 1912-style Ulster, inward-looking and isolated – and most Unionists know it' (BT 11.2.72). Many moderates as well as ultras expressed abhorrence of the idea of UDI for Northern Ireland: independence is thought neither desirable, nor economically viable, as the *Belfast Telegraph* once again reminded its readers: 'Everyone knows how essential the British link is to Ulster's standard of living ... the gap between income and expenditure ... is believed to be around £3 billion and rising' (BT 14.12.93). The same argument is, of course, used against Irish unity.

The unpopularity of the idea of UDI for Northern Ireland means that proponents of independence have to be cautious about using the term. Hence a number of letters insisted that Craig or Vanguard's aim was not UDI but simply full control of Ulster's internal affairs. One article displayed the problems of this stand: 'Those who [are determined that Ulster should go it alone] ... do not advocate a U.D.I. ... they would seek an agreed separation, Mr Heath notwithstanding' (OS Jan 1973). This presumably means that sections of the Conservative Party would lend support, as they had in the third Home Rule crisis. This problem of 'UDI' resurfaced in the wake of the Anglo–Irish Agreement, long after Rhodesia was no more ('20th Century Unionist' BTimes 17.7.86). One writer expressed the old abhorrence of the term UDI while proposing independence (Thomas Chittick CDS 10.4.86); three letters proposed UDI in unequivocal terms ('Concerned Unionist' PDT 28.3.86; R McKenzie PDT 22.8.86; 'Strategist' BTimes 17.4.86); and there were calls for a Provisional Government of Ulster (Rev Hugh Ross IR 24.9.87, 24.3.88), described as a 'mad scheme' (IR 8.10.87). More recently the Ulster Defence Association's (UDA) 'doomsday' plan based on re-partition was rejected by the *Belfast Telegraph* on the grounds that 'any new "Protestant" statelet would be shunned by the world, cut off by sanctions and reduced to absolute penury' (BT 17.1.94). Overall the comparison with Rhodesia, in the light of Rhodesia's rebellion, is a problematic one for Protestants.

The comparison which most enraged ultras is that with Algeria, which was discussed in a correspondence in 1972. As in academic writings on the topic (see Roberts 1986), it is notable that the validity of the comparison depends on the historical starting point: for two letter-writers, going back to pre-Stormont days, the two situations are similar and the logical solution is a united Ireland. Four answers are given to this, which essentially extract from the equation that part of Ireland which had been successfully settled: seventeenth-century Ulster was 'the least densely populated of the provinces and more like a wilderness'; Ireland had not been united before the Plantation; Northern Ireland is not a colonial situation;

and 90 per cent in modern Ulster want to stay with Britain (A Edwin D Fleming IR 4.5.72, 20.7.72). The Algerian analogy was raised again in 1994, when the MP for Upper Bann, David Trimble, 'drew a parallel with what happened in Algeria in 1962 when over a million "Pieds Noir" French settlers left ... [despite the fact that] all sorts of guarantees and promises were made to the French population ... about their culture and traditions being protected'. The difference, however, is that 'Ulster Protestants constitute a big majority in Northern Ireland' (OS Mar 1994).

A more favoured comparison was with the white Dominions. There have been three major periods when there has been a demand for Dominion status for Northern Ireland: the war years up to the Ireland Act of 1949; the period following the suspension of Stormont in 1972; and to a far smaller extent the period after the Anglo–Irish Agreement. Admiration for the progress and loyalty of the Dominions from the First World War onwards was not of course confined to Ulster, but an additional feature of such praise is that Ulster people (that is, Protestants) were among those who founded countries like Canada, Australia and New Zealand. Certainly the historically high rates of emigration have resulted in many cases of family ties within the white Commonwealth (as well as with South Africa and the USA).

It is clear, however, that while parallels with such as Rhodesia (and Algeria) were particularly close before 1921, no situation is exactly like that of Northern Ireland, with its large minority which resists the British link, its geographical closeness to the metropolis and its economic dependence on Britain. Nor was the nature of the link between settlement and metropolis so ambiguous in the other cases. So what is the nature of this link?

Local ideologists are prone to deny vehemently that Northern Ireland's situation is colonial: yet there is a wide perception that Britain sees things in this light, and there are implications that Northern Ireland under Stormont had corresponded to something between a Crown Colony and a Dominion. There are, for example, references to Northern Ireland being an 'outpost of the Commonwealth' (PDN 10.11.72) or 'this British outpost in Ireland' (OS Sep 1973) which clearly suggest a comparison with distant colonies separated from the motherland. The very constitutional position of Northern Ireland had a peculiarly imperial tinge, with the possibility for 'the minority party' to make 'a direct appeal to the Judicial Committee of the Privy Council' (John Kerr IR 29.11.79) and a Governor as the monarch's representative, whose removal was extremely unpopular in some quarters (OS July 1973) and 'an erosion of the rights' of the majority of the population (NL 20.7.73). It was Martin Smyth (OS Dec 1976/Jan 1977), the Orange leader, who in a speech at the Oxford Union most clearly outlined Northern

Ireland's position under Stormont, and hence the position of the unionist majority:

> Even where, under self-government in some part of the former British Empire, there has been scandal, oppression, bloodshed on a large scale, cruel and arbitrary dictators, the British government does not step in to withdraw that self-government ... Now it is obvious that the case of Northern Ireland is different from that of overseas member states of the Commonwealth, like India or Uganda. It is here in the British Isles and within the United Kingdom. The self-government given to it was a devolved self-government, limited in nearly all respects to internal affairs. It was a much less extreme, a much more muted grant of self-government than that given to any of the Commonwealth countries. The act setting up the parliament and government of Northern Ireland provided for the retention of ultimate Westminster control but this was not pursued in practice. The UK government made it a regular constitutional practice to consult the Ulster government about any Westminster legislation that would directly concern it, and as early as 1925 the British government let the Ulster government be a party to an agreement with it, which was subsequently registered at Geneva with the then League of Nations as an agreement between nations. And the last man who was appointed to the office of Governor of Northern Ireland, the Queen's representative there, has revealed that he was instructed, like the Governor or Governor General of one of the member states of the Commonwealth, to be guided by the advice of the Northern Ireland Government rather than by the Government of Westminster. So not only was the legal framework of the Northern Ireland Government established by Westminster but also the constitutional custom of treating the Northern Ireland Government as an entity in its own right was also firmly established by long usage, with all the obligations and expectations that this involved. In all the circumstances ... it is hardly surprising that when after half a century, the parliament and government of Northern Ireland were suddenly and very arbitrarily suspended and closed down, the reaction of a large proportion of our people in Ulster was rather like that of the people of Prague when they wakened one morning to find Russian tanks in their streets. Nor is it surprising that, though they have felt it necessary to tolerate what has been put in the place of their own government, they have never really regarded it as the lawful government of their country.

Intentionally or not, he outlined the differences and similarities between Northern Ireland and Southern Rhodesia. The main difference between Northern Ireland and the whole Commonwealth is geography; a secondary difference is that Northern Ireland's self-government was limited unlike that of the Dominions and the newly-independent nations; but both the principle of ultimate Westminster control and the fact of this principle being waived continued to exist in two entities, the white settler Crown Colony of Southern Rhodesia 1923–64, and the Protestant settler 'state' of Northern Ireland 1921–69, both of which in the main came to see the local government as the only legitimate one.

Whether by direct reference to settler origins or by reference to affinities with the people of Great Britain and with other states of settler origin, it is clear that many of Northern Ireland's ideologists have seen themselves as inheritors of a proud tradition of British settlement throughout the globe. It is notable that the substantial Irish Catholic contribution to this process was rarely, if ever, mentioned. Perhaps forced emigration through famine or hardship is 'passive', in contrast to the 'active' quality of the British imperial thrust. Certainly ultra propaganda seized upon whatever appeared to bolster its basic thrust, namely that Northern Ireland should stay British, in the contemporary circumstances. Thus the settler argument was used on occasion because it might appeal to the British conscience. This does not, however, invalidate the fact that the origin of Northern Ireland's Protestants lay in the conquest and settlement of Ireland, a fact acknowledged directly or indirectly by a number of editors and writers to unionist newspapers.

In contrast with aggressive ultra assertions, moderate acknowledgements of settler or Planter origin tend to be either apologetic or merely factual. One moderate expressed shame in his origins, being afraid to trace his ancestry 'in case I might find that some of my ancestors had participated in the butchery of fellow Irishmen' (W J Wright BO 23.7.70). Others who acknowledged and deprecated the settler origins of Protestants and the injustice of the Plantation blamed it on English imperialism and strategic concerns resulting in exploitation and atrocities (John Young Simms CDS 21.1.83; Edward Archdale IR 18.4.85; 'Disillusioned' LS 22.1.86), though for one writer this was sufficient reason to retain the Union and British protection (Paul J M Campbell CDS 6.6.69, 20.6.69).

David Armstrong, editor of the *Portadown News* from 1973, the *Portadown Times* and the *Craigavon Times*, accepted Protestant settler origins without apparent pride (PDT 27.11.74) but denied that the conflict was 'a planter versus native affair' as Ulster Protestants regard the province as their native land since they had settled there so long ago. It is long residence, not superior abilities and character, that give settlers their 'birthright' to stay in Ulster (PDN 18.2.77), and this means that there is no simple solution to the conflict:

> The Northern Irish have been in this province for nearly 400 years, much longer than the white man has been in the United

States, and there is no wish on their part to settle in any other country, however convenient that would be to the people who want a tidy solution to the Ulster problem ... The Protestants of Ulster are not going to be driven into the sea, nor will they conveniently disappear (PDN 29.10.76).

At the same time he sees the heritage of the Plantation as 'a divided community, which is the victim of 400 years of strife and bitterness' (CT 28.4.76). Nevertheless the US bicentenary and the unpopularity of the then British government led him to muse:

There's a lesson to be learned by the Mother Country, which provided the US with its foundations before the child rebelled and became the first of the English-speaking colonies to break the link with the Crown. In breaking that link ... America asserted the right of free peoples everywhere to go their own way. There is a lesson here for Ireland ... In seeking to find their own destiny, without political ties or dictation from Dublin, the Ulster people are merely following in the footsteps of their Scotch Irish fore-fathers who fought against the British to establish their right to nationhood (CT 7.7.76).

He did not, however, reach the apparently logical conclusion that Northern Ireland should break away from Britain, but concluded the argument as if the undeserving metropolis were the Republic of Ireland rather than Britain.

Like many ultras he expresses a dislike of the Foreign Office (PDN 19.3.82), but unlike them he recognises modern realities while criticising the Anglo–Irish Agreement:

Ulster MPs rightly expressed outrage ... some ... spoke about the past sacrifices of Ulstermen and women in two World Wars. But the harsh fact is that a Britain which abandoned the Empire concept years ago, and turned towards Europe in preference, is hardly listening to such arguments. They no longer carry any great weight in Britain (PDT 29.11.85).

This was not the first time that moderates had warned their readers that Ulster people should settle their differences peacefully as Britain's imperial days were over: 'Britain ... has been shrugging off appendages around the world at ... the least embarrassment or difficulty' (IR 16.10.69). The *County Down Spectator* gave a similar warning but expressed more confidence in British intentions: 'in similar circumstances, many of the European colonial powers have rid themselves of argumentative little offshoots [but] Britain has never been one to cop out and she will not cop out of Ulster' (CDS 13.11.81).

UNLIKE THE SETTLER colonies of the later British empire, the settlement of English and Scottish Protestants in Ulster was government policy, a fact which Protestants later used as an argument for continued British protection against Irish aspirations to recover the lost territory. Ireland was effectively ruled from Great Britain (unlike settlements in distant lands where metropolitan rule was more-or-less nominal) and Catholics had gradually acquired the same legal rights as Protestants. Despite these differences, Protestants, like settlers elsewhere, claimed that they had an eternal right to Ulster because it was their efforts, rather than those of the British government, which had transformed Ulster from a 'desert', allegedly underdeveloped by its former inhabitants, into a flourishing province.

Although direct references to settler origins become increasingly rare there is sufficient inferential evidence to show that these origins remained part of the political consciousness of Protestants. At different times a variety of writers compare Northern Ireland to regions which are held to be similar in specific ways: the USA, a great settler nation to whose independence Ulster Protestants had made a significant contribution (but which solved its 'native problem' through extermination and marginalisation); Gibraltar and the Falkland Islands, small British communities threatened by hostile irredentist neighbours (but without a 'native' problem); Kenya, South Africa and Rhodesia, white settlements faced by a combination of a majority of indigenes and a British government hostile to the settlers; and the white Dominions which had gained independence while retaining ties with the British motherland (and having, except for New Zealand, 'solved' the 'native' problem in ways similar to the USA). The comparison with Algeria is rejected, despite its similarity to Rhodesia: but it has been noted that the comparison with Rhodesia created difficulties. The affinity expressed with these societies of settler origin and the parallels drawn between Northern Ireland and the Falklands, and even with Catholic Gibraltar, suggest a continuing settler identity. Of course, many Ulster Protestants had emigrated to white settler states, the USA and the Dominions, and family ties still exist, but the affinity demonstrated is political as well as personal, and what all these situations have in common is that they were British settlements where settlers, initially a minority, took power over the existing inhabitants and/or took over territory claimed by another state or people.

The relationship between settlers and the British metropolis is also echoed in the Northern Ireland case. For example, the Oxford Union speech by Martin Smyth shows very clearly that, despite the stated difference between Northern Ireland and 'overseas member states of the Commonwealth', in practice the Stormont government had been able to act very much as if the region were 'an entity in its own right'. Although the speaker did not draw the parallel, the position of Northern Ireland that he described was precisely that of the white settler colony of Southern Rhodesia up to the late 1950s. Furthermore the habitual suspicion of settlers that the metropolis was planning to betray them into the hand of the 'natives' is also shown by the support for the settler rebellion in Rhodesia and the parallels drawn between the break-out from the Maze prison in 1983 and a 'Mau Mau' break-out in Kenya, which some see as a British government plot.

Ultras and moderates interpret the origins of the Ulster settlement differently. Some ultras have used Adamson's thesis in an attempt to deny the implications of settler origins, that is, to assert a natural right to live in Ulster. Others have drawn from settler origins the pressing necessity to hold on to what their ancestors won against the Irish Catholic threat, typified by such slogans as 'Not an inch' and 'No Surrender'. Moderates on the other hand accept that the Plantation was unfortunate but they believe that with goodwill on both sides Protestants and Catholics can live together in the remaining counties of Ulster, putting the past behind them.

3 Do Protestant Attitudes to Catholics Constitute Racism?

MANY ACCOUNTS OF colonialism see racism as a key dimension of settler–'native' relations. This may seem to be problematic in an Irish context, where skin colour is shared and where ideas of 'race' interact with ethnic and religious divisions, but abusive racial stereotyping of the Catholic Irish in the Victorian era has been well documented (Curtis 1968, 1971; Lebow 1979). The Victorian portrait of the Irish had a long history, for Henry II's conquest was justified by describing the Irish as lazy, treacherous, superstitious, ignorant, pagan, immoral, dirty and vicious (Rolston 1993:16), to which the Victorians added that they were uncivilised, violent, irrational, ungrateful, impractical, childlike, easily aroused and manipulated by self-serving agitators and content to be poor. The nature of the stereotype is of particular interest, in that it was the one applied to 'native' peoples everywhere. They were often compared with 'aboriginal peoples in Africa, the Antipodes and the Orient' (Curtis 1968:58) and were, according to Lord Salisbury, as unfit for self-government as Hottentots (ibid.:103). Another imperialist, Dilke, saw the Irish among the 'cheaper races' like the Chinese: 'both prolific breeders, hard workers and inveterate migrants' (ibid.:46). As is the common way with prejudice, there seemed to be no difficulty in accepting that the Irish could be both indolent and hard workers. By contrast, the 'Anglo-Saxon race', that is, the modern British, was deemed to be practical, individualistic, business-like, efficient and responsibly mature, an 'imperial race' which was industrious, frugal and adaptable, and essentially masculine. Attitudes such as 'reason, restraint, self-control, love of freedom and hatred of anarchy, respect for law and distrust of enthusiasm' were inherited and inheritable (Curtis 1968:11).

Within Ireland, Ulster Protestants identified with these attributes; for example, Anderson (1988:151) found that a key theme in Conservative unionist editorials in 1886 was the thrift and industry of Ulster Protestants as opposed to nationalists, even though Ulster ranked lower than Leinster in terms of income tax paid and per capita value of rateable property, and Ulster's richest county, Down, ranked only fifteenth of the thirty-two counties in average per capita income tax. Gailey (1987:11) noted that the 'innate sense of superiority [of] Ulster Unionists over the backward, poor, rural south ...

was almost racial in tone, even if religion tended to be the medium of this social Darwinism'. Curtis (1968:107) further noted that whereas the racial argument lost much of its popularity in Britain from the end of the nineteenth century, the arguments of the Ulster Unionists continued to display the same crude prejudices.

Most of the literature on Northern Ireland consigns racial stereo-typing to pre-partition days and 'ethnic division' or 'sectarianism' are preferred as explanations for ultra Protestant views of Catholics. To call such views 'racism' may appear implicitly to support the dangerous (as well as unscientific) notion of genetic and therefore immutable differences between groups of people, and 'ethnicity' and 'ethnocentrism' are more appropriate in focusing on culture and the imagined community – but these can also be used to ignore the historical origins of the divisions as well as still-existing inequalities. Similarly, the use of 'sectarianism' carries the danger of ignoring the politico/historical dimensions of religious difference and the inferior status of one major group. Which term is used is not, however, the main issue, and Mason (1970:3) is among those who see common-alities in all situations of dominance and inequality, colour merely adding 'a special sharpness'. What is important is that a significant section of unionists see Catholics as a group which is both distinct and inferior, and that the real and potential danger posed by this group has been met with structural domination through political exclusion and wide-ranging security legislation.

All the same, despite its problems, the term 'racism' seems more appropriate than 'ethnocentrism'. Rex (cited in Brewer 1992:356) believes that racism can exist separately from notions of race. Cer-tainly only the term 'racism' adequately implies the viciousness of the stereotype of the inferior group and the peculiar mixture of contempt, hatred and fear that characterises the feelings of members of the dominant (but insecure) group towards the inferior (but threatening) group. Examples of largely negative stereotyping in a mixture of quasi-racial and sectarian terms have been noted for Northern Ireland, and the data produced here supports this. Whether or not individuals still believe in biological differences between Catholics and Protestants, there is plenty of evidence of what Fanon (1967b:32–3) called 'cultural racism', and there has been little change in its content. The composite portrait of Catholics that emerges, however, goes beyond mere denigration for its own sake: it is informed principally by the political events of the times and by the need to convince the imperial power, Britain, of a par-ticular version of reality.

In the 1912–21 period the fight against Home Rule overcame any preference for bridge-building between the main contenders and in-sulting references are often found in most papers. A disproportion-ate number of these are in the *Impartial Reporter* and the *Londonderry*

Sentinel. Both represented areas with the largest percentages of Catholics on the borders of what was to become Northern Ireland, and they maintained lengthy and frequent editorial columns throughout the war years.

Overall, political labels predominate – 'nationalists' until 1916 with the addition of 'Sinn Feiners' and 'republicans' thereafter. An earlier assertion that there were no moderate nationalists (LS 20.1.14) was partly modified by an approving reference to the 'large section of Irishmen who are not Republicans' (LS 15.10.17). So Sinn Féin, 'that evil spirit ... that spirit of implacable hatred' (CDS 20.4.18) might be differentiated from the Nationalist Party, the death of whose leader, John Redmond, was marked by a eulogy from a most unexpected source: 'political life is the poorer by the removal of an Irishman of great eloquence, singular amiability and the highest honour' (LS 7.3.18). Essentially though, all political labels mean the same: 'Scratch a "Constitutional" Nationalist and you invariably find a Sinn Feiner' (LS 18.3.19), and the old habit of refusing to believe that Home Rulers could be moderates, or that moderates, if any, had any influence, persisted. Nevertheless these political labels at least conferred respectability on the enemy. Other epithets reveal a mixture of contempt and hatred. Terms such as 'Molly Maguires' and 'Hibernians', common up to 1914, are meant to convey the impression that nationalists were merely contemptible ruffians. In these same years the Others are more simply 'enemies'. That they hate England and/or the empire, is undoubtedly propaganda aimed at a British audience; more important is their historical enmity for Ulster Protestants: 'Ulster ... is not prepared to be handed over to the uncovenanted mercies of her hereditary enemies' (PDN 25.5.12).

There are fewer direct references to 'Roman Catholics'; but several editorials made it clear that Catholic equals Nationalist and/or Sinn Féin: 'the Nationalists ... hate England, not for any difference of race or language, but solely because of the difference of religion. They refuse to live peaceably under the Imperial Parliament because it is predominantly Protestant' (NL 14.2.12). The general perception of the divide between the 'two kinds of people in Ireland' conflates political and religious differences, which are at the root of the Home Rule campaign, the violence and the opposition of Ulster Protestants (IR 29.2.12, LS 15.7.19). In addition, past discrimination against Catholics was due to the Roman Catholic Church withholding good education from its people, and not to Protestant Ascendancy (IR 22.2.12).

Overt 'racial' labels are less frequent, but the *Impartial Reporter* almost exclusively used the terms 'Irish' and 'Celt', and in ways that clearly exclude Protestants. They are found in other papers too. It is a lone voice which declared that Home Rule would 'set men of a kindred race, though of different kinds of thought, at each other's throats' (PDN 20.7.12). More popular is Carson's slogan, derived from Thomas Macauley, 'two races in Ireland', that is 'the Ulsterman and the Irishman' (IR 22.6.16). The Ulsterman 'two-thirds Scotch and one-third of him English' is 'altogether a different man from the Irish Celt' (IR 15.3.17). He is of the 'same race as the men of Great Britain ... a race with a great ancestry' (LS 20.1.14), indeed an 'Imperial race' (IR 14.8.13). That the word 'race' has a biological connotation is shown by the editor's observation that nationalists hope 'to build up a successful Celtic nation while other Celtic nations have been decadent. In Ireland, Australia, England and the United States, the Celtic element has been a disturbing and pulling-down element' (IR 23.1.13).

This perception of racial difference is not always unkind:

> our Celtic fellow-countrymen are a courteous, familiar, charming people, often preferred by English folk to our Northern folk, with our Scotch coldness and aloofness ... We fully believe in their good desires ... good intentions and ... kindly motives, especially in the South where by their overwhelming majority they are free from the bitterness of race rivalry in the North (IR 10.10.12).

The charm and intellectual brilliance also reported by this editor were not, however, considered solid virtues at that time, and the main problem in the foregoing editorial is the lack of toleration by the Roman Catholic Church rather than the Celtic character. A later judgement is less charitable:

> The Gaelic race continues to show ... its incapacity for good government, and the other race, while not at all gifted with the same personal charm or intellectual brilliance as the Celtic, continues to manifest that strong, steady power of construction, organisation and grasp of methods and ways of building-up, along with thrift, prudence and industry, which the other unfortunately lacks ... There cannot be any subjugation of Ulster to the disturbers, spoilers, moonlighters, assassins, and outrage mongers of the south and west ... A progressive community like that of Ulster cannot have binding relations with a degenerate Ireland (IR 25.4.18).

The domain assumption is that the Other differs from good Ulstermen in religion and race, which in themselves are sufficient to explain their irrational and destructive pursuit of Home Rule for Ireland. The popular stereotypes reinforce this impression, and they are similar whether the reference is to 'nationalists', 'republicans', 'Roman Catholics', 'Celts' or 'Irish'. They are also typical of the stereotypes commonly used by settlers of 'natives' and an examination of these, contrasted with the self-perceptions of Protestants, shows a form of 'cultural racism' informing many judgements.

Basic to the image of Catholics is the claim that 'generations' residence side by side with the Nationalists' (PDN 13.9.13) means that Protestants know nationalists too well and understand Ireland 'better than Ministers can possibly do' (LS 19.10.20). What is principally needed is that the British government take unionist advice and exert 'Imperial control' (LS 3.9.12) or, in other words, colonial government; and the traits highlighted are precisely those which commonly legitimate colonial rule.

Laziness is one vice commonly attributed to 'natives' and that the trouble with Ireland was 'too much history and too little industry' (LS 5.10.16) was a common cliché. 'Industry' means 'hard work' as well as a sector of production, and the two meanings became conflated, so that 'industrial' implied hard-working. Nineteenth-century ideology equated progress with industry, so 'rural' and 'agricultural' were used as synonyms for lazy and backward. Thus it is unthinkable that 'industrial, Protestant, progressive Ulster [should be] placed at the mercy of the agricultural, unprogressive, mediaeval Hibernian element of the other provinces' (LS 13.9.13). The Fermanagh newspaper, serving a Protestant farming area, had to take a more qualified line, and pointed out that the nationalist majority of Tyrone is 'formed chiefly of farm servants and not of those who contribute most to the building-up of a nation' (IR 23.7.14).

Similarly, reminders that Ireland outside Ulster is not industrial carried the same message of backwardness and idleness. The horse-racing industry in the rest of Ireland was dismissed with contempt: 'The people in the North are too busy to cultivate the sport to the absorbing extent seen elsewhere. They believe in industry of a more wholesome and productive nature' (LS 5.5.17). Catholics are somehow unfitted for the progressive occupations of heavy industry and commerce. Those who establish new local industries and give employment to others are Protestants, and it is the 'atmosphere' of the Ulster towns which has attracted 'the captains of industry' (LS 5.10.16). This is a typical view:

> We have managed by our industrial enterprise and skill to make such progress that we are in perfect line with the industrial populations of England and Scotland. The rest of Ireland, where Roman Catholicism and Nationalism have been dominant, is admittedly far behind in its economic position (NL 16.1.13).

Catholics have had exactly the same laws, and hence the same opportunities, and yet it is 'the men of Ulster [who] flourished' (BO 30.1.14). So 'is there a particle of reason why all of Ireland should not have been as Ulster and Belfast are, if they had used their opportunities in like manner?' (BT 15.5.16).

These accusations of laziness served a double purpose: to justify both the Union and the greater wealth of Protestants. Unionist propaganda of this period focused on Ireland's growing prosperity in order to demonstrate the success of the Union. To counter the rejoinder that there were areas of endemic poverty, it was claimed that 'the backward condition of some parts of the country is not the fault of the Imperial Parliament or the British Constitution, but of the people themselves, and of the leaders whom they have followed' (NL 8.3.12). The blame lies with 'the idleness [and] thriftlessness of the section of the people which has allowed itself to dream of a time when no work will be necessary' (LS 20.3.17), in contrast with the 'industrious Protestant Irish people of all classes' (BO 27.9.12), who support the Union rather than letting the government subjugate them to 'the inferior elements which ... are the least industrious' (IR 16.7.14). This is why Ulster's 'prosperity' contrasts greatly with the poverty and illiteracy of the rest of Ireland, and why within Ulster it is Protestants who have reaped the reward of their 'lives of industry and integrity' (NL 21.9.12) in becoming the wealthy section of the community, in contrast with Catholics, who make up the majority of the slum-dwellers of Belfast (PDN 8.6.12). It is indeed to Ulster Protestants that Ireland owes its present prosperity, which has been won 'in spite of Nationalist members' (LS 18.10.13). It follows therefore, once exclusion was won, that Ulster's prosperity would be threatened by 'the thraldom of Sinn Fein' (LS 13.7.20), and that exclusion would lead to even greater prosperity within the province.

According to the liberal ethos of the times, prosperity was a matter for self-congratulation rather than a cause for gratitude. One editor attributed Irish prosperity to 'the considerate treatment the country has received at the hands of the British Parliament' (CDS 12.4.12), but more common, and contradicting the claim that the Union was indispensable, was the notion that Ulster Protestants had achieved it unaided, 'without the slightest aid, and with only the minimum of encouragement from the powers that be' (LS 18.4.16), thanks to their Northern habits of self-reliance: 'A simple, sturdy folk hitherto successful in their self-reliance and accustomed to look to themselves for all things' (PDN 13.9.13).

Catholics, by contrast, are devoid of such qualities, which is proved by their poverty; and further evidence of Catholic incompetence was extracted from the record of local government under Nationalist control. Sligo and Dublin were held up as portents of what would happen under a Dublin government, and Irish local government in general, especially compared to Ulster, was castigated as incompetent, inefficient and proof of incapacity for good government, as well as unjust and corrupt. In particular Catholic ideals are 'opposed to the principles of political economy' (LS 1.10.12) and inevitably lead to higher rates and taxes. Thus Protestants can claim they do not want rule by:

a band of men wholly unskilled in the arts of government and possessed of no real practical knowledge of the facts of the situation and management of the businesses in which we are so vitally concerned ... Ulster ... will not exchange the stately rule and ample protection of the Parliament of Great Britain for a bankrupt, intolerant and embittered assembly but little removed from the dignity and capacity of a parish council, and destitute of all justice and toleration (BT 16.1.13).

The new Northern government by contrast can show the rest of Ireland the way by setting 'an example of orderly, fair-handed, tolerant, progressive self-government' (NL 8.6.21).

A few references contradict this general portrait of Catholic laziness and ineptitude. The picture of Catholics either staying in Ulster or 'flocking in' in search of work (LS 13.7.16) does not suggest a preference for idleness, but it was taken rather as a compliment to unionist enterprise and Ulster's prosperity. In any case, industriousness was defined by material success, not by effort. The case of Derry is instructive. Catholics had no more ratepayers in 1918, it was claimed, than when the ward boundaries were previously fixed (which means that there is no need to change the boundaries) (LS 17.1.18), yet 'Unionist enterprise' means that 'a Roman Catholic majority has been created' (LS 26.1.18). If correct, this would mean that average Catholic income had fallen. Despite this possibility, an attempt at gerrymandering the boundaries was made, to include 'the valuable property lying immediately outside the boundary and the people living on that property', allegedly for the good of Derry as a whole, but undoubtedly to bring in more Protestant votes to counterbalance the growing number of Catholic ratepayers (LS 29.1.18).

A little of Londonderry Corporation's history also makes interesting reading. The *Londonderry Sentinel* favoured a new water scheme for the benefit of industry, which would raise the rates; this was favoured by Unionist members, some of whom 'pay more taxes than the whole of the Nationalist members put together' but impeded by Nationalist members (LS 10.1.18). The newspaper predictably campaigned against the Nationalists and Sinn Féin in the 1920 local election on the grounds that they would 'play ducks and drakes with the city's finances' (LS 8.1.20) and threaten 'the ratepayers and owners of property' (LS 13.1.20) – that is, by raising the rates. Catholics did become 'a nondescript majority' in the Corporation (LS 22.1.20), the water scheme was now voted to go ahead and the rates went up. The paper duly defended the Corporation, claiming that the economical management of previous members had too long delayed the waterworks, and making no mention of the present Nationalist/Sinn Féin control of the Corporation (LS 28.2.20). A year later this fact was also omitted from a report that the rates were to fall again (LS 19.2.21). In this case, where the facts were available to any interested reader, and where a particular project, judged to be useful to business, was involved, the stereotypes of extravagant Catholic management of local government could not be invoked.

The impression often given that all employers were Protestant is belied by references to wealthy Catholics and complaints that Catholic employers refused to hire Protestants; and the proclaimed self-reliance sits a little uneasily with the revelation that at least some of Ulster's railways were built by the state, that 'it is rich England which runs the Post Office for us at a loss to Great Britain every year of £300,000' (IR 15.8.12) and the fear that the suppression of the Union flag 'would synchronise with new taxes ... instead of financial assistance from a wealthy nation' (IR 19.9.12). Nor did the 'ingrained patriotism of the Belfast workmen' fail to withstand the foreign-inspired 'Bolshevism' leading to the 'deplorable, shameful and unprecedented' strike in the mainly Protestant shipyards which embarrassed unionist editors (LS 28.1.19). Despite these difficulties, the overall portrait of Catholic incapacity was maintained as proof that they could not rule Ulster.

There are other character defects: the *Impartial Reporter* for example portrayed the Irish as passionate, volatile, erratic, fissiparous, shallow, emotional, and given to imagination, enthusiasm and hysteria. As well as being unstable, they are impractical dreamers and visionaries: 'Ireland ... ever too unpractical ... Yes, our Irish people lack "the power of ordered thought"' (IR 10.6.15). A fondness for drink was hinted at too: 'the foolish people who have pictured Ireland under Home Rule as a land flowing with milk and honey, and in which everything will be free, including whiskey' (LS 4.2.13).

More serious was the claim that Catholics were incapable of thinking for themselves, but instead let priests and politicians manipulate them, particularly in elections: 'the average Nationalist has lost the power to think. He has so long had his thinking done for him that his faculty has passed away owing to disuse' (LS 26.11.12). In other words, Catholics would not vote Nationalist if they were intelligent and reasonable or if they were capable of independent action: 'The Irish people do not, as a rule, act individually on their own initiative. They go as a crowd. They wait to see what others are doing' (IR 1.10.14).

By contrast, Protestants present a rational and manly appearance. Although firmly united and disciplined, they nevertheless think for themselves: 'every Ulsterman is an independent unit – not part of a jelly mass which will all move the one way' (IR 18.5.16). Practical, straightforward and thorough in all their doings, Protestants are also manly and 'sturdy' (LS 31.12.18), possessing 'the tough and indomitable stubbornness of [their] Scotch ancestors' (IR 29.8.12) who were moreover 'thrifty, persevering and strong in character' (IR

3.8.16). The meeting in the Ulster Hall which set up an illegal Provisional Government 'was no gathering of fanatics ... it was a gathering of solemn, earnest men' (BT 24.9.13) whose 'temper, character and resolve' justified their actions (CDS 23.1.14).

Aside from the economic arguments for the Union, there were other reasons why the desire for Home Rule was held to be irrational and undesirable. 'English rule' has been generous, and has 'resulted in "studding" Ireland with happy homes and contented peasantry' (BT 24.4.12). Roman Catholics are better off ruled by Protestants than by their co-religionists (LS 19.2.20); but whereas Protestants are fit to rule Catholics, the reverse is not the case:

> it is far more reasonable that Roman Catholics should live under a Protestant Parliament than that Irish Protestants should live under a Roman Catholic Parliament, because Protestants believe in and practice the principles of civil and religious liberty, while Roman Catholics do not (NL 14.2.12).

This was supported by reports of Catholic discrimination against Protestants in employment and public offices, assertions of Protestant fairness and rectitude and examples of Protestant altruism and charitable donations to institutions which benefited mainly the Catholic poor and sick. The latter are given 'without expecting any return, even an acknowledgement of gratitude' (LS 3.7.17); on the contrary, Protestants' reward is to be called 'narrow-minded, bigoted and intolerant' (LS 26.1.18). Ingratitude is in any case to be expected from 'unthankful Ireland' (IR 28.12.16).

It is, however, the Protestant ideals of liberty and freedom which make them peculiarly fit to rule:

> The Northern Nationalist is certain of his liberty, of his security, of free speech and action, of his life with his Northern neighbours; neither his politics nor his religion are interfered with ... he will be as he is now, contented in the possession of what he enjoys at present (IR 18.3.20).

Indeed, 'we confess that we would feel hurt if there could possibly arise a thought of the need for any protection among Ulstermen' (IR 23.12.20).

A few more contradictions slipped into this picture. The 'emotional and unpractical Irishman' is thought to want Ulster because it is an asset to Ireland (IR 22.6.16), a practical enough reason. Nationalists are evidently clever enough to know that when their leaders urge enlistment, they know when they do and do not mean what they say (LS 21.9.14), and Derry Catholics are held to vote Nationalist against their own wishes (LS 4.1.19), which presupposes that they are able at least to form opinions. The portrait of fair-minded and tolerant Protestants was also marred by the trials in which the Protestant attackers of Catholics were acquitted, which according to the *Impartial Reporter* made them no better than similar cases in the West of Ireland (IR 3.4.13). Belfast was, however, generally scorned by the Fermanagh paper. The assertion that 'Roman Catholics find freedom in Ulster, as they always will do' was unselfconsciously juxtaposed with the 'refusal of Belfast shipyard Protestants to work alongside rebels', the justification being that:

the men excluded from employment were only asked to declare that they were not rebels in order to right themselves. Their refusal to make the simple declaration was probably due to the very terrorism in which the Republicans find their greatest power (LS 16.12.20).

Despite the contradictions in the portrait of Catholics, since the Union is beneficial to Ireland, it follows that the agitation for Home Rule must arise from defects of character, perhaps above all from the feebleness of character that allowed agitators to lead into violence 'decent Irishmen' (LS 23.12.20), 'one of the loveliest [people] in the world if let alone' (IR 22.4.20) with 'kindly and neighbourly ways ... if allowed to follow their natural inclinations' (IR 7.3.12):

It is a sad reflection upon the Irish race that a very substantial body of ostensibly sane men could be misled by a parcel of frothy ranters whose history is the very negation of commonsense conduct. Unhappily it is a glaring defect of the Celtic character, upon which the professional agitator has always been able to play at will. The wilder the language, and the more impossible and violent the programme propounded, the more certain was the agitator to secure a following. That fact ... is writ large upon every page of Irish history (BT 27.4.16).

The proper government of Ireland needs to take this into account, and if some express the need for 'fair, firm and sympathetic government' (BT 1.4.12), the *Impartial Reporter* from 1917 keeps repeating that firmness is the only prerequisite:

Ireland only respects the strong hand, and we cannot get the English statesmen to comprehend that fact. He tries his lollipops and his doles, for which he is laughed at; while the whole secret of good government in Ireland is firmness (IR 30.5.18).

As security became harder to maintain the same editor wished for 'a modern Oliver Cromwell' to censor the British newspapers which were sympathetic to Home Rule and make Ireland calm down (IR 22.1.20, 3.6.20).

Curiously enough, the dreamy impractical Irish reveal different qualities when dealing with the 'stupid' English, particularly when fighting against them, judging from the tributes to their quick-wittedness, organisation, resourcefulness and determination (IR 28.2.18). There is some ambivalence about their bravery: 'cowards' and 'shirkers' when they fail to volunteer from 1914 onwards (LS 6.11.15), 'Paddy' when in the British Army is 'by nature a fighter, and does not belong to a craven breed' (PDN 22.12.15). Even the *Londonderry Sentinel* admired the courage of the hunger striker Terence M'Swiney (LS 26.10.20). Wit and bravery, however, do not compensate for the effects of an unstable character:

> We do admit, however, that it would be possible to have a united Ireland if such a thing could be possible ... it will become necessary to put Ireland on her good behaviour for a term of years, to see if it be possible to such an erratic and volatile people to settle down to industry and to walk in the paths of peace (IR 15.1.20).

Thus Ireland outside Ulster was depicted, alongside its social inefficiency and irrational nationalism, almost entirely in terms of violence, terrorism, disorder and general lawlessness. It is roamed by murder gangs and typified by 'the disturbers, spoilers, moonlighters, assassins, and outrage mongers of the south and west' (IR 25.4.18). The violence is not politically motivated, just as the Home Rule campaign is not motivated by genuine grievances, and whether referring to the desire for Home Rule or to Catholics forced out of the shipyards, grievances were dismissed as 'imaginary woes' fabricated in the face of the Imperial Parliament's beneficence to Ireland. Those who recognised that cause for grief had once existed dismissed it as 'things that happened hundreds of years ago' (LS 23.11.15), notwithstanding that one editor sees the violation of the Treaty of Limerick as 'an act of perfidy which gave just cause to the Irish cry that no trust could be placed on Saxon faith' (IR 3.8.16). Even the Great Famine of the mid-nineteenth century was ignored by the *Londonderry Sentinel* in its slighting comment that the South does not want to export potatoes (LS 30.12.16) and in its many complaints about 'twopenny-halfpenny little Irish Nationalist constituencies [with] four and six times the voting power of the large English industrial constituencies' (LS 6.12.17). The original reason for this, the halving of the Irish population through famine and forced emigration, was never mentioned; and the violence implied by conquest is irrelevant:

> The United Parliament came to Scotland and England, and since then Scotland has prospered and abided by the compact. Scotland

, never was conquered. Ireland was conquered: yet [sic] she fumes and frets against a Union which has given Ireland comparative control of Parliament, which has extracted numerous concessions not granted to other portions of the United Kingdom; and utterly regardless of her (ought to be) proud position of being a governing factor of the greatest Empire in the world seeks the complete independence of a small island with a divided population (IR 23.5.18).

Since conquest has brought such benefits, political grievances are mere inventions, and the cause of dissent resides in the Irish character: irrational and easily led, many fall prey to agitators and the violence is perpetrated by 'gangs of wild men ... who have been either tempted or coerced into the ways of crime' (LS 1.3.21) or driven by 'unreasoning fanaticism' (LS 3.2.21). The terms 'rebels' and 'rebellion' imply not protest against a superior power but a basic character trait of 'the unruly Irish' who cannot be 'bought or tamed' (IR 28.2.18). The *Londonderry Sentinel* agreed that 'as Archbishop Alexander once remarked, the Celt is a born anarchist' (LS 12.2.18) and Irish risings, past and present, have been marked with 'fiendish cruelty' (LS 2.5.16). Even after the bloody 1914–18 war it was still claimed that the rebels are 'deaf to the instincts that cause civilised beings to revolt from shedding human blood' (BT 22.7.20). Indeed, 'the issue at stake in Ireland today is not one of party politics but of civilisation' (LS 10.7.20), and even in normal circumstances, it is significant that the majority of criminals and lunatics in Ulster prisons are Catholics (LS 24.9.12).

Not all Catholics were accused of involvement in violence. The *Londonderry Sentinel*, no doubt aware of local realities and perhaps its responsibility towards harmony in the Maiden City, absolved 'very large numbers of respectable Nationalists' in Derry of wrongdoing (LS 31.5.21). Nor could Ulster be painted as a place where disorder was likely, in view of the propaganda about Ulster's stability and bright future; but only when Ulster was safe from Home Rule could it be admitted that the majority of people in the South are tired of 'the devastating rule of the gunmen and the firebugs' (IR 9.6.21). The danger of stereotyping had perhaps been brought home by the excesses of the Black and Tans:

Lord Lieutenant Fitzalan ... felt it his duty to deplore, as all do, the serious indiscretions of which a few members of the newly-recruited force that has taken up duty in the martial law area have been guilty. But he did not fall into the Nationalist-Sinn Fein habit of condemning the whole membership of the new force because of the misdeeds of a few. It would be as unfair to do so as it would be to associate the bulk of the Irish community with crime because the criminals are of the same religion as the majority of the Irish population (LS 9.8.19).

Nevertheless this non-violent Catholic majority is not blameless: 'the great mass of the Irish people are not steeped in crime, but the deplorable fact is that ... they do not look with a sufficiently unfriendly eye upon criminality' (IR 4.12.19).

Two functions of this emphasis on violence, criminality and lawlessness as character traits are that no other explanation need be sought for them, and that it could be argued that violence would continue even if Home Rule were granted:

> Unionists have the fear that under a Parliament controlled by the Hibernians the system of intimidation, leading to murder, would be extended all over Ireland, seeing that there would be entire immunity from punishment for the criminals (LS 26.9.12).

Ulster Protestants, on the other hand, were asserted to be law-abiding, peaceable and orderly, indeed 'the most law-abiding people in the King's wide dominions' (LS 18.4.14). Expressions such as 'law-abiding Ulster' (BT 21.3.14), where 'fines for technical offences [unfortunately not defined] are the rule' (LS 26.2.18), referred to 'the loyal third of the population of Ireland, who stand for ... Ireland's peace' (IR 11.4.12). Evidence of this is their 'unbounded admiration for the British Army' (LS 7.5.14). Any trouble that occurs in Ulster is due to Catholics or to Catholic provocation, as it is clear from the criminal records that Protestants 'are not lawbreakers by instinct' (LS 10.7.20). Even though the *Impartial Reporter's* assertion that modern-day riots are confined to Roman Catholics (IR 4.7.12) is swiftly followed by an editorial strongly condemning Protestant attacks on Catholics in Belfast (IR 1.8.12), the editor soon offered the comfort that worse happens in the South (IR 8.8.12). The looting of several Protestant shops in Belfast by 'men and boys who call themselves Protestants' may not be excused by 'great provocation from Sinn Feiners with their wretched cry of "Up the Rebels"'; but the emphasis is placed on rioting:

> It is significant that all the rioting occurred in Nationalist centres except for the looting ... and it was as bad there as elsewhere. If the Nationalists or Sinn Feiners or whatever they may be, insist on creating trouble the soldiers and police will see to it that they are kept in their own districts. They will not be permitted to invade localities where they are not wanted (BT 22.7.20).

Further Protestant rioting and looting in Belfast, Lisburn and other districts (but not Portadown) (PDN 4.9.20) are illustrative of the

Belfast rather than the Protestant character. The bigotry of Belfast's artisan class has long been deplored in Fermanagh (IR 23.1.13), but all will be well once Northern Ireland is established as a separate entity: 'We in Ulster ... desire ... peace, all good neighbourhood ... a new Ulster will arise when freed from terrorism with the assassinating South' (IR 2.12.20).

Finally, there is an underlying assumption of the unchanging nature of Catholics, whatever superficial religious or political changes might take place: 'A Roman Catholic because he happened to have become more a Hibernian than a Roman Catholic would not be disposed to love his Protestant countrymen anything the more' (LS 3.9.12). Since Protestants have not caused any harm to Catholics, this hostility can be only a defect of character; and three Ulster counties have to be sacrificed because Protestants 'do not want to take the risk of having the Ulster Parliament dominated by Roman Catholics in the near or even remote future' (LS 11.3.20).

BY 1939 THE emphasis had shifted to defending a Northern Ireland 'state' now in existence for nearly two decades. The large minority of Catholics within had the potential support of an independent Irish state next door. 'Ireland-watching' was an obsession with many unionist editors and their readers, especially on the border; and the attitudes of the leader-writers of the *Belfast Telegraph*, *News Letter* and *Northern Whig* towards nationalist Ireland from 1919 to 1949 have been amply documented (see Kennedy 1988). To a large extent insulting and angry references were levelled now at the Free State (often referred to incorrectly as 'Eire' or prematurely as 'the Republic') rather than at Northern Ireland Catholics, but the general tone was not conciliatory. The need for eternal vigilance was the leitmotif of the period. Protestants must be 'ceaselessly on guard' and exercise 'the utmost vigilance', for 'there can be no relaxation of that eternal watchfulness against the foe, whether he be in the old garb or a new one' (LS 30.4.42). It was not always specified who 'the foe' was, but they are 'numberless' (LS 10.1.39) and they are Irish nationalists, whether within Northern Ireland, the Irish state or agitating in Great Britain for a united Ireland.

The foe within was, as in the 1912–21 period, usually given a political label, such as 'Nationalists', 'Republicans', 'anti-Loyalists', 'anti-Partitionists' or 'anti-British' or, more picturesquely, 'Eire's friends in the North' (LS 1.7.44). Editors did tend to use religious labels when referring to employment, but in most cases 'Catholic' and 'nationalist' were used interchangeably. 'Nationalist' clearly means 'Roman Catholic' in the report that: 'Many loyal Nationalists have responded to the call of the country' (IR 29.5.41), and when Nationalists did badly in the Fermanagh local elections, 'All Nationalists are not anti-Partitionists' (IR 9.6.49), even though the editor's defence against complaints that Unionist councils did not employ Catholics was that 'in this country "Nationalist" and Roman Catholic are synonymous terms' (IR 22.2.45). Letter-writers, on the other hand, nearly all used religion to identify the enemy. Racial labels were now rare and confined to the people of the Irish state. There were a few generalisations about 'the Irish' and 'Irish Celts' and Irish reaction to the Ireland Bill was described (borrowing from Disraeli) as 'the dizziest heights of Celtic impudence' and 'Celtic hysteria' (NL 7.5.49; LS 10.5.49). More often the terms 'Gael' and 'Gaelic' were used in mockery, the greatest scorn being reserved for Irish state attempts to spread the Gaelic language, despite some professed admiration of it as 'an ancient language ... a knowledge of [which] is a cultural achievement of considerable value' (LS 1.3.47). For 'Young Guard', however, the Irish language is 'pigeon Gaelic' (LS 1.7.39) and 'the "Irish race" is mongrel, as is the Gaelic language ... and this is the "historic Irish nation"' (LS 25.7.39).

Similarly the majority of insulting epithets was reserved for the Irish state. This was often referred to as 'Eire', which is the Irish word for the island of Ireland, but was used by editors such as those of the *News Letter* and *Londonderry Sentinel* to mean only the twenty-six counties. It is very rare for the editors of the *Londonderry Sentinel* and the *Impartial Reporter* in particular to refrain from reviewing the latest 'follies' of both national and local government in the Free State. To see the Free Staters as 'our Southern fellow-countrymen' (PDN 26.6.48) was unusual, but a continuation of the perception of the *Portadown News* in 1912–21 that all the inhabitants of Ireland belonged to one race. Instead the focus was on what divides the two parts of the island. Whereas Northern Ireland was cast as part of a great and prosperous British nation, the Free State was characterised as a petty self-important 'Republic' (LS 28.3.39), ridden with poverty and dependent on Britain for what little wealth it possessed. Nevertheless the Irish irrationally hate Britain. The *Londonderry Sentinel* in particular, with its usual ill-disguised gloating over the 'evidence' that the Irish have indeed proved themselves unfit for self-government, claimed that the Irish economic plight was due to 'native rule, the blessings of which "Irish patriots" have yearned for generations!' (LS 2.11.39); and that paper's reaction to Fine Gael's wish to seek more trade with Britain shows hypocrisy leavened with self-interest:

Ulster, of course, would welcome a prosperous Eire, but she must ever be watchful of developments in this sphere of lively Commonwealth membership on the part of Eire. It is certain to be used as an instrument to force Ulster into a united Ireland (LS 19.12.44).

The Irish state's inferior status and self-inflicted separation from the United Kingdom means that the Irish government has no right to 'interfere' in the affairs of the Northern state, or even express opinions about it: this is both 'sinister' and 'impudent' behaviour on the part of a state which can now be labelled 'foreign' and 'alien'. Much trouble could have been avoided had 'Britain and those who are supposed to serve her paid more attention to Ulster opinion concerning Irish affairs' (LS 14.2.42), for 'the hard-headed people of Ulster ... know the Southern Irish mentality' (LS 30.11.48). Nevertheless Britain's treatment of its 'noisy neighbour' is finally to be applauded:

> Britain has been most magnanimous. Costello and De Valera have been treated like naughty children. They have been left sitting on the mat, and are to be welcomed back again into the fold when they say they are sorry ... Professor Savory, for the Ulster Unionists, said: 'We would welcome unity, but it must be a unity within the Commonwealth of Nations. We would welcome Eire back to join us and become a part of the United Kingdom. That is the only way to bring about unity between the North and the South.' Unity cannot be visualised at the moment, but perhaps in a few years' time Eire, when she has learned her lesson, may return like the Prodigal Son (IR 19.5.49).

If the enemy without can be held at bay by Westminster, the enemy within is still there:

> Even more fantastic is the ... suggestion that advancing social progress in Northern Ireland might tend to reconcile the Northern Nationalists to their minority position ... the Northern Nationalist mentality ... is even more recalcitrant than the most extreme Republican in Eire (LS 24.10.44).

The term 'the minority', although clear in the above example, was often a device both to avoid having to use a specific label and to imply the inferior position of that minority. Despite the preponderance of political or non-specific labels, however, the differences between the opposing groups in Ireland were most often stated in terms of religion, as in the 1912–21 period. Sometimes religion was juxtaposed with 'outlook', 'tradition' and 'temperament' as dividers and also with 'race': 'that racial, religious and territorial tangle which none but the Irish themselves understand' (LS 9.10.48); but it is religious differences which form the primary division from which political differences emanate: 'In the political sphere, religion is the dividing line ... The Prime Minister [Brooke] rightly emphasised that the cleavage is centuries old and time has not altered matters' (LS 13.10.45). Catholics hate Britain and Ulster for being Protestant (LS 22.11.45), and 'Protestant' and 'Loyalist' are synonymous ('A Southern Loyalist' IR 30.12.48). A distaste for Catholics and Catholicism is evident from editorials about Protestant children having to attend Roman Catholic schools in the Free State, and Roman Catholic teachers in 'Protestant' schools in Northern Ireland (LS 14.12.44; IR 1.7.48).

The portrait of Catholics that emerges in the 1939–49 period is very similar to that of 1912–21. Dependent and profligate, volatile and lawless, ungrateful and rebellious, incapable of independent thought and instinctively favouring extremist leaders, they are clearly undesirable neighbours who should not be allowed to gain political power. The unemployed who prefer to 'loaf and live on the "'dole"'' (IR 29.4.43) are clearly Catholics:

> There is an element in the city who apparently consider that the hard-working and industrious rate-payer should feed, clothe and house them while they live in indolence and idleness and squander what money – sometimes big money – they earn and do nothing to help themselves (LS 1.3.45).

Despite the reference to 'big money', there was some sneering at Catholics' 'few shillings' ('Anti-Republican' IR 23.9.43) and a general picture was built up of Catholic dependency on Protestant employers and on the state for jobs, houses and state benefits: 'the vast majority of [Nationalists] derive their livelihood from Unionist owned and Unionist-controlled public and private undertakings' (PDN 21.7.45). Catholics also benefit from Protestant charity: 'Unionists have always been kind to their poorer Nationalist brethren' (IR 25.10.45). Some feel that Catholics are treated far too well: 'the Northern Government would do well to ... choose more frequently from their own supporters ... often too much consideration is given to the minority' ('N.J.S.' IR 6.4.39), and there is anti-Protestant discrimination even by unionist employers and the state:

> Our rural areas are being denuded of their Protestant manhood because they cannot exist on the wages paid to them, and Roman Catholics, content to work for less, are taking their places. The Northern Government is dotting the countryside with cottages mainly for Roman Catholic labourers ... If need be the Ulster farmer should be assisted so that Protestant rural workers would not be obliged to desert the farm because of low wages ... there is also the disturbing fact that considerable numbers of Protestant young men are leaving Ulster for Great Britain and the Dominions ... The supreme task [the Northern Government] should set itself is to endeavour to provide work for all who belong to Northern Ireland (LS 11.7.39).

At the same time Catholics (despite the general picture of their dependence) discriminate against Protestants in employment ('Lest We Forget' IR 1.4.43).

Much of the above was a response to repeated Catholic complaints of unfair treatment (the term 'discrimination' had not yet come into use). Only one paper, the *Impartial Reporter*, admitted any truth in this, but saw nothing wrong in it:

> Unionist bodies in the North always give preference to their political supporters. Why not? Public bodies in all countries do this ... why should the North be the sole exception and give its favours to those opposed to its Government and who desire its destruction. Such a course would not be common sense (IR 8.4.43).

This is nothing to do with religion, but only with politics (IR 1.4.48). This did not preclude comparison between Northern 'Nationalists' and Southern 'Protestants': the treatment of the latter, 'their persecuted brethren from Eire' (LS 15.7.44), provided another justification for any disadvantaged state of the former which was actually admitted. The dwindling numbers of the Protestants in the Irish state are also a warning to 'the Protestants of Londonderry and the rest of Northern Ireland' that they might be driven out of Northern Ireland as their brethren are being from the South (LS 10.2.45), and the corollary of this is that Protestant strength should be built up: 'We want to build up a strong and loyal Ulster, and the way to do it is to provide employment for Ulster's own loyal sons and daughters' (LS 28.2.46).

Though Catholics receive fair or even favoured treatment they continue to show no gratitude:

> In Ulster, if Roman Catholics do not get their own way in everything they cry out 'persecution'. They claim the right to be employed by Protestants, while they themselves give no employment in return ... They expect these persecutors to provide district nurses for their sick poor, to subscribe to their churches and their charitable institutions (IR 23.11.44).

The preceding portrait, however, is benign compared with the following:

> if the filthy conditions under which large families are being brought up in the back streets of Nationalist areas in our cities and towns is in keeping with Roman Catholic civilisation then we 'non-Christians' have very little to be ashamed of ... early marriage and indiscriminate breeding can become a means to [Irish

unity]. Consequently whether the offspring can be comfortably maintained on the parent's income must remain a secondary affair. Charitable organisations can do the rest, even should such institutions receive subscriptions from Protestant sources! ... Your reminder to 'Aire' as to who provides his co-religionists with their livelihood is the true position because the only Nationalist industries that I am aware of are public houses and racing dogs, and the number of Protestants employed in the former trade is very small indeed ('Ballinagone' PDN 28.7.45).

The term 'breeding' is more properly connected with animals; but since 'our Protestant people have failed in what is the most important factor in maintaining a nation and empire – an increase in the birth rate ... the breeding out of Ulster' ('Countryman' PDN 31.8.46) is possible, thanks to 'the numerically superior breeding qualities of the "children of bondage"' (LS 29.1.46). This is a new addition to the old stereotype.

On the whole, however, there is little innovation in the portrait, and the same contradictions can be observed as before. Catholics are unstable and prone to hysteria, fissiparous and, despite the constant political debate among nationalists that some unionists mocked, and their deviousness and subtlety, nevertheless unable to think for themselves. They are impractical dreamers, particularly when it comes to inventing 'mythical grievances ... imaginary political troubles ... their grievances are without a shred of foundation ... they enjoy the greatest freedom of any people in the world' (LS 14.3.40). Once again the *Impartial Reporter* admitted past wrongs in stating 'there is no parallel in this country for the persecution of the Jews in Germany, unless one goes back a hundred and fifty years or more' (IR 4.11.43) but this is no reason for 'harping on the dim distant past' (IR 22.8.46). The Penal Laws in Ireland are nullified by anti-Protestant laws in other countries (I L Montgomery IR 27.4.44); and inconvenient historical facts are met by outlining the post-1921 history of Ireland (LS 1.12.45). Opposition to partition then is animated by 'deep-rooted and unreasoning ... anti-British feeling' (LS 3.6.41), maintained by agitators who 'have always been loud-spoken and powerful, unfailingly influencing the course of Irish politics, because they represented the extremists, who, despite checks from time to time, have invariably dominated the moderate elements' (LS 27.2.41). This is no doubt because Catholics are by nature 'quarrelsome' (IR 25.5.39) and violent, as proved by 'outrages' continuing after the cessation of British rule:

It shed a bright light on all what has been called the political crime record of Ireland in the past and shows that much of it was due to downright criminal instinct ... [probably true that] this lawlessness has always been the work of a comparatively small number ... Despite the assumption of unfettered authority by native rulers the criminal element persists in Eire. It is root and branch the same as is to be found in Northern Ireland ... It is ... beyond doubt that the Republican apostles of physical force have very large backing in Northern Ireland by many who will not participate in active outrage and terrorism to the same extent and by many others who would not indulge in it at all, but who would be prepared to reap all they could from it in the achievement of their political aims (LS 13.7.43).

In contrast, Protestants, Northern Ireland's 'best blood, brains and character' (LS 29.1.46), are generally associated with enterprise, industriousness, competence in business and administration, progressiveness and prosperity. Claims to self-reliance, however, were under nationalist attack at this time and this is the context for the many claims that 'we pay our way in Ulster' (PDN 7.8.48) or even that Northern Ireland is a financial asset to Great Britain, especially after the war:

> If Great Britain prefers a type of government to which most of us in Ulster object, why should we have to subsidise her, as we have been doing and still are? Why can Ulster not conserve her monetary surplus for development and emergency? (R A Patterson CDS 28.2.48).

Particularly galling was the claim that Northern Ireland was benefiting from the South's food production: 'it is true that a good deal of foodstuffs are finding their way from Eire into Northern Ireland, but ... not by any means a one-way traffic' (LS 30.8.41).

Protestants are, as they have always been, 'on the side of liberty, truth and justice' (PDN 5.2.49); and unlike Catholics, they are united:

> The intricacies of the never-ending disputes between the manifold and variegated elements which go to make up the whole body of advocates of an All-Ireland Republic are too great for the Ulster mind, accustomed to adherence to well-defined vital principles and loyalty to tried and trusted leaders to fathom (LS 27.7.40).

This is somewhat contradicted by the constant calls for unionist unity every election, and the warning that nationalists always unite in order to try to drive unionists into a united Ireland (LS 30.4.42, 3.3.45); and some doubt is unwittingly cast on the Protestant character by the assertion that although the masses are 'sound and firm' they need 'strong and determined leaders' (LS 10.2.45). The innate lawlessness of Catholics is still contrasted with the law-abiding, peaceful nature of their opponents: 'those brought up under a Protestant civilisation ... won't run amuck' ('Ballinagone' PDN 11.8.45). Nevertheless, they are a sturdy race and men of steel:

> if some of the advocates of annexation had profited from the history of the Protestants of Ulster they would know that ... only the sternest resistance would be met with ... any effort at subjugation would bring only desolation and the loss of many lives (LS 9.2.39).

Given the contrasting portraits of Catholics and Protestants, the *Londonderry Sentinel*'s conclusion is neither novel nor surprising: 'the prospect of Ulster Protestants being dominated by a permanent Roman Catholic majority is ... abhorrent' (LS 31.7.48).

In the modern period, however, the fight to retain Northern Ireland, in the face of new challenges from within its large Catholic minority, shows much more variation in editorial policy. Some newspapers now refrain from political comment; even certain ultra editors initially expressed support for the spirit of reform personified by Prime Minister O'Neill (LS 11.12.68; PDN 7.2.69, 21.2.69; NL 10.12.68); and there are more attempts than before, even among ultras, to address both Catholics and Protestants, to take a fairly neutral stance on 'sectarianism' or at least to show a moderate face. Nevertheless many editorials and letters stress what divides Catholics from Protestants rather than what they have in common, and the term 'the minority' is still frequently used in this context, functioning both as a marker of division and as a reminder of Catholics' inferior position.

One new issue is the identity of the Other. Within Northern Ireland it is primarily the IRA and other militant republican groups which are execrated and blamed for the conflict, but there is considerable variation in views as to which groups apart from Sinn Féin constitute 'those upon whom the Provisionals most depend' (NL 6.12.75) and are therefore rightfully the hated outgroup. The 'enemies of Ulster' are ever-present (NL 13.7.85) – but in which guise today, and in what proportion?

On the political front, some consider both NICRA/PD and their successor, the Social Democratic and Labour Party (SDLP), little different from republican parties: '[The SDLP is] responsible ... for 95% of all the misery and trouble in Northern Ireland these last five years' ('Dubious' BO 13.12.73) and its members include 'the traditional enemies of the Province' (S Foster IR 1.10.87). Total integration is preferable to devolved government because the SDLP is 'of a purely Republican nature' and therefore cannot be trusted ('Lisnaskea Unionist IR' 28.1.88). More generally, nationalists and republicans combined are cited as the Other. However, even Catholics in the unionist Alliance Party of Northern Ireland (APNI) are secretly working for a united Ireland ('Spectator' IR 1.6.72) and the whole party has united Ireland aspirations because of its support for the Anglo–Irish Agreement (Raymond Farrell IR 20.3.86).

The *Londonderry Sentinel*, without being overtly papaphobic, commonly uses the term Roman Catholics to identify the Other, as do others who are less polite, and one justification advanced for dislike of Catholics is purely doctrinal:

> Who are our enemies? Well, right down through our history, the Roman Catholic Church was the enemy of the Church of God. How then can we love them? ... we do not hate the Roman Catholic but we do hate his doctrine. So the Roman Catholic is not my brother, and they are not my neighbours, but I still love them as my enemies in the love of God (Ben Richardson PDN 7.11.69).

Thus Protestant fundamentalists are well represented from early in the period:

> the Victory for Ulster will be wrought by the King of Kings and Lord of Lords, through servants wholly committed to Him and His Will. Such has been the case in the dark days of Ulster's History. King William was a Calvanist [sic], Lord Carson was a Brethren (Irene Brown CDS 4.8.72).

More commonly the overt conflation of religion and politics continues. Catholics are 'Anti-Unionists', and asking a correspondent who was in favour of the Ulster Defence Regiment (UDR) if he would feel happy doing night patrols with Catholics, one writer commented: 'perhaps when you have served three compulsory years alongside Roman Catholics you might not think so much about Harold or Big Jim' ('Uneasy Unionist' IR 5.2.70). The reasons for the divisions also show little innovation. 'Culture' is mentioned (without being defined) (NL 27.11.71), and 'people of diverse political and racial outlook' (PDN 26.9.69); but I found only one overtly racist remark: 'there are two races in Northern Ireland – the "human race" and the "minority Irish race"' (N J Swanston IR 4.6.70). A few state that the conflict is purely political and the *Orange Standard* even compares Ulster loyalists to the 'predominantly Roman Catholic Gibraltarians [with] a deep attachment to Britain and the British way of life' (OS Oct 1981).

The identity of religion and politics is used to excuse bigotry:

> I wish to admit to being bigoted, but maybe being a young man and being brought up in a hostile atmosphere ... and learning

from an early age in Londonderry that you could not turn your back on the 'rebel scum' that surrounded us, I think that my bigotry is understandable ('Londonderry Loyalist' BO 29.3.84).

It is notable that ultra letter-writers who express anti-Catholicism frequently come from the beleaguered City of Derry, some of whose inhabitants claim that 'there is a subtle, well organised campaign to de-Protestantise as many parts of the Province as possible' ('Londonderry Protestant, also educationally interested' LS 7.11.84). An attempt by the *Londonderry Sentinel* to win Catholic readers provoked one furious reaction:

> The *Londonderry Sentinel* has always been a loyalist paper, bought and read in every Protestant home in Londonderry and beyond. Now it has lost all the esteem in which it was held by the Protestant people. On Wednesday, October 10, what did we find? Bishop Daly [I have censored the remainder of your comments on the Bishop – Editor] and a horde of RC school children. We have had enough of prizegivings in RC schools and news about RC affairs which are of no interest to the people who buy the paper ... And did we ever think the *Londonderry Sentinel* would employ a RC reporter? ... I call upon all loyalists to boycott this paper ... until it alters to suit the loyalist people who buy it ('Watch Tower' LS 31.10.84).

The paper has since reverted to a more 'Protestant' line, since it lost many of its old readers without attracting Catholic ones.

Stereotypes of Catholics also reveal continuities, with minor changes. The 'minority' who in the past have not 'striven to work for the prosperity ... of Northern Ireland' (NL 6.4.82) can, now that the welfare state is fully in place, be accused of preferring to live on the dole: 'It would appear to me and many other people that a lot of RCs don't want jobs because of the benefits they receive by not working' ('Taxpayer' PDN 19.7.85). There are continued references to the higher Catholic birthrate (Beryl Holland CDS 24.12.68), sometimes still referred to as 'breeding': 'Why pay people to breed like rabbits?' ('Fair Play' IR 10.10.85). Catholics are also perceived as dirty: 'Generally speaking they create housing problems and slums in the areas they flock to' ('British Subject' IR 12.10.72). The *Portadown News* under Douglas Sloan quoted in full an article from a Chicago newspaper, calling the following 'an unbiased account' and 'constructive approach'. Claiming that Irish Catholics should not be up North in the first place but 'South, where they come from', the Chicago columnist goes on to ask:

> Who told them to have all those babies? ... Why don't they pull themselves up by the bootstraps and get some property ... the

Irish Protestants pay most of the taxes in Northern Ireland ... The industrious, prudent, frugal, ambitious Irish Protestants don't have any trouble getting jobs (PDN 24.1.69).

A new feature, however, was the 'discovery' of Protestant poverty, which is held to match or surpass the previously-despised poverty of Catholics. Since some Protestants are now admitted to be poor, poverty has become a matter for sympathy, especially when bravely borne: 'out of an inverted sense of loyalty to Great Britain few people in the majority community complained about their deprivation although it was just as real as among the minority' (NL 31.12.85). It also helps to make a useful political point: 'Working-class Protestants without jobs and in poor housing conditions must find it ironic to hear themselves described as the privileged community' (IR 21.4.88).

Furthermore the proud assertions of Protestant self-reliance somewhat decrease in this period. Despite Paisley's assertion that 'We Protestants of Ulster ask no favours or indulgences' (PT 22.2.69), even ultras tend to see this self-reliance as at least partly a thing of the past. Direct rule is blamed, mainly through presenting the fifty years of Stormont rule in a rosy light: 'For fifty years Ulster had a prosperous country run by Ulstermen and women Civil Servants' (Beryl Holland CDS 30.7.76). It should be noted that those who laud Northern Ireland's past come chiefly from east of the Bann, that is, the more prosperous part, and that the transformation of the Stormont years into a fifty-year-long golden age of prosperity is missing from the *Londonderry Sentinel*, no doubt partly because of the endemic depression in the region.

Dislike of dependency arises partly from a sense of shame and mortification: 'We are made to feel that we exist on British charity' ('A Ballymena Unionist' BO 10.2.77). This, allied with a fear of abandonment and annoyance at nationalist mockery over Northern Ireland's now publicly-proclaimed dependence on Britain, requires excuses. One such is the premiership of O'Neill, who announced in 1964 that his objectives were to make Northern Ireland more prosperous (through a large public spending programme) and 'to build bridges between the two traditions within our community' (Bardon 1992:622). Prior to this, it is alleged:

(During the forty-two years of) so-called 'Unionist misrule' up to 1964 this little state ... was able not only to run its affairs with financial buoyancy but also to contribute its share totalling £439,674,344 to the British Exchequer (OS Oct 1983).

Another solution to the shame of dependency is to assert, usually in the form of a rhetorical question, that no one knows how much money 'Ulster' gives the mainland, including taxes, export revenue and so on, the implication being that Northern Ireland under Stormont made a large net contribution to UK finances and that this is still the case (George Bulbrook PDN 21.3.68). In any case, '[most of] England's financial contribution to Ulster ... goes to Ulster's avowed enemies' (PT 22.2.69), that is, to Catholics, who are seen as the main beneficiaries of the welfare state, although they contribute nothing ('Fair Play' IR 3.10.85).

A further device is to claim that Northern Ireland had made its own indispensable contribution to the United Kingdom, making the Union of mutual benefit to Great Britain and Northern Ireland rather than merely a drain on British finances; and ultras tend to stress the Protestant contribution, when 'loyal Ulstermen ... steadfastly stood by Britain when her need was greatest in two World Wars' ('W.B.' IR 8.12.83). The metropolis is thus placed in a moral debtor relationship to Northern Ireland just as the latter is usually admitted to be an economic debtor to Britain. Hence the debts cancel out; but the implication of ultra selectivity is that whereas Protestants have paid their debt in blood, Catholics have not, remaining instead ungrateful dependants who refuse to 'show allegiance to the British Crown (only the half crown)' (Beryl Holland CDS 30.5.69). Once again then, Catholics display the sin of ingratitude.

Catholic allegations of political and economic discrimination are another manifestation of this ingratitude. Some admit that this had been the case, but excuse it by Catholic 'disloyalty' (NL 12.9.69). Others excuse discrimination by continuing to claim that Catholics themselves are the worst offenders, especially in Derry and in Imperial employment such as the Post Office:

> the parrot cry of 'discrimination' – despite the fact that the Protestant employers in Londonderry employ far, far more RC workers than Catholic employers do Protestants ... discrimination in employment that exists in this city exists against Protestants ('Veritas' TLS 2.5.73).

A sectarian dispute in a Scottish district council area proves the point in more general terms: 'whenever Roman Catholics have control of administration – Monklands, Londonderry, Liverpool, or Newry, Protestants can expect to come off worse in relation to jobs and investments' (OS May 1994). Yet others claim there is no discrimination: 'The Republican minority expect the majority of jobs and houses. If an RC applies for a job and is not up to the standard, he immediately cries discrimination' (Beryl Holland CDS 30.5.69). Whichever line is taken, the ultra message is that Catholics have no legitimate complaints about their treatment under Stormont (John Kerr IR 29.11.79), and the earlier history of Ireland is now irrelevant ('Disaffected Protestant' BO 9.4.81). Portadown in particular consists of 'a strong Protestant majority and satisfied, happy Catholic minority' ('British Subject' PDT 27.3.70). Not only are Catholics well treated in Northern Ireland, they are certainly better off than the Protestant minority in the Republic (Wilfred Breen IR 2.12.71).

A further excuse for economic dependency is the violence of this period which justifies special treatment: 'Northern Ireland has been living in virtual war-time conditions since 1968 ... The people of Northern Ireland are not seeking charity; they are seeking a greater appreciation of their plight' (LS 28.7.76). The violence is perpetrated by Catholics, and is the only reason for the need for British subventions: 'Only for the nationalist campaign over the past seventeen years we wouldn't have needed any large grants' ('Concerned Unionist' PDT 28.3.86). Hence Catholics are at the root of the destruction not only of Northern Ireland as represented by Stormont, but also of the Protestant virtue of self-reliance. Above all, of course, ultras see them as the source of all violence, as is suggested by their pre-colonial history of 'almost continuous internecine strife' ('John the Horse' IR 20.7.72). Protestants by contrast are law-abiding and peaceful ('Disgusted Ulsterman' IR 11.9.69), though men enough to be able to defend themselves (Kenny Allen LS 29.8.84).

Ultras certainly assume that all troublemakers are Catholics (Thomas Bothwell IR 9.10.69); but are all Catholics troublemakers? As cited above, the SDLP as well as Sinn Féin is often equated with the campaign of violence, the two parties together representing a majority of Catholics. Even the APNI has members 'who are IRA at heart' (Bertie Connor IR 1.6.72). In certain areas all Catholic males are probably members of republican paramilitary units:

> As for the politicians being silent when 'Wee Seamus from the Falls' gets shot down you could nearly be 100% sure that Wee Seamus is active in either the IRA or the INLA [Irish National Liberation Army]' ('Londonderry Loyalist' BO 15.3.84).

The SLDP's plans to erect a plaque to the dead of Bloody Sunday mean that it will 'commemorate the IRA sympathisers who were killed on Sunday, January 30, 1972, when they reaped the consequences of their lawlessness that day' ('Drumahoe Loyalist' LS 13.2.85). In addition, the long-held belief that Catholics are unable to think for themselves surfaces in claims that they are manipulated, misled and brainwashed by their politicians ('Peaceful Unionist' TLS 24.1.68).

The election of Bobby Sands, the IRA hunger-striker who won the Fermanagh by-election, proves the truth of the stereotypes:

Those 30,000 Roman Catholics in effect told the IRA that they fully supported that organisation's attempts to drive all Protestants out of the area. They have clearly stated that every time the IRA creates widows and orphans the Catholics of Fermanagh/ South Tyrone will gleefully rub their hands. Every time a defenceless woman collecting census forms is shot dead, 30,000 Catholic hearts will beat a little faster in joy. Is their hatred of their fellow countrymen pure sectarianism, or do they hope to get their hands on cheap farms and businesses if the Protestants are forced to leave the area? ... One can only assume from the election result that the votes of the 30,000 IRA backers is representative of the Catholic community as a whole and that the 'moderate' Catholic is indeed a rare animal ... how can the British Government expect a Protestant from Ulster to trust a Catholic from Cork when that Protestant has found out so shockingly that the local variety are so blood thirsty? ('Disillusioned' IR 16.4.81).

The *News Letter* describe the voters as acting both deliberately and mindlessly:

The grave implications are ... that more than 30,000 people in this country, with deliberation and in full recognition of the consequences, have aligned themselves with violence as a political solution ... the violence to which the 30,000 mindless voters in counties Fermanagh and Tyrone have given their blessing ... let those 30,000 electors be assured this morning that with them there cannot be, nor is there ever likely to be, unity of spirit. They have placed themselves beyond the boundaries of our civilisation (NL 11.4.81).

The implication here is not only that Catholics tend to be republicans but that they support the IRA (or INLA). At least one ultra, however, would not have been surprised by the election result:

As for trusting our RC neighbours, the majority of Fermanagh Protestants would not trust them as far as they would trust old Nick himself ... the barbarous deeds carried out by the IRA in this area could not have succeeded without the help of the local community ('A Loyal British Protestant' IR 5.2.81).

It is safer, then, to assume that all Catholics are violent or support violence; and if the course of Irish history has not changed, it is clearly the fault of its people, who have not changed either. This might be due to their adherence to 'Roman Catholicism which can never change' (Wesleyan PDN 10.8.79). Certainly Catholics cannot ever be trusted to share power:

I would suggest that the divisions of this community will never be healed by bowing to pressure imposed by men who supported the murderous campaign which has terrorised this province during the last five years. I refer of course to Messrs Fitt, Devlin, Currie, Hume and Cooper who have ridden on the back of this campaign to the positions which they now hold. Examine their past record and ask the questions, 'Can a leopard change its spots or an Ethiopian his colour?' (John McAuley BO 14.2.74).

Although there have always been moderates seeking reconciliation between Protestants and Catholics rather than the perpetuation of division, their views were rarely reflected by the editors of the Unionist local newspapers until the advent of O'Neill in the mid-1960s. This period marked a change in that a number of editors demonstrated moderate attitudes. At the same time many more readers wrote to their local newspapers expressing the need for reconciliation and engaging in debates with ultra letter-writers.

Moderates take the view that accommodation is both desirable and possible within Northern Ireland and hence take on the role of conciliators. They pursue a basic policy of focusing on what unites the people of Northern Ireland and associate the majority of Catholics with the Protestant majority in their desire for peace and friendly relations, excluding only Sinn Féin and republican paramilitaries.

Although it is occasionally stated that politics and not religion is the issue (PDN 2.9.77, 17.3.78), moderates lay the main blame, especially in the early days, on Protestant bigotry and sectarianism:

The threat to Northern Ireland's future is not Mr Wilson or Mr Lynch or the IRA or even Nationalism. It comes from Protestant Ulstermen who will not allow themselves to be liberated from the delusion that every Roman Catholic is their enemy (BT 5.11.68).

It is sectarianism which leads to discrimination and makes Northern Ireland an abnormal society which needs O'Neillite reforms to make it truly democratic:

The inescapable choice for Northern Ireland is between accepting reform and becoming a normal Western European Democracy, or remaining a political and social slum, with no friends, and in which: People are refused jobs and houses on account of their religion; obscene sectarian slogans on gable walls are regarded as folk art; honest and forward looking politicians are intimidated out of public life; such instruments for influencing children's minds as Junior Orange Lodges are accepted as ordinary features of society (L H Liddle CDS 17.10.69).

Many Ballymena Protestants are particularly disgusted at the idea that denomination determines politics or virtue:

> On both sides of the fence, Catholic and Protestant, there are good Christian people. People who think right; people who love one another and who love their country, not for what money, power or other gains they can make out of it (Name and address supplied BO 26.5.83).

Some moderates refuse to blame either side for 'the general misery caused by our wretched sectarian squabble' (PDT 21.12.84). Northern Ireland is 'an already far too divided community' (PDT 31.12.82) where 'normal politics have never had a chance ... with the religious-political divide separating people who have more in common than they will admit' (PDT 9.8.85). What is needed is 'a spirit of compromise and reconciliation' (PDN 23.3.73). In similar vein all local politicians are blamed for their failure to agree, thus 'condemning the one-and-a-half million inhabitants [that is, all of them] of Northern Ireland to an indefinite spell in the political, social and economic wilderness' (PDN 10.10.80). Contrary to ultras then, moderates assert that there is no essential difference between Catholics and Protestants and therefore union between them is possible. The notion of race is largely dropped or transmuted: 'The Armagh man is basically a mixture of two racial groupings – English planter stock and native Irish' (PDT 27.11.74).

Some ultra stereotypes are specifically rejected. For example, moderates assert that the great majority of Catholics are against violence and only paramilitaries should be blamed and targeted by the security forces. Hence intensified security measures should be designed to 'make life more difficult for the IRA activists and not to hold an entire Catholic population responsible' (BT 12.11.81). Even a reaction to the election of Bobby Sands was relatively mild:

> support for Mr Sands ... must be an unreliable guide to the level of support for violence. Fermanagh South Tyrone is real border country, where attitudes are unreservedly tribal ... [but] Fermanagh Protestants understandably ask: 'How can we trust neighbours who side with murderers of our kith and kin?' And it is a difficult question to answer ... A hunger striker is an MP, because tribal loyalties of Republicanism were stronger than a sense of right and wrong (BT 11.4.81).

On one occasion even the IRA was credited with a conscience, on the bombing of the Abercorn which was (correctly) attributed to it:

> Even the IRA ... deny responsibility. They know when there has

been an offence not just against law and order, which is part of their stock in trade, but against humanity on a major scale, and they cannot face it (BT 6.3.72).

The same source commented: 'Violence is written into Ireland's history and we are all a part of it, to some degree' (BT 22.11.74). The stereotyped picture of Catholics as dirty, over-fecund and unchristian is explicitly rejected (William S Dryburgh CDS 3.1.69). Moderates are also prone to assert that very many Catholics are content to remain within the UK (IR 9.4.70) and to remind readers that Catholics from North and South had voluntarily served in Britain's wars, whatever ultras, especially those who boycotted inter-denominational Remembrance Day ceremonies, might try to imply (CDS 10.6.77).

This tolerance does not, however, mean that all Catholic political parties are acceptable. Protestants must work with 'moderate Catholics like Oliver Napier [APNI]' (PDN 29.11.74), and the SDLP is accepted as a respectable political party, democratic and constitutional (BT 25.10.73), especially members like Lord Fitt, 'that respected politician' (PDT 21.3.86) – but only as long as it refrains from making 'arrogant and bullying requests' (CDS 16.7.71), does not push for a united Ireland (BT 22.9.72; PDN 17.1.75; PDT 16.10.74, 26.7.85), supports the RUC (IR 7.11.74; PDN 17.1.75, 22.8.75), accepts the right of British royalty to visit Northern Ireland (BT 8.8.77) and does not engage in such 'disloyal steps' as attacking 'respectable institutions such as the flying of the Union Jack, the description "Crown Courts" and ... the word "Royal" from the designation of the police force here' (PDT 23.8.85). In other words, it must not behave like a nationalist party. Sinn Féin on the other hand is not respectable and only one editor concedes that its five successful candidates for the Assembly have a democratic right to speak for its constituents and engage in political discussion with the Northern Ireland Office (NIO):

Mr Prior ... and the rest of us, must acknowledge their right to speak for their constituents ... scrupulous evenhandedness from Westminster may not solve the Irish Problem, but it's the only way to avoid compounding it (CDS 29.10.82).

The *Belfast Telegraph* has moved from its earlier more even-handed optimism to the perception that the Northern Ireland problem, including the violence, 'is based on the conflicting aspirations of two politically-divided communities' (BT 19.11.93), divided too in that 'Nationalists of all descriptions have learned to promote their aspiration in the most subtle fashion, around the globe, keeping everyone in suspense and never quite revealing their full political intent' (BT 21.3.94). Even among moderates, then, the old habits of denigrating

Catholics and seeing them as enemies are not always shaken off. For this reason the *Impartial Reporter* editors have to be considered self-styled moderates. Just as they oscillate between favouring and rejecting power-sharing, they also oscillate between moderate and ultra views on Catholics. On the one hand they claim to dislike sectarianism and hope for reconciliation, welcome the idea of a papal visit to Northern Ireland (IR 26.7.79), support integrated education (IR 28.1.82), and agree that 'Ireland's troubles stem largely from the partition of our country. The only difference between the majority and the minority is how the problem may be solved and peace brought about' (IR 14.3.85). On the other hand, they label NICRA/PD 'a campaign by a violent anarchistic minority' (IR 30.3.72) and claim that partition is irrelevant: 'Root causes do not matter: militancy is the same' (IR 18.8.77). This paper also finds it hard to shake off its historical antipathy to the Roman Catholic Church (IR 20.7.72, 29.11.84), and like most ultras conflates religion and politics. Hence the troubles are caused by 'a sizeable number of Nationalists, Republicans, Roman Catholics, call them what you will' (IR 11.9.70). When the divisions between the 'two kinds of people who inhabit Ireland' (IR 11.12.75) are spelled out, the favoured explanation remains race: 'It is still a case of two large racially opposite populations bitterly opposed' (IR 10.10.74). The editor clearly feels constrained to defend this terminology at one point:

> It is the racial, nationalist outlook which must be nurtured ... as adult nations have learned, keeping their cultures alive and thriving, even as part of a wider identity. Wales and Scotland are much further ahead than Ireland (IR 26.10.78).

Nevertheless, the general picture is of two opposed groups of people with little in common: 'the tangle of religious and political hatred, distrust and fear, which distorts life and living in Ireland ... ethnic loyalties, Celtic or British' (IR 23.10.80).

Other differences are implied. Some Catholics prefer to live on 'easy dole money' (IR 12.8.76). The Protestant ideal of self-help is particularly strongly expressed in the *Impartial Reporter*, which is even more dubious than most ultras about the value of the welfare state and public spending (IR 18.3.76), and similarly seeks to explain away the current economic dependence on the British state, but at the same time to stress the economic value of the Union: 'As for Ulster, it has been on the receiving side of regular grants and subsidies, even though it has always paid its way in full' (IR 10.2.77). The situation of the Irish Republic is still useful as a weapon, notwithstanding insulting the Irish state might offend some of the Catholics with whom reconciliation is supposedly sought. This 'poor off-shore dependant of Europe' is similarly dependent (IR

13.8.70) and is moreover still dependent on Britain (IR 28.11.68, 20.7.78).

The *Impartial Reporter* also shares ultra views of Catholic incapacity and disloyalty:

> While the Unionists did very well for fifty years, and expanded the economy of the country ... they did it without the help of the Roman Catholic minority, and in spite of many of their more militant anti-British elements (IR 31.5.73).

On the issue of discrimination this paper is indistinguishable from ultras. It claims variously that Catholics themselves are the worst offenders (IR 31.5.73, 18.8.83), that there is no discrimination against Catholics (IR 26.8.76) and that if it had existed it is normal political practice everywhere and in the Northern Ireland case is excused by Catholic 'disloyalty': 'No wonder they were not popular when it came to jobs and influential positions' (IR 2.11.72). The ultra claim that Catholics are by nature violent is also echoed:

> the searches and 'discrimination' were directed against Roman Catholics, because the Protestant community was until then loyal and law-abiding. Ireland is still a place of tribal superstitions and witch-doctors, and the body of the people have a morbid conservatism which deadens progress. It has proved the perfect seed-bed for treachery and sedition, anarchy and lawlessness (IR 11.12.75).

It is for this reason that the formation of Northern Ireland has had no effect on:

> the basic and underlying attitudes of the Roman Catholic minority in Ulster, the refusal to recognise and encourage cooperation and a new understanding ... the inflexibility which has shut out all hope of cooperation and partnership in all avenues of life from government to local administration, from cultural activities to sport, ever since 1922 (IR 7.11.74).

Fortunately Protestants are a match for them, thanks to 'the basic Protestant instinct, forged in centuries of war, rebellion and hardship' (IR 18.7.68).

ON THE FACE of it it is not surprising that editors in the border areas of Derry and Fermanagh, with large numbers of Catholics and a high incidence of violence, should tend to focus on division; but editorial policy rather than area seems to be more important in the case of the Morton-owned Portadown papers and the province-wide

Belfast Telegraph. Letters from both ultras and moderates come from all areas. Moderates on the whole avoid stereotyping Catholics, focusing instead on what Protestants and respectable Catholics have in common and seeing Catholic violence as an aberration by a small minority; but the greater number of references to Catholics comes from ultras.

Although letters from ultras on the political situation in Northern Ireland form only a small part of all letters to the editor, it should be noted that editorial policy plays a part not only in selecting which letters to print, but also in cutting out of printed letters the more offensive sections (see for example CDS 28.7.78, whose editor in 1990 and again in 1994 confirmed that certain letters in their original form were unprintable; and TLS 31.10.84, editor's emendations to the letter from 'Watch Tower'). This understandable policy means that at least some anti-Catholic opinion is not accessible in the letters columns; but there is no shortage all the same. Further, there are many continuities between the three periods, and much of the data is redolent of the settler racism described in chapter 1. Fanon's perception that settlers see themselves as good and the 'natives' as an evil power against which an eternal battle must be fought seems peculiarly appropriate as a description of much ultra thinking. All ultras hold that there is a deep division in Ireland between Protestants and Catholics, and the Other is always there, a potential enemy, whether under the Union until 1921 or subsequently. The doctrinal difference between the two groups is used to maintain the boundaries and as an important element in the denigration of Catholic culture. That the issue is, however, the question of which group will hold power, rather than a 'religious' conflict, is suggested by the conflation of religion and politics common to the three periods, and political labels are preferred on the whole. Despite this, the reason for Catholic disaffection is never admitted to be genuinely political: just as settlers in other societies claimed about 'native' demands, Catholic 'woes' are either imaginary or merely past history, invented by violent agitators for people who are easily manipulated and unable to think for themselves.

Other features of the portraits of Catholics and Protestants show notable continuities. It is true that Catholics also stereotype Protestants in a denigratory way, but there is a fundamental difference in the content of the stereotypes: Protestant stereotyping of Catholics is similar to the stereotypes of 'natives' held in settler colonial societies: they are groups considered both inferior and threatening. It is the threatening nature of the existence of large numbers of Catholics and the well-founded fear engendered of their eventual dominance that creates the 'siege mentality' often observed in settler societies as well as in Northern Ireland. Of the elements of the portrait of the colonised drawn from the literature, the following are also found in the stereotype of twentieth-century Irish Catholics described above: laziness, inefficiency, lack of ambition, ingratitude, deviousness, moral laxity, emotionality, superstition, thraldom to manipulative leaders and violence. Childishness may perhaps be inferred from the above. By contrast, Protestants portray themselves as hardworking and competent, peaceful and law-abiding but manly and resolute.

There are changes in the discourse about Catholics as the century progresses. The 'minority' emerges as a label once Northern Ireland was established with its carefully-devised Protestant majority. Race as an explanation of the division and the denigration of the 'Celtic race' become increasingly rare; and descriptions of the Irish as volatile, impractical dreamers are missing from the modern period, perhaps because these interpretations are too benign to apply to people who achieved the fall of Stormont. The mocking epithets of 1912–21 are largely confined to the Irish state after that period. Nevertheless, the widening gap between Protestant and Catholic birth-rates, which had differed little up to 1911, allowed a new stereotype to emerge, that of 'dirty' Catholics 'breeding' too many children. Poverty and prosperity also become problematic from the 1920s. Although Catholics are stigmatised as poor and Protestants lauded as prosperous up to the 1939–49 period, there is increasingly less certainty about the latter, who of course also suffered the Depression and the economic need to emigrate, if not to the same extent as Catholics; and by the modern period prosperity is viewed retrospectively, as belonging to the days of Stormont rule. Protestant poverty is now proclaimed. Conversely Catholic poverty is no longer asserted, as this is precisely one of the things Catholics are complaining about. A related change is seen in the decline in assertions of Protestant self-reliance. This is still seen as a basic character trait, as it is in settler societies in general, but the obvious dependency of Northern Ireland has stifled claims to self-sufficiency. Catholics do serve, however, as a reason for this loss.

The continuity of the portrait and the consistent determination to resist not merely rule by Catholics but even the sharing of any degree of power with them suggests that an underlying assumption is that they will never change, and the nature of the stereotype allied with this assumption and with the fear of eventual Catholic 'domination' constitutes a form of racism little distinguishable from settler racism. These attitudes and attempts to paint a derogatory picture of Catholics seem certain to persist for at least as long as the British government continues to propose power-sharing or appears ambivalent in its project for the future of Northern Ireland.

4 From Ireland to Ulster

DURING THE THIRD Home Rule crisis Irish nationalists had a powerful propaganda base in the House of Commons, and more than ever before Protestants had to attempt to manipulate British opinion in favour of 'Ulster's cause'. Unionist newspaper editorials were an important part of the propaganda battle. Local newspapers naturally addressed the local readership, encouraging supporters of the Union and persuading Protestant waverers and doubters to support it too. More unexpectedly, they also attempted to convince cross-channel readers of the rightness of Ulster's cause, for even local papers were (and still are) sent to the many migrants to Great Britain and further afield who, it was hoped, would play their part in 'educating' their neighbours. Local newspapers were also anxiously assiduous observers of the British political scene, sensitive to every nuance, which they conveyed to their local readership. However, there was one section of the population they rarely addressed, or even mentioned: Ulster Catholics. These indeed remained largely invisible, and the casual reader might think Catholics in Ulster were few, highly localised and politically apathetic. It was largely Catholics in the other three provinces who were routinely portrayed to the Protestant and British 'audience' as unfit to contribute to the government of Ireland.

Along the way, the arguments altered to suit the circumstances, but there were many continuities, and many of the arguments were repetitions of claims made in the first Home Rule crisis, when rural Conservative/unionist newspapers argued that Home Rule would be Rome Rule; that it would be economically disastrous for Ireland and threatened the integrity of the empire; that there were two 'Irish nations' and that Ulster should have a separate assembly; and that unionists in Ulster should resist Home Rule with armed force (Anderson 1988:150–1). The 'two nations' claim and the still-repeated assertion that Ireland was never united except under British rule have long been used to counter the argument that unionists should accept the will of the majority in Ireland.

A distinct shift in ideology, however, involves identity. It is a widely-held, though not universal, idea that Northern Ireland Protestants have an 'identity problem', in that they do not truly know who they are, though Hennessey (1993:23–8, 30–4) has documented the

84

complex of territorial identities which Ulster Protestants held in the 1886–93 period without discomfort or contradiction: county, Ulster, Ireland, United Kingdom and empire, all bound by the Crown. From 1912, however, the shifting of Northern Protestants' 'imagined community' from Ireland, first to Ulster and the empire and subsequently also to Britain, can be traced.

If there is an 'identity problem', it perhaps arises from the dubious nature of 'British' as a nationality (Lijphart 1975:86). After all, the term 'British' arises from a legal (from the English point of view) union of formerly separate territories, the United Kingdom of Great Britain and Ireland, which then went on to form an overseas empire of British subjects, both settlers and 'natives'. The empire has gone and the union has changed with the establishment of the Irish Free State. Further changes are legally possible. So the term 'British' is an inherently unstable identity, as well as a slippery category (as many British subjects denied entry to Great Britain could attest to – not to mention British citizens from Northern Ireland excluded under the Prevention of Terrorism Act [PTA]). On the other hand people born in, for example, England or Scotland of English or Scottish forebears cannot be legally deprived of calling themselves 'English' or 'Scottish' respectively whatever happens to the Union which makes them all legally 'British'. Being 'English' or 'Scottish' involves an imagined sense of continuity with the past and with the territory that predates the modern nation-state and the Union.

From a different angle again it has been pointed out that it is, at the very least, disingenuous to conceptualise the current conflict merely in terms of different national identities and allegiances that can be reconciled simply by evolving constitutional arrangements which recognise the value of both 'traditions', as this wrongly assumes that 'the conflict can be mended through the symbolic inclusions of the embattled communities in expressive institutions' (MacDonald 1991:85). This is no solution because, as is often pointed out, Protestants' sense of political identity is formed through opposition (often in a concrete sense as in the confrontational behaviour of the marching season) to that of Catholics. Nevertheless the question of national identity in Northern Ireland cannot be ignored since it gives rise not only to a literature based both on surveys and on impressions but also to autonomous (if politically-motivated) assertions of national identity by the actors themselves.

Major attitude surveys were carried out in 1968, 1978, 1986 and 1989. Even taking into account differences between them (for example, 'Northern Irish' was an option only in 1986 and 1989, and 'British/Irish' was offered only in 1989), there has been a notable change since 1968, when only 39 per cent of Protestants chose 'British' and fully 20 per cent 'Irish', with 32 per cent opting for

'Ulster'. In subsequent surveys 'British' ranged between 65 and 68 per cent, with 'Irish' having plummeted to 3 per cent by 1986. 'Ulster', however, when combined with 'Northern Irish', shows much more stability with between one-fifth and one-quarter of respondents choosing this regional identity. The two terms do, however, have different connotations, shown by the finding that APNI members were more than twice as likely to choose 'Northern Irish' as either Democratic Unionist Party (DUP) or Ulster Unionist Party (UUP) members. There were also class differences, with Protestants in class 1 being more likely than any other class to choose either a 'British' identity (82 per cent) or an 'Irish' one (18 per cent) (see Moxon-Browne 1991:25–9 for detailed results).

Such surveys do not necessarily reveal what the chosen terms actually mean to the actors or how important they are. For example, Trew (1983:29–31) found not only that different methods of investigation led to discrepant conclusions, but also that faced with the open-ended question 'What are you?' only 4 per cent of Protestants in her 1981 sample mentioned nationality, and none in her 1982 sample. Todd (1987:3, 11, 17), exploring meaning through a survey of literature by and about Northern Ireland Protestants, found that the primary imagined community of Ulster loyalists consisted of Northern Protestants, whereas that of the group she designates 'Ulster British' was Greater Britain. Two interviews which explore the meanings attached to identity reveal the complexity of the issue. The UDA leader Andy Tyrie explained that he had been educated to think of himself as a 'British subject', but when he went to Britain he found both that he was treated as if he were Irish and that he found he 'had more in common with lads from the Falls than with the English' (Bell 1985:3). His eventual solution to his newly-found identity problem was to turn to Adamson's theory of the Cruthin, which gave him ancient historical roots in Ulster. The poet John Hewitt on the other hand discerned different levels of identity according to context:

> We've always had a strong association with Scotland ... the people who worked in North-East Ulster were working for the British imperial market ... so they were British. It wasn't the Irish market so they weren't Irish. So that has made our national identity a difficult problem ... Ireland is part of the British Isles. I was born in the North of Ireland before partition, so I'm an Irishman in that way ... I speak English and I know no other tongue, so I'm British. And because we're an archipelago to the west of Europe, I'm European. So that's my hierarchy: I'm an Ulsterman, an Irishman, British and European (Levine 1985:16).

Local newspapers too provide an alternative means to surveys of assessing the identity of Protestants and the changes in that identity at critical periods in the twentieth century, and they also reveal the complexity of the process. The distancing of Ulster from the rest of Ireland and the shift towards an Ulster identity required the invention of Protestant (as opposed to British) rights to Ulster. This entailed the usurpation of Ulster both from Ireland and from Ulster Catholics, a process which continues today.

THE PROCESS OF distancing Ulster from the rest of Ireland did not begin as early as many claim. In the early years of the third Home Rule crisis, there are many signs of identification by Protestants with Ireland as a whole. For example, there were many claims that the 'Betrayal of Ireland Bill' would 'sacrifice the best interests of Ireland' (BO 11.7.13), and Ireland's prosperity would be ruined by the inevitable disorder. The country can prosper only under British rule:

> We have a land system, thanks to the generosity of England, unequalled in the world. We lean upon the strong arm of Great Britain in our hours of need; her laws are equitable; her generosity is unstinted; she alone is adequate to the task of enforcing obedience and respect for law and order, and public safety (BT 15.3.12).

Ireland is lost if it is placed 'at the mercy of the Ancient Order of Hibernians' (LS 11.5.12):

> Unionists ... wish to keep Ireland generally free of the terrorism which has devastated large areas of it ... Ulster Protestants believe themselves justified in doing everything in their power to avert these evils, which they maintain would come upon Roman Catholics in scarcely less marked degree than upon themselves (LS 26.9.12).

It is therefore Protestants who best know what is good for Ireland and Catholics who should be excluded from its governance, if necessary by:

> The loyal third of the population of Ireland who tomorrow take their solemn oath and covenant not to submit to the betrayal of their country into the hands of the Irish Nationalist Party (CDS 27.9.12).

This early concern with Ireland as a whole did, however, begin to diminish as the Bill proceeded through parliament: if Ireland could not be saved from its nationalist majority then perhaps Ulster could, and the welfare of Ireland gave way to the welfare of Ulster. The Northern Province was given the characteristics of its Protestant people: peaceful, law-abiding and progressive, while the rest of Ireland was identified with a violent and backward people. The rural nature of much of Ulster was ignored in its portrayal as 'the prosperous business province of the country' (LS 31.12.12), and its fragile garrison, dependent on metropolitan troops, was transformed into the claim that 'Ulster holds the fort; and again Ulster will have saved Ireland for the United Kingdom' (IR 3.8.16). Its high position means that the exclusion of Ireland from conscription would be 'a bitter pill for Ulster to swallow' (NL 30.12.15). Ulster then began to be portrayed as a place apart, frequently personified, in the tradition of nationalism: 'She is not prepared to be handed over to the uncovenanted mercies of her hereditary enemies' (PDN 25.5.12) and will 'remain apart ... until the rest of Ireland be fit for Ulster to recognise as capable of self-government' (IR 2.10.13).

The nationalist case that Home Rule should be granted to the whole island under one parliament has to be countered: 'Ulster does not care for an "Ireland which is indivisible" ... what she does care for is peace and security within her borders' (IR 15.6.16). One device is to claim that 'Ireland' does not mean the island of Ireland but the people who inhabit it: 'Here, as always, there are two Irelands, and the Ireland which is opposed to Home Rule has done more to win the war than the Ireland which demands it' (NL 13.5.16). Hence 'Ireland' is stripped of meaning: '"His [Lord Northcliffe's] Northern friends" have nothing in common with the rebels of Dublin and Enniscorthy, except the accident that they both live on the same island' (LS 20.3.17). Another device is to separate the island into 'Ireland' and 'Ulster': 'Ireland (as we may now call the 26 counties of Ireland)' (IR 29.6.16), although the term 'Irish Ireland' used by the same newspaper suggests that this separation was not complete (IR 21.6.17). Southern Protestant Home Rulers are rejected along with the rest of Ireland, on the grounds that Southern Protestant dioceses are 'quite different in religion and race' from Northern ones (IR 3.8.16); and their abandonment on partition is dismissed by one paper on the grounds that they would probably suffer no more under Home Rule than they already did and the important thing is that 'in cutting the painter that even now binds us to the Irish barque we are serving our own interests' (CDS 30.11.18).

There appears a willingness on the part of unionists to define themselves as a nation when circumstances favour this. One thrust of their argument is that Ireland is not a nation but a mixture of peoples (BT 24.2.12), but it is simultaneously argued that 'our "nation" is that of the United Kingdom, in which there are several peoples, kindred and tongues' (IR 4.4.12). The right to constitute a nation is clearly selective, and denied to Ireland because, even if it stayed within the empire, it would become effectively independent

(IR 28.3.12). The alleged reason for the outbreak of war in 1914 was, however, the defence of small nations and this led to a change in direction. Ireland, rather than being an integral part of the British nation is composed of two nations: 'The partition proposals ... represented an attempt to give a sort of recognition to the existence of the two nationalities' (LS 12.8.16). The corollary of this is that 'Protestant Ulster is as much of a nation and has as much right to be considered a self-determining unity as has Nationalist Ireland' (CDS 20.4.18). The careful choice of wording suggests that assertion of an Ulster nationality is partly a reaction to the Irish nationalists' prior claim to nationhood and partly a rhetorical device to claim separate treatment from the rest of Ireland, but there is no protest against Lloyd George's assertion that the two parts of Ireland 'differ in race, religion, temperament and outlook – in everything that constitutes the fundamental essentials of a nation' (NL 23.7.19).

For some, Irish unity remained an object to be desired, and there is recognition that Southern Irishmen were fighting alongside Ulstermen: 'They died together, men of Antrim and men of Clare' (BO 24.8.17); but in view of the character of nationalist Ireland, such unity can exist only under British rule. Advocating a tunnel link between Ireland and Great Britain, one editor thinks that 'the closer incorporation of Ireland in the life of Britain ... would wreck our insularism – would destroy Sinn Feinism' (CDS 23.3.18). Even with partition safely complete Carson's wish was echoed: if the rest of Ireland peacefully enters its new parliament, there should ensue 'the unity of Ireland, with the accord of all its people, within the unity of the Kingdom and the Empire under the Crown and Constitution' (NL 22.6.21). Ulster, then, though separate from the rest of Ireland, is still perhaps Irish in its own way.

THE ROAD TO partition reveals some interesting aspects of the separation of Ulster from Ireland. The official view is that Home Rule of any kind is undesirable but that the exclusion of Ulster, even under its own parliament, is the lesser evil:

> Some Liberals have made the desperate suggestion of a separate Ulster Parliament as an escape from the national assembly proposed. Ulster wants no such compromise ... It is only in the event of a forced expulsion that she will fall back upon an Ulster Parliament as the sole defence left to her against the intolerable tyranny, but that in the last extremity she will do so there can be no doubt whatever (BT 4.1.12).

Any exclusion should be of all nine counties or none (IR 9.5.12, 12.3.14); and the later 'sacrifice' of three counties and the exclusion of only six is made patriotically, if reluctantly, for the sake of the empire and the nation (BT 13.6.16). The partition of Ireland and proposed establishment of two local parliaments is, if necessary at all, caused by 'natural' factors such as differences in race, creed or nationality or by the intransigence of nationalists, and not by any actions of Ulster unionists (LS 12.8.16) (who to prove this abstained in the final vote on the Government of Ireland Act). One aspect which is clearly heartfelt rather than propaganda is that any exclusion must be permanent (NL 13.2.14), and to ensure this all loyalists must vote Unionist in the 1921 election (CDS 12.2.21).

This version of the path to partition is belied to some extent by the variations in the contemporary accounts. Only the *Londonderry Sentinel* began the period arguing against any type of partition (LS 4.5.12) and it remained relatively unenthusiastic about a Northern parliament (LS 19.5.21). The cautious support for exclusion of the North Down paper, on the other hand (CDS 25.7.13, 30.11.18), gave way to optimistic fervour, if only on Imperial grounds:

> With Lord Londonderry we believe that in 'the great new departure – the Ulster parliament – lies the consummation and eventuality' for which all true men hope, namely, a peaceful Empire to which we all belong (CDS 29.1.21).

The *News Letter* went further, despite its later reversion (NL 8.6.21) to the line that the old Union was preferable:

> In the Six Counties we are masters of our own fate now; our political, social and economic future is in our own hands now, and we are content to take whatever risks that may entail, believing we can do better for ourselves in the matter of real progress than the Imperial Government has been able to do for us, with the wheels of reform clogged by Irish Nationalist obstruction and obscurantism (NL 27.5.21).

The newspaper whose editorials reveal most clearly the twists and turns in the process of extracting Ulster from the Irish menace is the *Impartial Reporter*. Although later conforming to the official line that Ulster did not want its own parliament and joining in the chorus of 'all Ulster or none', the paper in fact was an early enthusiast both for partition and a separate parliament under the Imperial Parliament (IR 2.1.13), and it early considered the choice between a separate legislature either for a six-county or a nine-county Ulster (IR 16.5.12). In a county whose Catholic majority might make it expendable, the local concern, rather than for Protestants throughout Ulster, was to fight against the proposal of four-county exclusion: 'Fermanagh and Tyrone are just as antagonistic to Home Rule as Down and Antrim' (IR 14.8.13). Finally, after the 1921 election, the editor excitedly declares:

The Union Jack has swept Ulster! Not one Unionist candidate has been defeated! ... an outstanding victory, so complete and so over-whelming, that it is bound to have had tremendous effect in England. The net result of the great rally of Empire Day, is that the North has put itself outside the bounds of all English party politics. The North is now independent, and nothing can rob her of her parliament ... the Union is dead, the North is free (IR 2.6.21).

There is no doubt that, as this editor states so openly, at least some Ulster unionists felt that they had shaken off metropolitan interfer-ence and had won for themselves a 'state' in which, as a substantial majority instead of a minority, they could at last exercise direct control in favour of their own interests *vis-à-vis* Catholics.

Since the excluded area was to consist of only six counties, Ulster had to be re-defined. From the sixteenth century the province had consisted of nine counties: Antrim, Down, Derry, Tyrone, Armagh, Fermanagh, Donegal, Cavan and Monaghan, of which all but Antrim, Down and Monaghan formed the official Plantation of Ulster. The greatest number of settlers, however, was attracted to Antrim and Down, and so the distribution of Protestants was uneven. Initially, therefore, the idea that counties would be allowed to vote individu-ally on the Home Rule issue was unpopular, and the greatest area could be excluded by considering Ulster as a whole:

> Geographically and historically Ulster is a distinct unit in Ireland, while the counties are purely arbitrary areas ... In only four of the nine counties of Ulster – Antrim and Down (including Belfast), Armagh and Londonderry – are Protestants in the majority. Yet, taking the whole Province, the Protestants number 890,880 and the Roman Catholics 640,972 ... county option ... would be not only illogical on geographical and historical grounds, but it would be grossly unfair to the Unionists of Ulster outside the four North-Eastern counties (NL 9.3.14).

However, particularly if the North was to have its own parliament, the Protestant majority was dangerously slender, and despite the warning that 'for the Unionists of the North-East to desert the Unionists of [Donegal, Tyrone, Cavan and Monaghan] now would be an act of infamy' (LS 23.7.14), the 'all Ulster or none' stance gave way to the 'reluctant' decision (LS 8.6.16) in 1916 to accept Lloyd George's plan and agree to the exclusion from Home Rule of the four eastern counties, plus Fermanagh with its slight Protestant minority and Tyrone with which, despite its substantial Catholic majority, it is impossible to part, as it is 'the heart of Ulster' (IR 23.7.14). The City of Derry, also with a Catholic majority, is also 'saved' for the Union. There is some metaphorical hand-wringing over the loyalists of the abandoned counties:

> We shall make no pretence of enthusiasm ... We could not save Cavan, Monaghan and Donegal, because of the changed attitude of the Coalition Cabinet ... It is mainly at their instance that we have to wring the hands of our brethren of Donegal, Cavan and Monaghan in agony and regret, and bid them good-bye if we are to save ourselves ... Nothing but absolute loyalty to the Empire and Sir Edward Carson has made this last, and in some respects greatest sacrifice of all, possible ... Ulster has for the sake of the Empire made the supreme sacrifice asked of her ... Having given her sons, now she has given her very soul (BT 13.6.16).

In 1920 the Ulster Unionist Council twice rejected a motion for a nine-county Ulster for, as Carson pointed out, of the 890,000 Protestants in Ulster, 830,000 lived in six counties: better sacrifice 60,000 Protestants than risk eventual Catholic domination of an Ulster parliament – and even a large Catholic minority would be politically troublesome (LS 11.3.20). A pamphlet issued by the Unionists of Cavan, Monaghan and Donegal pointed out that the six counties legislature would be too small and parochial and that 'it would be unwise that the Northern Parliament should have too great a majority'; but it was summarised without comment (LS 24.4.20).

Again the *Impartial Reporter* makes an interesting study: 'We admit that but for a slice of North Monaghan and a slice of West Cavan, neither of those counties belong to our Ulster; and the same thing applies to three-fourths of the County Donegal' (IR 8.6.16). Acknowledging that the main sacrifice involved was made by the abandoned counties, rather than by 'Ulster' or by Ulster Unionists in general (BO 16.6.16), the editor was not abashed to point out the great advantage of such a 'sacrifice': 'By that act a stronger Ulster is built up ... Practically, the new Ulster of the Six Counties of the Plantation will contain two Unionists to one Nationalist' (IR 15.6.16). He later turned his attention to the new boundaries, proposing changes which would exclude as many 'Nationalists' and incorporate as many 'Unionists' as possible to make 'our Ulster completely homogeneous' (IR 13.5.20).

'The area to be known as Ulster' (LS 6.5.20) was not therefore historic Ulster; 'our Ulster' was Protestant Ulster, even if its redefinition entailed the exclusion of 60,000 Ulster Protestants. Protestants from the abandoned counties and other parts of the Free State continued long after partition to send letters to Northern Ireland newspapers protesting about their fate and the plight of the border Protestants is often mentioned in editorials. Generally though the abandonment of Ulster Protestants is subsumed under the lot of 'their persecuted brethren from Eire' (LS 15.7.44), with the aim of reinforcing the rightness of partition and as a weapon to refute local Catholic complaints. 'Ulster' comes generally to refer to the six counties excluded from the Union, although Northern Ireland Protestants are quick to claim Montgomery (whose Ulster connections were with Donegal) as their 'fellow-countryman' (LS 20.8.42). Ireland or 'Eire' consists of the remaining twenty-six.

THE PROCESS OF separation seems to be completed by the Ireland Act of 1949, which, it is foreseen, will make the rest of Ireland 'a foreign and independent nation' and its inhabitants foreigners and aliens (IR 28.10.48), so there is annoyance that 'in their generosity the British propose not to treat Eire as a "foreign" country' (IR 12.5.49). This turned to anger, above all for ultras, when successive British governments began consultations with the Republic over Northern Ireland, and references to Eire as a foreign country multiply from Sunningdale through to the Anglo–Irish Agreement. Such talks constitute 'appeasement' ('Birches Loyalist' PDN 25.4.75), parallel with Chamberlain's agreement that Germany should take over Czechoslovakia in 1938. 'Eire' has no right to interfere or even to express an opinion. With the threat of Irish unity apparently backed up by a British government, Irish government, central and local, long merely a subject for mockery, becomes 'alien', 'hostile' and 'foreign', and the result of the Anglo–Irish Conference is a 'foreign invasion' (Raymond Farrell IR 7.11.85). The British seem not to realise that the Irish are essentially anti-British ('A True Ulster Loyalist' IR 17.10.85), and have forgotten that, like Argentina, they opened their ports to the German navy and 'assisted fascist Germany in its war against Britain and her allies' (Charles Quinn BO 20.5.82).

Under certain conditions cooperation with this alien state might be welcome:

> Only extreme Irish republicans could object to closer links between Eire and the United Kingdom, per se, to the mutual advantage of the peoples of both countries ... An Eire in a Siamese-twins link-up with the United Kingdom – and an Anglo–Irish Intergovernmental Council to be the first of several intended fleshly bonds, with possible electricity and gas interconnections, and intimate cooperation in many spheres, and neither side regarded as 'foreign' – is far removed from the Gaelic speaking 'ourselves alone' atavistic dream of Pearse-type fanatical republicans ... That having been said, however, Unionists in Northern Ireland will have to ensure that, if Eire is the 'returning prodigal', its trip back home will not be rewarded with Ulster as the sacrificial 'fatted calf' (NL 7.11.81).

The term 'returning prodigal' implies penitence and clientship on the part of the Republic, rather than signifying a relationship between two sovereign states; and Northern Ireland is still to remain safely separate – unless the island is unified within a restored United Kingdom (OS Apr 1986).

Even social relations with the Irish south of the border are unpopular. 'Twinning' is usually done with foreign towns, but a proposal that Ballymena should twin with a town in the Republic is indignantly rejected:

> True Loyalists will totally reject any concept of teaming-up with a town South of the border. It is repulsive and acrimonious to the majority of people in the Ballymena area. The Borough Council [DUP] were quite right in throwing out Castlebar's offer to strengthen ties. The less we see and hear of Southern citizens the better. Our aim surely is to strengthen ties with the mainland, not with some foreign source ('Loyalist' BO 1.3.79).

Irish sport is also a thorny issue. Defending his refusal to support a civic reception for a Catholic Olympic canoeist on the grounds (subsequently refuted) that he had participated under the Irish tricolour, a DUP councillor went on to complain about Ulstermen playing rugby for Ireland: 'If we are British and Unionist we must be seen as such and not acting as half-baked Irish baps to the Irish Republic in the field of sport' (Bert Johnson IR 26.3.81).

There seems little doubt that labelling the Republic a foreign country is a way both of expressing hatred for that country and by implication pointing to Northern Irish nationalists as traitors. The aim is therefore two-fold: to persuade the British government to resist all demands for Irish unity and to stop treating Catholics as if they have any right to consideration for their national aspirations. Moderates, however, display rather different attitudes from ultras. In general, they differentiate between attitudes to the Irish government and constitution on the one hand, and feelings about Ireland and the people of the Republic on the other. For example, although the issue of 'racial difference' surfaces even in the moderate *County Down Spectator*, it is of little importance in comparing the Irish North and South:

> And the differences between them? Harder to define. Some variation in the admixture of racial characteristics – though the constant influx of alien blood on both sides and the frequent exchange of genes across the border has made happy nonsense of any pretentions towards a pure national type north or south... A rather small difference of religious approach, comparable with that between Sephardic and Ashkenazim Jews ... for much the main part the same mother-tongue. In fact, no differences greater than cheerfully co-exist in most modern societies ... Indeed, there is no good reason

why the natives of any part of these islands should mistrust those of any other (CDS 12.12.80).

All-Ireland sport, especially when the opponent is England, is popular with moderates:

> the Ulster people (do not) want to live in perpetual war with their neighbours of the South. The Northern Irishman is proud of the fact that he is a son of Erin. Whether it is when Ireland beats England at Windsor Park at soccer, or when Bill McBride and Mike Gibson play their part in a Landsdowne Road triumph, he takes pride in the achievements of the boys in green. The Ulster 'exile' in Toronto, Melbourne and Wellington feels the same affection for his country (PDN 5.4.74).

Generally, however, relations with the Republic of Ireland, a state which claims jurisdiction over the North, are a matter for caution, and a few moderates also dream of the Irish state returning to the British fold, but as part of a federation with Northern Ireland separately represented in a 'United States of Britain' ('Peacemaker' LS 26.11.69). Talks between the British and Irish governments are usually welcomed because of the practical advantages, especially in the security field, of cementing the 'special relationship which exists with the Irish Republic because of our joint land frontier' (BT 5.7.74), but on condition that the North's future within the United Kingdom is not endangered. Hence the *Belfast Telegraph* approved of the Council of Ireland (as long as the Irish state did not use it to dictate to Northern Ireland) because it was promised that there would be no change without the consent of the majority in the North (BT 18.9.73); but this paper, wrong-footed by Protestant reactions to Sunningdale, had changed its approach by the 1980s. Friendly Anglo–Irish relations are to be commended but it would be unwise to 'risk institutionalising relationships between North and South' (BT 8.11.83) and after the New Ireland Forum report it began to talk about the issue of 'sovereignty':

> In practical terms, if the RUC or Garda were authorised to cross the border on duty, London or Dublin would be accepting responsibility for the actions of foreign nationals on their territory, which is inconceivable (BT 8.5.84).

The paper's rejection of the Anglo–Irish Agreement then had been foreseeable at least since 1983. Now, like most of the other moderate papers, it objected to the way the Agreement was implemented without the consent of 'the people':

To a people whose instinctive distrust of the Republic has been cemented by a sustained and vicious terrorist campaign by the IRA, the stakes now are unacceptable ... Even those who, like this newspaper, can see benefit flowing from closer consultation with Dublin, must draw the line at such institutionalised links between the two countries. This is on the pragmatic grounds that there is not consent from the people to be affected by the arrangement (BT 25.11.85).

The only newspaper which supported the Anglo–Irish Agreement was the *County Down Spectator*:

The fact that, for the first time, a formal role has been afforded to the Republic of Ireland in the affairs of Northern Ireland is not a minor change – but nor is it a threat to British sovereignty. The British government reserved to itself the power to make all decisions affecting us ... It is impossible not to sympathise with Unionists who strongly resent a foreign power having any formalised say in their affairs. Yet even this should be seen in the context of the UN, of NATO and the EEC, all of which may be considered to infringe national autonomy. We enter into such pacts in the hope of gaining more than we lose, and that principle applies here too (CDS 21.11.85).

THE COMMON CLAIM that Ulster Protestants have 'always' held a British identity is demonstrably false. In the 1912–21 period, five broad categories of self-assigned identity existed, Irish, Ulster, Protestant, British and imperial, and these run concurrently to quite an extent. Not only are there variations over time but also between newspapers.

An Irish identity survived throughout this whole period. The *News Letter* and the *Londonderry Sentinel* in particular continue to identify with 'Irish Unionists' long after the formation of the Ulster Unionist Party and the *Belfast Telegraph*, *News Letter*, *Londonderry Sentinel*, *Ballymena Observer*, *Portadown News* and *County Down Spectator* all identified with 'Irish Protestants', in opposition to either English Protestants or Irish Catholics. Other terms that express a particular brand of Irishness are 'the loyal Irish' and 'loyalist Irishmen' (BO 23.2.12), and in one case 'loyalist Irishmen of every class and creed' (BO 26.1.12); but by and large this 'section of the Irish population' (LS 15.7.19) consists largely of the Protestant minority or 'the loyal third of the population of Ireland' (BO 27.9.12), rather than to the people of 'Irish-Ireland' (IR 22.4.20).

Protestants as well as unionists are 'patriotic Irishmen' (NL 2.1.12), and even in the North-East corner of Ulster it is proclaimed: 'Whatever our political differences we are all Irishmen' (BO 21.1.16). Of the Irish divisions, only the Ulster Division (which

contained only about ten Catholics [Boyce 1990:246]) is 'truly Irish
in its composition' (BT 5.1.16); and even after the 1916 Rising there
is 'comradeship between the English and Irish in the ranks', the
Irish being 'soldiers from North and South' (BT 23.8.17), while
strike-bound Belfast is 'our quandam Irish city' (CDS 1.2.19). The
Impartial Reporter, which uses 'Irish' both to include and exclude
Protestants in the same editorial (IR 4.4.12), nevertheless hopes that
every Ulsterman will pray that North and South together can make
Ireland 'truly "First gem of the ocean, first isle of the sea"' (IR
23.6.21), while even just before partition the fiercely loyalist Derry
paper refers to Catholics and nationalists as 'fellow-countrymen' as
does the Fermanagh paper in the context of the Easter Rising (LS
23.9.20; IR 27.4.16).

The majority of 'Irish' self-appellations, however, are found in the
period up to 1916, the year of the Easter Rising, which is seen as
forming a decisive break within Protestant ideology, after which
identification with Ireland is largely reduced to that with the province of Ulster and eventually with the six excluded counties. Some
time after the Rising, 'Ulstermen may be deemed to be Irelanders,
but not Irishmen, in the sense in which that word is generally
understood' (IR 3.8.16), and 'the Irish' or 'the Irish people' specifically exclude Protestants (LS 20.3.17; IR 18.4.18).

The focus on Ulster is not new: 'Ulster' and 'Irish' identities run
concurrently from the beginning of the period. Party political identity is more common than religious labels, as in 'Ulster Unionists',
'Ulster Unionism' or 'the Unionists of Ulster'; but whereas the more
grandiose phrases such as 'the Unionists of Ireland' or 'the Protestants of Ireland' are rare, they abound in the context of Ulster,
particularly in the *Londonderry Sentinel* and *Ballymena Observer*. Sober
'Ulster loyalists' and 'loyal Ulstermen' are outnumbered by 'the Loyalists of Ulster' or more striking phrases such as 'the Loyalist electors of the six counties' (LS 15.1.21); and 'Ulster Protestants' are
less impressive than 'the Protestants of Ulster'; but often more
homely terms are used, such as 'Ulstermen' or 'the Ulster people',
particularly by the *Impartial Reporter*.

The British identity is also found quite early in the period, but it is a
limited one. Protestants are anxious to proclaim their British citizenship: 'The British people are not in the least inclined to wage war upon
loyal British citizens' (BO 18.4.13), with an emphasis on the 'rights
and privileges' of such citizenship (PDN 27.5.16). It is quite possible
to be British citizens as well as Irish: 'Irish Protestants are not aliens
... They are Irishmen, but they are also British citizens' (NL 2.1.20).
Hence British citizenship is not the same as being part of the British
people. 'British', as in 'British constituencies', 'the British electorate',
'the British people', 'the British public', 'the British nation' and even
'the British world', in the earlier part of the period means only the

English, Scottish and Welsh, and in one case the 'British' people are explicitly contrasted with the 'Ulster' people (BO 23.1.14). 'The British people' are the last resource for the 'friends of Great Britain' (LS 2.1.13); 'Irish Unionists ... only desire to stand in with Britain on equal terms' (LS 6.1.16); and 'with the new parliament we retain all our old associations with Great Britain' (BO 24.6.21). Ulster is in a minority *vis-à-vis* not only the rest of Ireland but the whole United Kingdom with its 'preponderating British and Irish majority' which can 'force an adventure on us' (IR 15.6.16). The most telling evidence of the perception that 'British' refers to the mainland comes during the IRA campaign:

> It is only when the war is carried across the Channel, and the methods of the leaders are shown to include the destruction of British, as well as Irish, property, that Lord Northcliffe's organ finds it necessary to reflect British indignation (LS 30.11.20).

Emotional bonds with the British people are rarely expressed. They are 'fellow-subjects' with whom Ulster competed in patriotism (NL 1.1.19), and the Ulster people are members of 'the same race as the men of Great Britain ... a race with a great ancestry' (LS 20.1.14); but only two editors refer to the British as Unionists' 'fellow-countrymen' (BO 23.8.12; CDS 26.9.13). For these two Britain is far more of the 'imagined community' than for any of the others in the sample (in the case of the *County Down Spectator* this may have been because the owner-editor was a Scotsman, as well as because of its location in North Down), and the 1914–18 war brings this out quite strikingly. Apart from a single reference in the Fermanagh paper (IR 27.1.16), only these papers fell into the way of using 'we' to refer to the British in general rather than to Ulster Protestants. That this was an effort to begin with is shown by the following, which mixes 'we' and 'they' in referring to the British people:

> We are not the same people ... that we were a year ago ... we seem much more approximated to that older and hardier race of men who crushed Napoleon ... A great change has unquestionably come over the British people ... They have shaken themselves free of many foibles and trammels ... The soundness of the nation's heart stands proved to the world ... We have been slow to gather up our scattered energies, but every day now sees those forces coming more strongly into play (BO 30.7.15).

On the whole though it is clear that 'our dear, peaceful Britain' (CDS 10.7.20) is indeed our own. Hence: 'Ulstermen are British' (BO 14.12.18); but the *County Down Spectator* early observes that there is a problem, and part of its cause is the Irish Sea: 'until our insularity is overcome, Irishmen will continue to think themselves as less British than the English, Scotch or Welsh' (CDS 23.3.18). Nevertheless, the result of the post-war general election, which brought a coalition government which was not dependent on Irish nationalists or Labour, surely means that Ulster people, though remaining distinct, can both take pride in their Britishness and feel confident in their cross-Channel brethren:

> the British have made a splendid choice ... They will not sell their birthright ... Such is the attitude of the British nation, and we in Ulster are British in heart, blood and sentiment. We are with them in their noble ideals, not that we follow them but because we walk abreast with them (CDS 4.1.19).

By the time of the Second World War the *County Down Spectator* and the *Ballymena Observer* identified as British in an unforced way: 'Whatever faults we British may have ... we do not worship brute strength ... We are a nation of ordinary citizens' (BO 23.2.41, 16.7.43). The *Londonderry Sentinel*, however, used Britishness with a notably strenuous insistence as a weapon against the Anti-Partition League:

> we in the North are the inheritors of so much deep-rooted British tradition that it makes us cling with strong tenacity to the Throne and all it stands for. Not even the removal of the Border, Crown and other physical Imperial symbols can eradicate British sympathies from Ulster hearts, or banish British blood from Ulster veins (LS 16.12.48),

culminating in the notable praise of 'the Ulster people who are more vigorously British than some of the people of Britain themselves' (LS 19.2.49).

Elsewhere there is a sense of distance from Great Britain. The *Londonderry Sentinel* refers to the 'citizens of Northern Ireland' (LS 1.8.42) and describes financial relations between Northern Ireland and Great Britain as 'Ulster's external trade' (LS 20.5.39); and although the people of Northern Ireland are part of 'our United Kingdom' (IR 17.8.39), expressions such as 'the British connection' (BT 26.6.45) and pride in standing 'by the side of Britain ... as an equal partner' (LS 20.4.39 and 12.10.39) suggest a degree of separation. Once again there are frequent references to the British people, public, nation, troops, ministers and statesmen which specifically mean those of England, Scotland and Wales, which is quite explicit in the following: 'The British people [will respond] to any call for sacrifice, and we have no doubt the people of Ulster will be ready to share fully in it' (LS 23.3.39).

At the same time an Irish identity lingers on:

When the Irish Republican Press write about 'the Irish race at home and abroad' they mean only the Roman Catholics, because, of course, there are tens of thousands of Ulstermen and Eire Protestants abroad as well as hundreds of thousands of Loyalists in Ulster who are utterly antagonistic to the views of this 'Irish race at home and abroad'. When the same Press want to claim Ulster as part of an 'indivisible Ireland' they condescendingly admit that Ulstermen are Irishmen, though in their anger at times they refer to them as aliens (LS 9.5.39).

Protestants inhabit an Ireland united not only by rugby (LS 11.2.47) but also by ties of history and emotion. There are still 'internal Irish affairs' ('Observant' IR 16.2.39) and the 'English' Education Bill is 'in some respects unsuited to rural Ireland' ('Protestant Manager' IR 5.12.46). Ireland is not to be confused with that neutral part called 'Eire' (LS 22.2.41); and it is inhabited by 'Irishmen north and south of the border' (LS 17.4.48, PDN 26.6.48), from the Northern Ireland prime minister down: 'Sir Basil [Brooke] is Irish by birth and rearing' (IR 3.2.49). There is no conflict between loyalty and Irishness: 'One of the main objects of social service is to make boys grow into good men, good Irishmen, and good citizens, loyal to the King' (IR 20.9.45). Nor is there any conflict in multiple identity: '[Craigavon] was a great Briton. He was a great Irishman. Above all, he was a great Ulsterman' (LS 26.11.40).

Essentially then the Ballymena and North Down editors see themselves as British, the Fermanagh and North Armagh editors as Irish, and the Derry editor as Irish and British but above all as an Ulsterman. The creation of Northern Ireland has had its effect on identity, but not as much as might have been expected.

MUCH OF THE academic writing on 'the identity problem', as well as 'ordinary' thinking, refers in fact to the modern period, while frequently assuming that the past was the same as the present. That this is false has already been demonstrated, but observers believe themselves to be on surer footing about the present, thanks to modern survey data about perceptions of identity. There are, however, some surprises in the local newspapers. One of these is the complexity and diversity among ultras, who are often perceived as proclaiming a British identity in opposition to an Irish one. Membership of an organisation such as the Orange Order or any unionist political party is not necessarily a predictor of perceived identity, and the same individuals may express different identities at different times or even at the same time.

There are certainly claims to British citizenship and the rights appertaining thereto:

I have always regarded myself as a full-blooded British citizen ...
voting for someone who would best represent my views and interests at what we regarded as our parliament at Westminster, a place
where I thought my right to remain a British citizen would be
respected and where my interests in maintaining my civil and religious liberties would best be maintained in the absence of our own
devolved Parliament at Stormont ... I demand, along with thousands
of other citizens of British Ulster, to be allowed to decide my own
future and to have a right, as majority citizens, to be fully British
and not in a diluted form (Raymond Farrell IR 17.4.86).

Cultural and kinship ties also bind Protestants to Great Britain:

The Ulsterman's desire to be British is not less than previously.
He is oriented towards the land and people of his roots. The
racial and cultural tastes are similar, and agreeable, too, are the
hopes and fears, ambitions and expectations of people who have
so much in common that they are all and always British together
(OS Dec 1981).

Again, Protestants are more British than the British: 'Whatever is
the English, Scottish and Welsh view of us ... the Ulsterman is often
more British than they are' (OS Jun 1984).

The obligations attached to being British are unclear: 'By not
following step by step with Britain on the "One man one vote"
issue, does not make us less British' (Beryl Holland CDS 30.5.69),
and what is meant by 'the maintenance of the British way of life' is
not always specified; but an important aspect for those like Martin
Smyth, Grand Master of the Orange Order in Ireland, is the association of Britishness with Protestantism:

From 1979 a pragmatic Conservative Government was prepared
again to play politics with the lives of British people ... the 'No
Surrender' spirit is very positive. It is not a so called siege mentality. Rather it is the expression of a positive choice ... they
chose William III as king ... they embraced the faith and freedom
enshrined in Protestantism (OS Nov 1986).

For some Protestantism rather than Britishness is important: 'a mass
exodus of Protestants may be necessary. We might be compelled to
seek another land where freedom to live and worship in peace
would be ours' (W A Norris PT 22.2.69), and it is marginally more
important than Ulster: 'if Ulster is to remain Great through God's
blessing, her battle must always be for God and Ulster – God must
always be first' (Robert Bamford BTimes 23.10.86). Those who are
confident of God's preference for their cause do not need British

help: 'Fear not, God has His chosen people. We will surely see a great deliverance' ('Steadfast' PDN 11.2.72); and for one 'Bible Protestant' a British identity is positively wrong:

> It appears the name of Protestant is fast disappearing from the vocabulary of most of our politicians and clergy. The most important term would now seem to be 'British'. This is a complete reversal of values. Protestant ought to be primary, British secondary, very secondary (William Roddy CDS 17.11.72).

Indeed, the connection between Britain and Protestantism is now tenuous and Paisley is 'Ulster's and indeed Britain's only unfettered and fearless Protestant voice in the Strasbourg parliament' (Thomas Greer BO 7.6.84).

'British' is still used in a way that excludes Northern Ireland and its people, as when Martin Smyth speaks of 'British politicians' (OS Jul 1974), so assertions that suggest an Ulster identity are not unexpected:

> We are Unionists. We are British, but we like to feel that our Ulster Government will govern us and tell us what requires to be done, not drive us into the future by getting outsiders to tell us what we must do under pressure (Muriel Lawson IR 6.2.69).

It is not surprising that an Irish identity is rejected, as in the definition of loyalism as 'being British and not wanting to be Irish – ever' (NL 25.5.74). Thus one writer states: 'As a British subject I refuse to be known as Northern Irish but prefer to be known by one of three descriptions: (1) British (2) Ulsterman or (3) Ulster-Scot' ('Against Action' OS Jun 1977). What is surprising on the face of it is the evidence of an Irish identity among some ultras. Some of the claims to be Irish arise from Adamson's theory that the Ulster-Scots were the original inhabitants of Ireland, but there are a few references, especially by Orangemen, which owe nothing to this theory. On Smyth's election as Imperial Grand Master he is described as an 'Irishman' (OS Aug 1973); and it is possible to be both British and Irish: 'Whatever the Ulsterman may feel about Irish nationalism, and he has a sense of Irishness which is in no way a contradiction of his Britishness, he is kin to the Scots, the English and the Welsh' (OS Jan 1973). With total integration the people of Northern Ireland could 'live together as Irish people within the British family' ('Lisnaskea Unionist' IR 28.1.88). Even in 1994, in a speech to a peace and justice group at Navan in which he defended partition, Martin Smyth, in similar terms to John Hewitt, called himself:

> an Irishman – in that I live on the island of Ireland ... an Ulster-

man – my family have lived in the Province for several hundred years ... Scottish in that my religion and cultural background come from those roots. And finally I am British by heritage and way of life (OS Jul 1994).

It would be wrong though to assume that ultra expressions of an Irish identity augur eventual acquiescence in a future united Irish Republic. The forty-nine members of the Ireland's Heritage Orange Lodge (Oidreacht na Eireann) in Belfast who are 'proud of being Irish' advertise for someone to teach them the Irish language, but specify that the teacher should not be a Catholic and warn that they have no intention of drawing closer to Catholics (OS Jul 1975). A more plausible explanation of expressions of 'Irishness' is disillusionment with Britain and the British, as well as the claim to have a right to stay in Ireland. Nevertheless it is a reminder that Ulster Protestants had considered themselves Irish up to the third Home Rule crisis and in some cases beyond.

THE ISSUE IS EVEN more complicated for moderates. For many of them their British citizenship is a matter of fact which needs no defence and perhaps for this reason many are able to continue to express friendly feelings towards the twenty-six counties rather than seeing it as a hostile foreign land, and to retain an Irish identity along with British citizenship. In this they face opposition from both republicans and ultras, and the latter's suspicions of moderate loyalty lie behind the moderates' protestation that Ulster supporters are no less British because they combine with the Southern Irish to cheer the Irish rugby team against England (CDS 17.1.75).

Although moderates refer to 'Ulster folk' and so on, they do not emphasise a non-Irish Ulster identity. More typical is a shifting use of national labels, different appellations usually being used at different times. In the following, however, three labels are, apparently unconsciously, used in the same editorial:

the suffering and misery inflicted on one-and-a-half million British people ... How can [the IRA] claim that the murder of innocent Irish victims does anything to further the unity of this island? ... the Ulster electorate has only one message ... to end this nightmare (PDN 20.4.79).

It is not uncommon to find moderates claiming both British and Irish identity:

I am a Northern Irishman and I am British. I am usually proud of the British label ... [but] any British Ulstermen who cannot also be Irish, and proud of it, are suffering from a very severe sickness of heart or mind ... They belong nowhere ... Large numbers of Ulstermen, who respect and value their British passports, also have as much pride in their shamrock as any tricolour-toting extremist (Anthony C Cowdy IR 7.8.69).

Often, however, 'Irish' refers to all the people of the North, largely but not exclusively in the border counties. The *Impartial Reporter* for example routinely uses the appellation 'Irish' and not always as defensively as here: 'For eight years the sufferers have been Irish institutions and Irish prosperity – if Northern Ireland is considered to be Irish' (IR 30.3.78). The Portadown papers also frequently use such terminology:

A million Irish people of different cultural, political and religious differences from the majority of their fellow countrymen believe that they are merely pawns in the Provisional IRA game of taking power in Ireland (PDN 21.12.79).

One identity is rejected both by ultras and moderates:

Mr Bulbrook's letter, an excellent one, [was] inaccurate in one respect. He stated that we in Ulster are English! ... I must disagree. If we are born in the Six Counties, we are Irish, whether our ancestors were English or Scottish planters, Huguenot refugees from France, native Irish or Normans ('British and Irish' PDN 14.3.69, and see George Bulbrook PDN 7.3.69).

WELL BEFORE PARTITION there was a process of 'ideological usurpation' which mirrored the actual expropriation – the usurpation of Ulster from the Irish, including its own Catholic inhabitants, by the Protestants of Ulster. Contrary to the impression often given, Ulster was never wholly Protestant, and Catholics always constituted the largest single denomination. Nor was Ulster's much-vaunted prosperity evenly spread: rather there were three economic regions, the west, the southern and mid-Ulster and the two north-eastern counties. Only Antrim and Down had a large majority of Protestants and economic development was concentrated here. Thus this part of Ulster was used as a metaphor for the whole. As a sixteen-year-old Protestant girl told a researcher: 'I don't think Ulster is meant to be a place ... it's just meant to be the Protestant people' (Bell 1986:37).

Throughout the 1912–21 period and whether six or nine counties, 'Ulster' and its Protestant inhabitants are synonymous. It is 'Ulster' that is hostile to Home Rule and whose interests are at stake: 'Home Rule involves for Ulster ... the vital question of her birthright and her national allegiance' (BO 23.8.12). The 'whole-souled devotion of Ulster to her liberty' (PDN 13.9.13) means that she will 'neither be cajoled nor coerced to her own destruction' (IR 25.4.12). It is therefore 'Ulster' that is grimly, proudly and confidently determined to fight, if necessary by force of arms:

> Ulster will fight with no one as long as she is left alone. All she asks is to be allowed to remain an integral portion of the British nation ... To be governed by John Redmond she will never submit (PDN 25.5.12).

It is likewise 'Ulster' which acts patriotically in the 1914–18 war, although the passing of the Home Rule Act might give her pause for thought: 'Ulster ... is not so likely now to volunteer for foreign service ... for our young men ... it is Ulster first' (IR 13.8.14); and it is 'Ulster' which, having fought off her 'betrayal', accepts self-government; and the 'gratifying' election results show that 'the heart of Ulster is still in the right place' (BO 3.6.21).

All in all, 'what Ulster considers her peculiar interests' (CDS 13.4.18) was identical with what Protestants or 'Ulstermen' considered their peculiar interests: 'What Ulstermen prefer is the maintenance of the United Kingdom as one nation ... What Ulster rules out as impossible ... is its subjection to a Dublin Parliament' (NL 22.7.19). 'The voice of Ulster' (PDN 13.4.12) was clearly a Protestant voice; and this use of 'Ulstermen', implicitly excluding Catholics, is common: 'Ulstermen can claim the full rights of those who have inherited the British privilege of being governed by the Parliament that British history made' (IR 2.5.12). Sometimes the contrast between 'Ulstermen' and Catholics is explicit: 'Ulstermen [enlisted] in thousands, as they recognised their first duty ... The Nationalists recognise no such thing' (BT 8.4.18), and certainly not all inhabitants of Ulster would have concurred with this sentiment:

> The popularity of the members of the present Royal House has been one of the chief characteristics of Ulstermen ... at least in the six counties of Ulster the monarchy is the pivot which moves all our aspirations (BO 24.6.21).

So 'the people of Ulster' do not include Catholics:

> to the people of Ulster, the future governance of Ireland is an issue as burning and ever-present as the future of life itself ... a simple, sturdy folk ... that Ulster will fight is a commonplace to all who know its history and its people (PDN 13.9.13),

and when Bonar Law 'advised the people of Ulster to defend their birthright' (IR 24.3.21) he did not have Catholic interests in mind. Catholics do not even exist in Ulster: the proclamation forbidding the import of arms to Ireland 'has come much too late to prevent the arming of the whole population [i.e. northern Protestants] should that be the course decided upon by-and-by' (BT 6.12.13).

Once 'Ulster' was reduced to six counties, there was still a substantial Catholic minority, one-third of the population as a whole but a majority in some areas. At the time of partition there was little reason to suppose that this proportion would change as birthrates were high regardless of sect and the 'fact that for months past ... Roman Catholics have been flocking into Ulster in larger numbers than ever before' is proof that they know they will be better off in Northern peace and prosperity (LS 16.12.20) rather than a threat. Nevertheless there are conflicting ideas about Northern Catholics. On the one hand they are against the exclusion from Home Rule of the six counties (LS 9.7.14, 8.6.16, 2.12.20), but they know that their material interests at least are best served in the North (IR 18.3.20). Although their decision was clearly of vital concern to the future of the North, only the *Londonderry Sentinel* takes much interest in it. Thanks to the ambiguity in the original Lloyd George scheme on the permanence of exclusion, 475 delegates to the Tyrone Nationalist Convention voted to accept the terms, to the editor's jubilation (LS 27.6.16); but when nationalists realised that exclusion would be permanent they came out against it. No compromise is offered, however: if nationalists do not like it they can leave:

> This is a free country. Nationalists are not compelled to live in the excluded area. If they find the 'serfdom', the 'tyranny', the 'slavery' of Unionist employment in Ulster too intolerable ... they can move into the new Ireland, and, perhaps, get well-paid and entirely congenial employment from people of their own politics and religion ... it is their patriotic duty to migrate to 'Ireland' in order to prove their faith in the panacea for which they have so long and so heroically struggled – always in the chains of slavery to Unionist employers (LS 13.7.16).

That Catholics might also regard Ulster as their native province is not part of this particular mindset; rather they are to be regarded as clients of unionist patronage and allowed rights as long as they behave themselves:

> the Roman Catholic must feel as safe and secure under the new condition of things as under the Imperial Parliament. If, on the other hand, any attempt be made to upset the Government of the six counties, it must be sternly suppressed. If reforms be desired they must be presented in a constitutional way, and the methods ⌐ the South, if introduced into the North, will meet with prompt ⌐ drastic punishment (IR 10.2.21).

Their good behaviour, however, is unlikely without Protestant volunteers working alongside the official security forces (LS 14.9.20), even though there is no excuse for rebellion: their position as a minority under a Protestant parliament is their own fault as it is 'the Nationalist demand which raises' the religious question, and consequently the question of partition' (NL 2.1.20).

Nevertheless in the euphoria generated by the certainty of partition there is also some optimism and magnanimity. Moderate nationalists can help make a great success of the new parliament (BO 11.2.21). Catholic and Protestant will 'live and thrive side by side' (IR 2.12.20) with no cause for irreconcilable division and under a government which will guard Catholic rights 'to the utmost' and recognise that 'they have their rights as well as other people' (IR 23.12.20). Catholics can even be good citizens: 'Loyalists, both Protestant and Roman Catholic, see that you vote early and give every assistance to the loyalist candidates ... This is the last and only chance' (IR 19.5.21).

Northern Catholics, then, are not completely ignored; but that a six-county Ulster had been accepted to make the new Province 'homogeneous' and 'one in spirit for the most part' (IR 18.3.20) might seem almost unnecessary, for in the common rhetoric of the time Ulster is already 'Protestant' and in helping the Protestants organise their resistance to Home Rule Carson 'roused the soul of Ulster' (LS 26.5.21).

This usurpation of Ulster proceeded apace once Protestants had their own government, and continued after its abolition in 1972. Although fewer editors in the modern period take such a hard-line stance, and a plainer style tends to replace the rhetoric, there are no important differences between this and the 1939–49 period, and much continuity with that of 1912–21. In essence the threat has always been the submergence of 'Ulster' into a united Ireland through the activities of Catholics and the incomprehension, incompetence and bias of the British government.

The rhetorical device of personification continues to portray Ulster as a woman – fair, loyal, besieged by enemies but strong. If there are 'two kinds of people' in Ireland, there is only one kind in the North, and 'the interests of Ulster and the Protestant faith are synonymous' (LS 21.12.48). 'Those whose outlook and ideals are truly representative of the spirit of Ulster to-day' are those 'who show a full consciousness of Ulster's position, peril and needs', that is, neither Catholics nor British ministers but Ulster Protestants (LS 20.4.46). The 'voice of Ulster' still excludes Catholics; and as it also specifically excludes the 'numerically infinitesimal' Protestant anti-partitionists (LS 11.2.39) her interests are identical above all with Unionist interests:

No bond of convenience ties Ulster to Great Britain. It is a bond of kinship, of hardships borne together; the self expressed desire of a free and loyal people. That bond can never be broken by the stroke of a pen at Westminster (IR 2.1.47).

Hence 'the people of Ulster', variously described as 'Ulster folk', 'Ulstermen', 'the ordinary Ulster citizen', 'the Ulster mind', 'Ulster's sons and daughters' or simply 'our people' are the Protestant and unionist people and no others. The heritage of 'Ulster Loyalists' is a 'Protestant heritage' (LS 20.4.48) and 'it is up to all true and loyal sons of Ulster ... to be in the ranks of the Orange Order' (LS 2.3.46). Only Protestant interests matter and 'Ulster's ministers ought only to be responsible to their own people' (LS 10.4.47), that is, to Protestants. The way to 'build up a strong and loyal Ulster' is to 'provide employment for Ulster's own loyal sons and daughters' (LS 28.2.46), especially since the Unionist government is 'in the long run mainly dependent on the support of Loyalist workers' (LS 4.5.43). It is stressed that loyalists must be registered to vote, not that everyone must assert their democratic right to do so.

Only one editor in the 1939–49 period includes Catholics among the 'people of Northern Ireland' but only those who are anti-republican (PDN 11.6.49). The *Londonderry Sentinel* in particular paints a picture of a region inhabited by loyalists 'rooted to the soil of Ulster for centuries' (LS 30.9.43), but with 'Roman Catholics' for some unexplained reason 'living in our midst' (LS 31.10.40) and conspiring against Ulster's British connection (LS 10.7.43). Thus, contrasted with 'the people of Ulster' are 'the people of Eire and their noisy friends in Ulster' (LS 28.11.40). These 'forces of evil' (LS 12.8.48) are not people with an equal right of residence but 'unwelcome elements who are agitating for the overthrow of the Northern Government's Constitution ... it would be for the good of Ulster if they departed' (LS 3.4.47). This perception of Northern Ireland Catholics as the enemy within, whose departure would be welcome, has survived amongst ultras in the modern period: 'Do they forget that while living in Ulster they have to respect our colours? If they do not like this they should go down south where they belong' ('Law abiding Third Force supporters' BO 4.2.82).

The claim that Loyalists form 'the overwhelming majority of the people of Northern Ireland' (LS 12.1.39) justifies the legitimacy of the majoritarian form of democracy, so they must remain a majority, showing unity and virility in the face of the Catholic threat. This was first voiced on attaining the Northern Parliament (LS 15.1.21) and echoed at every election. Calls to 'close the ranks' and stand firm (LS 12.10.43) assumed a new urgency in the light of new internal threats in the 1939–49 period: on the political front, the success among the Protestant working class of the Northern Ireland Labour Party (NILP) and some apathy among traditional unionist supporters; and on the demographic front the grant of resident permits for Free State citizens and the fall in the Protestant birth-rate, which endanger '[the Ulster people's] numerical strength ... which is the surest safeguard of their freedom' (LS 14.5.49), and the purchase by Catholics of Protestant property leading to the dilution of Protestant areas. These threats need to be met by 'a more militant Protestantism in the North ... We want more patriotism among our people, a patriotism that will be prepared to make sacrifices for the Cause' (LS 29.9.45).

The Catholic 'breeding' of large families is one part of the 'subtle design' to overthrow the Stormont government through 'a prolific birthrate' (PDN 11.1.47). In fact, large families had been the norm among Protestants too but now they are, unfortunately, smaller: 'our Protestant people have failed in what is the most important factor in maintaining a nation and empire – an increase in the birth rate' ('Countryman' PDN 31.8.46). Too many Protestants are also indulging in 'mixed' marriages, in which the children are brought up as Catholics. The Protestant majority would probably have come under threat sooner than it has had it not been for the higher Catholic emigration rate, but this is never mentioned; rather 'there is ... the disturbing fact that considerable numbers of Protestant young men are leaving Ulster for Great Britain and the Dominions' (LS 11.7.39). One 'solution' to this potential threat is to change the rules of majoritarian democracy. The Unionist parliament must 'effect legislation which would make it impossible to alter Ulster's constitutional position, unless, and until, a two-thirds majority were obtained in both Houses and in the Six Counties' ('Interested' IR 10.2.49).

A more immediate threat is posed by immigration from the twenty-six counties. Set against the million Protestants of Northern Ireland the actual numbers of immigrants were not very great. From 1939 to 1944 there were 30,000 applications for residence permits, of which over 25,000 were granted and by 1947 3,942 men and 10,096 women remained legally. These numbers are exaggerated to 'over 50,000 refugees from Southern Ireland' ('Regional Committee Member' IR 13.4.44) but usually less precise terms are used: 'the infiltrating masses from Eire' (LS 13.12.47) are 'swelling' the non-Protestant, anti-loyalist population by 'flooding into the North' (LS 16.9.44) in 'very large' numbers (LS 1.8.42). In all, there has been a 'Roman Catholic invasion of Ulster during the last thirty years' (LS 10.8.48), a repeat of claims made at least as early as 1885 (Patterson 1982:12). It is no accident that the majority of these references come from the Derry paper, as Catholics are 'triumphantly gloat[ing] over the fact that this once Protestant city has now a growing Roman Catholic majority' (LS 11.7.39). Furthermore, Southern Protestants are not being given residence permits whereas 'Roman Catholics and IRA' are:

And how can a man, invalided, sell his small farm in Eire, buy another farm in Northern Ireland and is now living on it with his family? Neither himself nor his family would be expected to improve or help any locality they go to, and Protestants or Loyalists are rather left out. It looks to us like allowing any kind of an Eireite into the North to vote the Border away when the time comes ('Fed Up' IR 13.7.44).

Other undesirable Irish types include Axis agents and collaborators who have been 'given work by the Imperial Government, who seem to learn nothing in regard to disloyal elements' (LS 26.3.42). The British government is partly to blame, but the Northern government, which should know better, also seems blind to the danger of 'the suicide of the Ulster state' (LS 11.7.44). There was, however, some propaganda value in this immigration, for it is proof both that Archbishop Griffin's accusation that Catholics were persecuted in the North is false and that the Southern economy is in a sorry state (LS 27.5.43, PDN 18.11.44).

The growing political militancy of Northern Catholics is blamed on the immigrants:

The influx of temporary labour from the South is at the bottom of this agitation; the solid and rooted Nationalist is heart and soul with the Northern Government. He has no complaints ('Northerner' BO 21.3.47).

Far more important, however, is the threat to the Protestant hold on the six counties, that is, 'the cost of the integrity of the State' (LS 30.9.41). This threat was delayed by adopting different legislation from Great Britain, such that seven years' residence in the United Kingdom was required before voting in local elections, a measure 'designed to frustrate citizens from Eire dominating Ulster political life' (LS 10.2.45). This did not, however, apply to the majority of Northern Ireland Catholics. Many of these (as well as many poorer Protestants) were unable to vote in local council elections because of the property qualification. A further threat then consists in the purchase by Catholics of 'Unionist-held property' (PDN 11.1.47), a trend that requires 'steady hard work all the year round, watching every opportunity of making votes, seeing that property is not sold to the enemy' (IR 9.11.44) by short-sighted Protestants. There is also the danger that the usurped land might revert to its original occupiers as Catholics 'got into districts where not for generations had there been Roman Catholics before' (LS 15.3.47).

This threat to the physical usurpation of Ulster led to the campaign for Dominion status, one of whose features was an early claim: 'Ulster is not theirs [Nationalists] to take, nor England's to give: it is our own to possess' (IR 4.7.12). The only paper in the sample which supported or even mentioned the campaign was the *Londonderry Sentinel*, other editors presumably sharing the views of the Unionist Party that its existing powers were sufficient and the Union should continue. From 1944 the paper repeatedly stressed the need for greater powers for the Northern government to combat the alleged shrinking of the Protestant majority. There is therefore a continuation of the early implications that 'our Northern State' or 'our Ulster State' not only belongs to its Protestants to the exclusion of its Catholics but that the British state has no right over it either: and claims that the Northern government should have 'absolute and unfettered control in their own State' (LS 15.7.44) and be 'complete mistress within her own borders' (LS 29.11.47) suggest that Northern Ireland's territory as well as rights of residence belong to the Protestant people.

The election of the Labour government in July 1945, followed by the formation of the Anti-Partition League, leads to 'a growing feeling that Ulster should have powers equal to that of a Dominion' (LS 4.9.45), which the editor reported in an approving tone rather than openly endorsing it. Ulster no longer has a proud status as a self-governing 'state', but is 'a puppet state' (LS 29.9.45) which should have more powers, in effect, full autonomy. The number of editorials complaining about British interference increased, and the demand that there should be 'far less interference [and] fewer services should be reserved' (LS 24.2.45) gave way to a more strident tone: 'The Ulster Government should have unfettered control of the Post Office, the Customs and Excise, broadcasting and all other departments operating within the Northern State' (LS 25.8.45). There were more frequent complaints of interference, not only by civil servants (LS 2.10.45) but by Westminster MPs, especially by 'ill-informed, spiteful and malicious Socialist Members of Parliament indulging in unjustified attacks on our Government' (LS 10.4.47); and relations between the Labour government and Stormont are 'impertinent dictation from Westminster' (LS 9.3.46).

The language of this newspaper campaign, with its 'demands' and statements of what 'must' happen, is that of a people negotiating from a position of strength, supported above all by an unshakeable sense of the rightness of their cause: 'Ulster's statesmen should demand this of right, and should not let it be imagined that there is any compliment or favour about it' (LS 15.2.45). In fact the rhetoric conceals a deep insecurity. Ulster might by right belong to the Protestant people, but that 'right' was constantly under threat from Irish nationalism and the unknown quantity of a Labour government at Westminster. In the event the idea of Dominion status was rejected by the Standing Committee of the Ulster Unionist Council, the Ulster Parliamentary Party at Stormont and the Ulster Unionist Conference, whose confidence was rewarded by the Ireland Act of 1949.

SINCE MODERATES PLAY a conciliatory role they rarely exclude Catholics in references to Ulster, and one editor rejected an Orange Master's call for an annual 'Ulster Day' precisely because it was intended to exclude non-Protestants, who by and large object to the term 'Ulster' for Northern Ireland (CDS 18.7.75). Hence 'Ulster' and 'Ulster folk' are used to include Catholics. The *Impartial Reporter*, however, is characteristically ambivalent, using 'Ulster' and 'Northern Ireland' interchangeably throughout the period. On a few occasions the 'Ulster people' are clearly Protestants, on others certainly both Protestants and Catholics, as when Barry McGuigan, a Catholic from Monaghan who made his home in Fermanagh, is celebrated as 'Ulster's favourite son' (IR 13.6.85).

Among ultras, however, the notion that Northern Ireland belongs only to its Protestants survives (Robin Stirling BO 28.8.69); but the renewed campaign for Dominion status led by William Craig had no more success, despite a stream of enthusiastic letters from a Vanguard supporter (Campbell McCormick CDS 16.6.72), and nor did later revivals of the idea. By this time important changes had taken place. It is regrettably clear to most Protestants that the ideal of self-sufficiency is only a dream. Northern Ireland might belong to its Protestants but it can survive economically only within a larger entity. Furthermore the threats from Irish nationalism and British untrustworthiness were by now joined by a split in the Unionist Party on a scale never before experienced, and appeals for unity to save Ulster from 'an impending United Ireland' took on a new force (William J Wilson BO 7.3.74). Only a united effort can restore Ulster to her rightful position as a quasi-independent Protestant state:

> At present, we speak with many voices, and alas even our politicians cannot agree among themselves – one says one thing, another says another thing, and we hear the clear voice of the Ulster people saying to the politicians, 'a plague on all your houses' ... Ulster must awake! ... Ulster Unionists must have one goal – to bring back strong devolved government in our Province, where there shall be majority rule ... Give us the unity we need and let's get on with the job ('A Ballymena Unionist' BO 10.2.77).

Although the DUP and UUP remained separate, the Anglo–Irish Agreement did much to restore Unionist unity of purpose, and it is perhaps significant that the slogan for the campaign against the agreement was yet another example of the usurpation of Ulster: 'Ulster Says No'. The more recent decision by many ultras to claim that a large number of Catholics wish to remain in the Union gives a legitimating gloss to their claims to speak for 'Ulster'.

5 Usurpation of the Empire and Monopolisation of Loyalty

THE DISTANCING OF Ulster from the rest of Ireland in the campaign to manipulate metropolitan opinion was accompanied by two further usurpations: since the bridge away from Irishness consisted of the British empire and loyalty to this empire, both the empire and loyalty were usurped to the 'cause of Ulster' and Ulster became the 'Imperial Province'. The usurpation of Ulster, the empire and loyalty by the northern Protestant population were together aimed ultimately at legitimating the exclusion of the six counties, both in British eyes and in their own. The 'imperialist message' in Ulster Unionism survives even today and plays an important part in ultra ideology:

> The Protestant imagined community is not a nation. It remains what it has always been – a beleaguered garrison loyal to the Crown and Empire, defending an Imperial interest in a hostile and rebellious land (Bell 1986:12).

Very little detailed work, however, has been published on the relationship between Ulster Protestants and the British empire, despite the plethora of references to the empire, which continued to a notable extent even after it had dwindled to a few islands. Of course, pride in 'the generous splashes of red which indicate upon a map of the world the greatest empire ever known' (BO 29.10.15) was not confined to the north of Ireland: most people born up to the 1940s in Britain no doubt saw such maps and had fathers and grandfathers who had fought in the various attempts to retain that coloration; the military adventures of Suez and the Falklands were supported by many, as was the Smith regime in Rhodesia. It is the use made of the empire that is worthy of examination. If the 'Orange card' has been played for local consumption, the 'Empire card' was played for the British audience too. During the Home Rule crises religion was fused with imperialism in the claim that Ireland separated from Great Britain would be ruled by the Pope, an argument which appealed to unionists such as Balfour and Milner who claimed that 'loyalty to the empire' rode above elected governments (Porter 1975:230). Ulster Protestants, however, having claimed in the first Home Rule crisis that Ireland's co-partnership in the empire was threatened, came to claim that they played a special and eventually an exclusive role in it.

It was a powerful propaganda weapon. Carson's role in image-building has been noted before, and it was observed at the time too. The right-wing *National Review* in November 1915:

> praised Carson above all for the hold he had over working men in Belfast ... He asked them to devote their wages, their time and their energy to their ideals: freedom, national unity and the defence of the British Empire ... The overwhelming majority of loyalists understood that the prosperity of the industries which dominated the city and provided their wages depended on the existence of a strong British Empire ... Carson never failed to remind his flock that the Empire belonged to them ... they must love it and, if necessary, be willing to die for it. 'So, gradually, the Empire came to rank second only to God in Ulster hearts, and in living for and giving to their Empire these people came to believe they were living for and giving to their God.' Sharing such an ideal transcended all class division (Goldring 1991:117–18).

Certainly Carson made a large contribution to editors' use of the empire, and many of the oft-repeated phrases used in newspaper editorials emanated originally from Carson's lips. It is ironic that Carson was not himself an Ulster Protestant, but a Dubliner.

What though did the term 'empire' mean to Ulster Protestants? The empire of colonial dependencies is mentioned infrequently, not so surprisingly in the light of the general lack of knowledge of or interest in conquered peoples. The empire was perhaps more an attitude of mind than a fact, and Joseph Chamberlain is to be praised because he 'thought imperially' (LS 4.7.14). However the empire of white settlement was better known, and constituted the 'real' empire:

> The old type of Empire, consisting of a paramount Mother State and dependent Colonies, could not suffice to give the powers of vigorous life and growth to the institutions of the British race. The Empire must be the voluntary union of free peoples in the bonds of common allegiance to the Crown and of that kinship of spirit and purpose which outlasts every laboured type of formal constitution (LS 14.6.21).

Hence, for all that Westminster was known as 'the Imperial Parliament', since the white settlements had their own parliaments, 'the British Parliament is to them "imperial" only in name, not in actual working' (IR 15.2.12). Nor was this mighty empire as strong as it might be. The lesson of the Boer War is that guarantees to British settlers proved worthless, as they would in Ireland (BT 6.2.12), a prophesy borne out later, when 'the Britannia that can rule the oceans of the world has to haul down the Union Jack before the tricolour of Sinn Fein!' (IR 22.4.20). The fault lies not in empire but in the men who make imperial policy, and Free Trade was particularly unpopular.

So given this less than rosy view of empire, the claim that Irish Protestants would be 'ruthlessly cast out from their citizenship of the Empire in the glories of which they claim the right to share' (LS 28.9.12) needs investigating, when all that was proposed was a limited amount of Irish autonomy, far less than the white Dominions already had. If the overseas dominions could have self-government, why should not Ireland be allowed, in John Redmond's words (NL 20.3.12), 'to enter loyally the great sisterhood of self-governing States that make up the British Empire'? One defence is its location in home waters. Commenting that the Imperial Veto was not used in the Dominions, one editor claims:

> This works well because of the vast distances which separate us from the Colonies ... to put the Veto of the Imperial Parliament into force against legislation by the Irish Parliament would be as dangerous as to enforce it against any of the Colonial Parliaments (NL 12.4.12).

So a common parliament for the British Isles is necessary; but more reliable than an elected body is the (Protestant) monarchy: 'The Monarchy is one of the Empire's brightest assets, and if ever Britain's love for Monarchical institutions within constitutional limits should decay the end of the Empire will not be far off' (BT 6.5.12). In this context this 'empire' to which Protestants cleave is little more than the United Kingdom, with Ireland its extreme point, including 'that outpost of Empire, county Donegal' (LS 4.10.13); and the interests that are threatened are not those of the empire but of Irish Protestants:

> Here we are in Ireland, a minority, a fourth of the population, Irish Protestants – set amidst an ultramontane Roman Catholicism, our country within the Union under the rule of an Imperial Parliament that is based on Protestant principles. It is proposed by this Bill to take from us the protection which the Union with Great Britain gives us (NL 16.1.13).

The empire was much more than the sum of its parts; it evoked a reassuring grandeur which rode above the irritations of the actuality of British rule and economic policy in Ireland, the machinations of British politicians, the hostility of the British press and the unpredictability of the British electorate. The British in their imperial role picked up dependencies rather than casting them off. Nevertheless it is hard to avoid the conclusion that much use of the 'empire' is little more than rhetoric: 'The situation is unparalleled in the history of the Empire' (BT 24.9.13) sounds better than 'in the history of the United Kingdom', given that the latter was no more than a collection of off-shore islands. Similarly, expressions like 'the Kingdom and Empire' sound grander; it makes the situation sound more dramatic and dangerous than it might really be, and Home Rule and the 'inevitable' civil war that would result from forcing Protestants under a Home Rule parliament can be claimed to be 'disastrous for the whole Empire' (CDS 28.11.13). It also enabled Ulster Protestants to claim that far from fighting for themselves they are struggling to maintain a noble ideal, that of 'imperial unity', unlike 'the Irish rebels' who, as Carson told the prime minister, are part of a Bolshevik conspiracy to destroy 'the British Empire ... the greatest element of solidity in the civilised world ... the greatest conservative force for the stability of society' (IR 5.8.20).

If there is some ambiguity in what the empire actually was, there is ambivalence about Ireland's place in this empire. What, apart from its obvious strategic position, was this? Since the Act of Union, Ireland is technically Great Britain's 'partner': 'Will you even now realise your partnership, and rejoice in the fact that you have a share in such an empire?' (IR 20.8.14). After the Easter Rising, however, it is more appropriate to view Ireland as a colonial dependency. General Dyer's vindication by the House of Lords is approved of, and appropriate lessons learned:

> We agree with [Lord Finlay] that 'if lives must be taken ... he would rather they were those of the criminal mob than of people who were loyal to the law, the Crown and the Empire.' This is a sound principle, but the present Government has not the courage to apply it, either in India or in Ireland ... The present Government would recover some of its waning popularity if it showed in Cork and other rebel cities something of the courage and resoluteness that General Dyer showed at Amritsar (NL 21.7.20).

Whatever they meant by it, the 'empire card' was clearly one that Ulster Protestants thought worth playing, and long before the Easter Rising they had begun the process of turning the north of Ireland into the 'Imperial Province'. The term is widely used, with scattered references to Protestants' imperial birthright and membership of 'the Imperial race' (IR 14.8.13). Ulster unionists are 'the Imperialists of the Six Counties' and there was an abortive move to change the name of the party to 'the Ulster Imperial Party' (LS 5.2.21).

These claims are justified in a variety of ways. Not only had 'the Empire's best friends' (LS 13.8.12) gone out to colonise distant lands, but 'the great turning-point in the history of the British Empire [was] the Battle of the Boyne. Without its Protestantism what would the spirit of England be?' (BT 24.1.12). Orangeism is 'the bulwark of Protestantism ... its ramifications are to be found performing their useful functions of welding more firmly the bonds that knit the Empire together in every part of the globe' (CDS 17.7.20). There is also Ulster's 'magnificent response for the call of men to defend the Empire' (LS 15.2.16). The carnage of the Somme, whose full horror did not emerge until the following year, is a cause of grief to many families but useful to the cause:

> The Unionists of Ulster deplore the losses sustained and sympathise with the sufferers and the bereaved, but they hail with joy the proof which their fellow-Unionists at the front have given of their right to be reckoned loyal sons of the empire and of their title to retain the full status of citizenship (LS 6.7.16).

Once the full extent of the disaster was known one editor praised all the Irish troops, for 'all the correspondents pay tribute to the valour of the Irish soldiers from North and South' (BT 23.8.17), but this generosity is rare, and the more usual claim is that 'no part of the Empire has been called upon to make such sacrifices and endure such trials as the Province of Ulster, in July last year' (BO 6.7.17).

The comparison with nationalists proves useful too: 'Nationalism ... is not concerned for the glory of the Empire, which the manhood of Ulster has splendidly rallied to support. Its friends are the King's enemies' (LS 13.7.18). In contrast with 'those who are loyal to the Empire' nationalists are 'Empire-wreckers', 'Empire-haters', 'enemies' or 'foes of the Empire', involved in a 'conspiracy against Ireland, Great Britain and the Empire' (BO 27.9.12). Nationalists who proclaim loyalty to the empire are untrustworthy liars with 'a horror of being called upon to discharge one of the first duties of citizenship' (LS 12.8.15), and 'dislike of the Empire and a firm conviction that all enemies of England are deserving of sympathy and support are important and necessary parts of Irish Nationalism' (LS 3.8.15). Further ammunition for this view was the nationalist refusal to countenance conscription:

> The British people will know that while the Nationalists deserted the Empire and the cause of civilisation in the hour of peril, Ulster was ready to take its stand with England and Scotland and accept any Bill which was applied to them (NL 10.12.15).

The falsity of this claim, in view of the nature of the opposition to the Home Rule Bill, is equalled only by that of the assertion that 'Ireland outside Ulster has never been really tapped for military purposes' (BT 8.4.18).

Most useful was the unlooked-for help from the Easter Rising. This 'puny rising against the might of the British Empire' (LS 2.5.16) nevertheless lends credence to Carson's expressed view that 'no concession can be made to the forces of disloyalty and sedition in Ireland without gravely increasing the danger to the security of the Empire' (LS 27.5.16), especially when the aim of the Rising is to 'assist the Germans to bring about the downfall of the Empire' (PDN 29.4.16). Hence Home Rule is 'really more an Imperial than a purely Irish question' and handing over 26 counties to Sinn Fein would endanger the security of the kingdom (LS 24.6.16), or even of the entire empire: 'We have won the war, but if Ireland is lost we shall lose the Empire, and that is why Britain's enemies, not alone in Ireland, but everywhere, are leaguing themselves with Sinn Fein' (BO 6.8.20). Hence this alleged contrast between the loyal Protestant imperialists of Ulster and the Catholic empire-haters of nationalist Ireland laid the basis for claims that Home Rule would 'dismember and disintegrate the Empire' or otherwise weaken it or impair its honour (BT 12.3.12). Although one editor wrote that even if the exclusion of Ulster were conditional upon review after five years, 'If it is in the interests of our beloved Empire that we sacrifice still more, we feel that the Ulster people may be persuaded to make this further sacrifice' (CDS 18.5.17), a more typical attitude is that of the *News Letter* which having said that as 'true Imperialists' unionists would consider favourably the new plan for Ireland 'in the interests of the Empire' (NL 18.5.17), then rejected the proposal of five-year exclusion.

Clearly Protestants would act in the interests of the empire only on their own definition of what those interests were; and the nobility of the imperial stance is somewhat impaired by the transparent self-interest of the claim that Home Rule threatens not only the empire but Irish Protestants, and by the unconcealed threat that service in the imperial armies means that after the war 'Ulster Unionism will have an army corps of seasoned soldiers to give it the same faithful service as in the meantime they will give to the Empire' (LS 5.9.14).

The empire also legitimates Ulster opposition to Home Rule: 'We are fighting for our own freedom and our own liberties in Ireland it is true ... But we are fighting for something more, for the preservation of the unity of the Kingdom and of the Empire' (NL 28.9.12). Ulster is to be held 'in trust for the Empire' (BO 26.1.12), so the Ulstermen are 'not ... fighting a selfish battle ... but the battle of the Empire' (PDN 25.5.12). That this fight on behalf of 'the Empire, which [Ulster Unionists] have never done anything to disgrace' (LS 19.9.14), involved illegal activities such as drilling and gun-running is justified by reference to the empire: 'The Government [should] realise what an asset to the Empire [the UVF] is' (LS 28.4.14).

Omitting to mention the fact that the Irish Volunteers were formed ten months after the UVF and in reaction to it, editors warn that Home Rule would bring civil war, '[not] some petty tribal raid in India or Africa, [but] a conflagration that will convulse the Empire and rapidly spread across the Channel' (LS 11.6.14). The value of the UVF is of course borne out when many of them 'having first made Ulster strong to defy the menace to her liberty' (LS 1.6.16) volunteered, forming the 36th Division. No doubt many were void of the ulterior motive hinted at here:

> When [the Ulstermen] sacrificed their domestic defence organisa- tion to the call of loyalty to the Empire they put their trust in the British people in a spirit that the British people will never suffer to be requited by betrayal (CDS 4.5.17).

The UVF, Carson warned after the war, should be restored, as the government is 'flirting with the avowed enemies of the Empire by its cowardly attitude' (IR 4.9.19). Carson himself, the leader of the Ulster rebellion, is the supreme patriot, the epitome of devotion and loyalty to the empire: 'He is too fine a character and actuated by too high feelings of patriotism to put politics for a moment before the welfare of the Empire, which he loves with whole-hearted devotion' (LS 19.10.15). The empire combined with the war also justifies the accept- ance of the exclusion of only six counties: 'Ulster has for the sake of the Empire made the supreme sacrifice asked of her' (BT 13.6.16).

Editorials are sprinkled with many more imperial references than are cited here, and empire provided a useful rallying-point for Prot- estants. Ultimately it ceased to be a propagandist exercise and en- tered into the mindset of Protestants, as is perhaps shown by the outburst of imperial fervour once partition was assured and the King opened the Northern Parliament. It still, however, proved a useful spur, this time to persuade Protestants to vote Ulster Unionist, as it is inconsistent with loyalty to King and empire to come forward even as an Independent Unionist (CDS 7.5.21), and the election results are both a triumph for the imperial spirit and a guarantee of Ulster's place in the empire.

This place in the empire is more than as a mere part of the Union:

> We Loyalists of the North of Ireland give precedence to no others in the British Empire. It may be that, like the peoples of the overseas Dominions, we labour under a sense of detachment from the centre of the national life and government, and that, like them, this feeling engenders in us a fonder and a keener apprecia- tion of what the Sovereignty stands for as the binding link in the nation and the Empire ... our loyalty ... is much more decisive

[than that of the people of Great Britain] ... in directing our outlook upon the affairs of the Empire (NL 22.6.21).

There was nothing new about the idea that the British government was incapable of 'guiding the destinies of the Empire in connection with questions arising in remote places' (LS 21.6.17). Now the empire was usurped, not only from the rest of Ireland, but even from the people of Great Britain whose support Protestants had earnestly solicited.

HOW MUCH TRUTH is there in these claims? Ulster Protestants certainly played a major part in the settlement of the United States of America, and fought on both sides in its War of Independence. Important numbers of Irish Protestants also went to other white settlements, though a factor excluded from the Protestant imperial discourse is the large contribution of the famine-induced Irish Catholic diaspora of the mid-nineteenth century. There were Irish colonial administrators too, usually Anglo-Irish and including Ulster Protestants. Most of the Irish officers in the army of the East India Company were Protestants, whereas most of the Irish soldiers were Catholics, and though the proportion of Irish soldiers fell dramatically, that of Irish officers fell very little. Protestant volunteering to the British forces in the 1914–18 war provided an added fillip to the claim that loyalty to empire was confined to Protestants, especially when the substantial amount of Catholic volunteering declined from 1915. One result of this was a decline in Ulster volunteering (CDS 13.4.18). Nevertheless, of the 170,000 recruits and reservists supplied in total, Ulster provided proportionately more than the other three provinces combined, especially if we discount the thousands who went from the other provinces to work in British munitions factories and the further thousands of British-based Irish and descendants of Irish immigrants who joined the army; but to describe it as the imperial province is both misleading and a disservice to the men, Irish Catholic and Anglo-Irish Protestant, from the other provinces of Ireland, and, given the usurpation of 'Ulster' by Protestants, to the many Catholic volunteers from Ulster. The later focus on the disaster of the Somme, when many of the Ulster Division were killed, hides the dreadful attrition of lives from men of all creeds and parts of Ireland (and indeed, from the whole empire) that went on throughout the war.

THESE ATTEMPTS AT legitimation continued in the Stormont years, and the 1939–45 war and its aftermath provided new opportunities for playing the empire card, for Protestants could portray themselves as holding 'Ulster' for the empire. 'This western outpost of Empire' (PDN 19.4.47) is a bulwark of imperialism against 'the foes of the Empire, especially in Ireland' (LS 13.7.39). The terms 'the imperial

Province', Ulster's 'Imperial birthright and traditions' and the 'Imperial race' which inhabits it excluded the large numbers of Free Staters who volunteered for service, and who are rarely mentioned. Instead Eire's 'sullen neutrality' (LS 20.6.40) is frequently contrasted with the Ulster loyalists who are 'proud to stand by Britain and the rest of the Empire' (LS 12.10.39). Even the German air-raids are a 'savage revenge upon Ulster for her loyalty to Britain and the Empire' (LS 22.2.41).

Loyalty to the empire, however, goes only so far. Gough's proposal for an All-Ireland Parliament in return for a military alliance, and the argument that by agreeing Northern Ireland would 'show her devotion to British and Imperial interests', is predictably unpopular (LS 22.2.41); but it proved a useful reminder that the position might be precarious and still required vigorous defence. 'Imperial interests' might decree the sacrifice of the six counties, if it could not be made clear that their retention in the United Kingdom served those interests better. Hence 'the situation can still be saved, but only by the strong united resolution of all the Protestants of Ulster to get together under the banner of Empire' (LS 7.11.44).

The election of a Labour government apparently dedicated to a 'policy of surrender' (IR 2.1.47) as the colonial empire began to disintegrate, and Eire's departure from the Commonwealth, spelled further danger until the Ireland Act was passed. Until that, Ulster's imperial role was aggrandised still further by one writer who, as happened in the 1912–21 period, usurped the empire not only from the rest of Ireland but from the rest of the United Kingdom as well: 'Until the Socialist Government in Britain is replaced, there are many in England who look upon Ulster as the guardian, in these Islands, of the greatness of the British Empire' (Ralph Stone IR 12.8.48).

As in the 1912–21 period, it is largely the white settler empire which counts: 'the Empire – or Commonwealth as it is now more generally called – is an association of free peoples, and free peoples have the right of choice' (LS 22.2.49); and again the role of Northern Protestants, this time in the 1939–45 war, when Northern Ireland was not subject to conscription, needs to be examined. Volunteering began at a rate of 2,500 per month but soon fell to under 1,000, and despite recruitment drives and an upsurge after Dunkirk, recruitment rates continued to fall. Apathy was observed 'amongst both religious groups' and among civil servants and politicians as well as the general populace (Barton 1989:49–50). Industrial productivity too was poor and absenteeism at the Harland and Wolff shipyard was two times higher than at the worst yards in Great Britain. Far from the outbreak of war arousing an instant response to the need to save the empire, it was widely felt that the war was far away and Northern Ireland would not be attacked. Even after the air raids which shattered the prevailing complacency, recruitment remained low. Conscription was considered but rejected: there seemed little doubt that Catholics would reject it, and there was evidence that many Protestants were at best half-hearted about it; it would also have stemmed the flow of recruits from the Irish state, which went far towards making up the shortfall caused by the lack of conscription. The total number of volunteers over the whole course of the war was 30,664 from Northern Ireland and 28,774 from the Irish state, despite the neutrality of the Irish government.

Certainly many Ulster Protestants did volunteer, uncomplainingly accepted rationing and worked for the war effort; but Northern Ireland's main usefulness during the war was its strategic geographical position, for if its war effort was unimpressive, its role in the Allied victory was vital as a naval base and as a launching pad for US forces, particularly given the neutrality of the Irish state. It was this that inspired Churchill's letter of appreciation, so often quoted in later times by ultra writers. Northern Ireland was the 'imperial province' in that its territory was still a full part of the British empire, being part of the United Kingdom, unlike the Free State; but to have called Ulster 'the imperial province' on the basis of its military record or even the whole-hearted support of its Protestant population, was unjustified.

THE DEMISE OF the empire removed an important plank from Protestant propaganda and despite a few, mainly early, references which assume that there is still an empire to be defended against Rome, the European Economic Community (EEC), communism or NICRA, there is a not-surprising nostalgia for 'the late lamented British Empire' (OS Feb 1984). Some of the earlier usages survived for a while, including the 'Imperial Government/Parliament/General Election/MP/Civil Service' and the Orange Order still retains 'Imperial' in some of its titles. Readers are occasionally reminded of the role of the 'Ulster Imperialists' who 'exercised a prominent role as Empire Builders, on the battlefield and off it, for generations' (PDN 7.3.69), unlike the rebel Irish:

> It was not the Ulster loyalists who in 1922 took the first practical steps towards the eventual break-up of the British Empire; it was not Ulstermen but the Connaught Rangers who rebelled on the field of battle in India; it was not an Ulster loyalist who endeavoured to form an Irish Brigade in Europe during the 1914–18 War (OS Jun 1984).

There was also an attempt to portray the DUP as the guardian of the old values, in the naming of local branches such as the 'Armagh/South Down Imperial Democratic Unionist Association' (Chairman PDN 10.1.75).

In many instances moderates are on the face of it indistinguishable from ultras on the subject of empire. Anachronistic usages are as common among these 'people of Ulster who value the Imperial connection' ('Immoderate' IR 30.10.69), and Westminster elections and the British government continues to be 'Imperial'. There are also nostalgic references to the greatness of the empire and muted regret at its passing:

> A 'Yes' vote [in the EEC referendum] would be an acknowledgement by the British people that their unique role as a proud, independent, trading nation with large overseas commitments has ended. In a military and political sense this has been happening since 1945, as the Union Jack has been hauled down in country after country, and as Britain's forces have been scaled down to a comparatively minor European role ... Britain is now regarded as the economic 'sick man' of Europe – and that is a measure of the nation's decline from heights of power and wealth ... so many people at home and abroad have 'knocked' all the old virtues and standards which made Britain great ... Britain and the British people will have to re-discover their ideals – that role in the world which they have turned their backs on for so long (PDT 4.6.75).

There are also references to Ulster's role in empire 'Ulster has given some of its greatest sons to the cause of Empire – Nicholson the hero of Delhi, Rollo Gillespie of Comber, and Portadown's own son Sir Robert Hart of China fame' (PDN 8.9.78). However, 'Ireland's marvellous tradition of service in the Forces' is not neglected (PDT 8.11.85).

THE EMPIRE SERVED a useful purpose in much of the 1912–21 period, and even in 1939–49, as a 'noble ideal' to unite Ulster Protestants and differentiate Ulster from the rest of Ireland in the eyes of the British. It was abandoned with reluctance, especially by ultras, for with the end of empire the underlying notion of Northern Ireland as an 'imperial garrison' was no longer as credible as it had been. Britain's greatly diminished role as a military power similarly decreased Northern Ireland's strategic importance, and the Falklands affair turned out to be a passing phase rather than a new start. One ironic twist in the imperial story is the transformation under direct rule from Westminster of proud settlers, who had participated in governing a world-wide empire and protecting imperial interests in Ireland, into colonial subjects with as little autonomy as 'natives' in the old colonial empire. This subject empire with its deep injustices, long ignored in Protestant historiography in favour of the self-governing white settler empire, has now been placed on the agenda.

The colonisers have become the colonised, and they do not like the experience; but they do not draw any conclusions favourable to those who had earlier endeavoured to gain their freedom from the empire.

IF THE EMPIRE was usurped then so was 'loyalty'. It has, of course, often been observed that Protestant loyalty is conditional and that it is still conceived of as loyalty by Protestants when they are disobeying the law of the country to which they profess loyalty. There is, however, nothing abnormal, unusual or irrational about loyalty that is conditional: as Hirschman states, the very existence of loyalty is predicated on the possibility of exit (Hechter 1975:268). Loyalty is usually claimed to be to the Crown and Constitution, which appear to support appeals to retain the status quo in favour of their interests. It is explicitly not to any government (defined as the Cabinet and the House of Commons) which appears potentially dangerous to those interests. When aspects of the metropolis which appear not to tolerate the status quo come to the fore, protestations of loyalty increase. It is then not the conditional nature of loyalty that is so much of interest, but that loyalty should be such an integral part of the Northern Ireland political discourse, and particularly at times when the relationship with Great Britain is strained over the role and position of Catholics. The fear of being cut off from the shelter of the metropolis and left to the mercy of the 'natives' in a united independent Ireland has been a powerful incentive to cry ancient loyalty. The meaning which 'loyalty' assumes is also of interest. In fact, the definition of loyalty has changed, and it was probably the first Home Rule crisis which added to the absolute meaning of 'loyal' as 'faithful in allegiance to the sovereign, or constituted government' (1531) the more relative 'loyal, as opposed to disaffected, subjects (1885)' (Shorter Oxford English Dictionary 1959).

Since Protestants have often pursued aims opposed to those of the British state, they need to claim loyalty to something higher than the government or parliament. The idea of the empire, as previously outlined, is a useful focus for Protestant expressions of loyalty, especially when Catholics are deprived of using imperial precedents to advance their own interests. Similarly, expressions of loyalty to the Crown or the United Kingdom are monopolised by Protestants, while Catholics are 'disloyal'. This process has been seen as a necessary strategy to maintain Protestants' historic advantages arising from their role as a 'garrison' for British power in Ireland (MacDonald 1991:81–2), as necessary now as it was throughout the Home Rule crises of 1885, 1893 and 1912–20:

> Ulster loyalists 'need' disloyal nationalists to demonstrate their own loyalty ... Even when 'natives' give their consent to a consti-

tutional compromise, their newly proclaimed loyalty is seen as suspect and merely instrumental to their long-term goal. Loyalists, on the other hand, demonstrate their own loyalty ostentatiously (O'Dowd 1990:40).

After all, if the 'natives' are loyal, there is no need for the metropolis to privilege and protect settlers. Hence protestations of Protestant loyalty and charges of Catholic disloyalty are largely directed towards the metropolis, and in the 1912–21 period formed an important part of the campaign to convince the British audience that the Protestant minority in Ireland had a right to fight against Home Rule by any means available. It was the good fortune of the survivors that the 1914–18 war provided an opportunity to 'prove' this loyalty while the Easter Rising in later years 'proved' Catholic disloyalty.

Catholic disloyalty is in any case axiomatic: those who are against the British connection and want to withdraw from the Union, namely nationalists, are automatically 'disloyal', despite the insincere 'loyalist utterances' of John Redmond and other nationalists; those who are for 'the British connection', namely unionists, are by definition loyal. Doubters should note the past, for example, 'the Nationalist cheers that greeted the news of Boer victories in the South Africa War' (BO 12.4.12); and comparisons with Quebec suggested that disloyalty is a Roman Catholic trait.

If Protestants are loyal, what exactly are they loyal to? Despite the many references to loyalty to the empire, to 'the Throne and Constitution', 'the United Kingdom and its flag' or 'England', loyalty is ultimately to Protestant interests:

In Ulster to-day all loyal men are making preparations ... for a death-grapple with whatever forces may be employed ... to coerce them under an intensely disloyal and hostile Parliament ... under a Home Rule parliament the loyal minority would have no power ... Thus an Ascendancy would be created in favour of those ... who have threatened to wreak vengeance on the loyal minority in Ireland when they get power (LS 11.6.14).

By this time there was an additional need for protestations of loyalty: the undoubtedly illegal acts of drilling, setting up a provisional government and smuggling arms into Ulster. All of these are defensible because they are approved by 'tens of thousands of the King's most loyal citizens' (BT 24.9.13) who are 'fighting the battle of the nation' (BO 27.9.12), unlike those 'men who have made no secret of their disloyalty to and hatred of all that the British people hold most dear' (CDS 28.11.13). There is no contradiction between words and actions:

[Carson's] loyalty is the centre force of his action, just as it is
with every Ulster Unionist. We are told it is conditional loyalty.
Not in the smallest degree, so far as the Crown is concerned.
This Radical Government is not the Crown (NL 23.9.13).

That the King later signed the Home Rule Bill into law, despite some
certainty that he would not, does not challenge this conception of
loyalty, for by then the 1914–18 war had started. If England's difficulty
was Ireland's opportunity, it is not only Catholics who might benefit;
from 1914 Protestants have a chance to 'prove their loyalty by their
magnificent rally to the colours' (LS 16.5.16), even if this is explicitly
conditional in some quarters: '35,000 Ulster Volunteers have ... volunteered if the Government do not violate their pledged honour in regard
to the Home Rule Bill' (IR 27.8.14). At the same time the war was an
opportunity to 'prove' Catholic disloyalty. From the beginning the
impression was conveyed, not simply that Ulster provided more recruits than the rest of Ireland, which was true, but also that Catholic
recruiting figures were much lower than they really were and Protestant, especially Ulster, figures much higher. The term 'shirking' was
generally reserved for Catholics: 'the glaring fact that wholesale and
systematic shirking is going on amongst the great body of the Roman
Catholics in Ireland' (LS 24.10.14). This is not necessarily due to
cowardice: 'Large numbers of Nationalists who have refused to join
the army have done so solely through feelings of disloyalty to the
Crown and Constitution' (LS 29.6.15). The editor of the *Londonderry
Sentinel* painted a picture of Ulster unionists volunteering while
nationalists stayed at home and took their jobs but in the face of the
evidence, well-known locally, grudgingly had to admit that many
Ulster Catholics had also enlisted (LS 7.10.16).

In war conditions, 'disloyalty', which really meant general hostility
to British rule, could, happily, be translated into 'sedition', that is,
attempts to inspire rebellion against the British state, and hence to
'the existence of a strong pro-German feeling' (LS 1.7.15) or even to
plotting with Germany. The Easter Rising itself, especially given the
coincidence of its timing just before the first casualty figures from
the Somme started to arrive, provided further ammunition for Protestant claims; but at that time the rebels were not seen as representative of the Catholic population, and though hindsight declared
it 'inevitable' (NL 20.5.18), it clearly came as a surprise. Despite the
fact that it is supported only by a small minority, everyone must
take sides: 'At the present juncture the community knows but two
divisions – loyalists and rebels. To seek any middle course is to be
disloyal, for there can be no neutrality' (BT 28.4.16). Nevertheless
the blame was placed, partly at the door of German intrigue, but
mainly at that of 'the slack feeble government which has cursed our
country ever since Mr Augustine Birrell became head of the Irish

Administration' (NL 4.5.16). The importance that the Easter Rising would assume in history, both for Protestants and Catholics, was not foreseen. The Irish rebellion 'will presently be little more than a memory, though it will long be a bitter and aching memory to many' (BT 2.5.16), and its only significance for one editor was that it provided good practice for the troops who dealt with it (BO 5.5.16).

IN FUTURE PERIODS of tension, however, both the loyalty shown by the Battle of the Somme and the disloyalty shown by the Easter Rising were used as ammunition for the Protestant cause. The 1939–45 war provided a further opportunity, through volunteering, to claim a monopoly of loyalty as well as devotion to the empire. Civil defence was based on the Ulster Special Constabulary (USC) and consisted largely of internal security duties (Harkness 1983:83–4). Hence Catholics were effectively debarred from showing loyalty locally, although some did volunteer for the British armed forces.

The official line was that conscription should have been levied in Northern Ireland, but reluctance was expressed in unionist circles at the possible training in arms of the subversive element of the population – that is, the 'disloyal' Northern Ireland Catholics whom informed readers would have recognised in the following:

> The best of our men have already volunteered. One-third at least of the men conscription would have called to the colours would have been traitors to the success of the cause for which they would have been forced to fight (CDS 31.5.41).

In some quarters there was in any case little incentive for Catholics to be 'loyal':

> Mr Justice Megaw ... rightly called attention to the point that, while disloyalty at any time is a crime, feigned loyalty is even more dangerous. There is no doubt that loyalty is being feigned at the present time by numbers of people whose sole desire is to see the enemies of Britain and Ulster triumph ... His Lordship, however, issued a warning ... Pointing out that, while there may be no immediate outward manifestations of activities on the part of those whose purpose is to subvert the State, overthrow the Constitution, and aid the enemy ... it may very well be only a momentary lull, and he hopes that such a lull will not create a sense of false security (LS 27.7.40).

The 'blood-soaked pledge' (LS 26.4.45) of Northern Ireland's war effort may be proof of Protestant loyalty but this did not always apply to Catholic ex-servicemen, as the Cassidy case in Fermanagh shows.

Far from his service and disablement showing loyalty, his application for a job is a mere propaganda exercise (James Ritchie IR 14.9.44). Servicemen irrespective of sect often had a hard time finding work on discharge.

There are generous acknowledgements by moderates of Southern volunteering, but more frequently the contrast is between loyal Ulster and disloyal neutral 'Eire', which refused to hand over the ports it was given back before the war. For all the self-righteous indignation at Irish policy, however, it clearly helps Northern Ireland's case: 'Ulster's loyalty has been brought into sharper focus because of the neutrality of Eire' (LS 23.11.43); and the Protestant record was by no means as unblemished as some writers portray it, as Barton (1989) demonstrates. There are contemporary complaints about the Northern government's 'supineness' and the USC had to be defended against nationalist jibes that they were not volunteering on the grounds that many were in reserved occupations. Protestants too complained of backsliding among their own people, especially in Bangor and Fermanagh. Other factors that marred Ulster's record tended to be played down or treated leniently. One of these was the prevalence of strikes and absenteeism. Dislike of Belfast usually got the better of the Fermanagh editor and, apart from blaming one strike on 'the republican element spreading disaffection' (IR 8.4.43), his general verdict was that the absenteeism ('three times as bad as England') and strikes showed the disloyalty of Belfast (IR 22.10.42, 18.2.43). They were, however, condemned by the Belfast papers with far more sorrow than anger. For example, the strike at the mainly Protestant Harland and Wolff shipyard, condemned in Fermanagh as 'rank treason' (IR 13.4.44), merely evoked this comment as part of a mild exhortation to return to work: 'The patriotism and loyalty of the men of our shipyard are not in doubt' (NL 6.4.44). It is hard to imagine such a reaction if the strikers had been Catholics.

The blemishes on Northern Ireland's record are, however, more than counterbalanced by the ignominy of Southern neutrality, and the contribution of individuals from the South was typically ignored, played down or nullified, as in the following comment on Churchill's speech praising Northern Ireland's loyal aid:

Then Mr Churchill contrasted Eire's neutrality and its consequences with the temper and instinct of thousands of Southern Irishmen who hastened to the battlefront to prove their ancient valour. It is well to remember the decision of the Dublin Government that Eire should remain neutral was in accordance with the wishes of the vast majority of the people of Eire, whose anti-British instincts are as strong as ever. Moreover, it was against the wish and the will of Mr De Valera and his Government that these Irishmen joined the Fighting Forces of the Crown (LS 15.5.45).

As the relative lack of condemnation of Protestant war-time strikers shows, loyalty is a part of character as much as a way of behaving. Hence loyalty can be claimed even by those aiming to break away from the Union: 'In Ulster Britain would have the most loyal Dominion in her Empire' (LS 13.2.47). This raises the question of what 'loyalty' actually means, apart from supporting Britain in her various wars. I found only one definition for this period:

> An Ulsterman's greatest virtue is loyalty; personal loyalty to his friends and a higher spirited loyalty to his principles and his Faith have always been a characteristic and cardinal virtue of the native of Ulster, especially the members of the Orange Order (LS 15.7.47).

If self-interest is missing from this statement, it is certainly present in the following: 'Ulster has taken her stand by Britain, and the least that we can expect from Britain is that she will reciprocate our loyalty' (LS 15.2.49). Instead the House of Commons extended 'Eire' citizens' Westminster voting rights in Northern Ireland, an 'inexplicable anomaly ... concession to disloyalty' (LS 31.3.49). Fortunately the 1949 Ireland Act made it safe to be unconditionally loyal again – until the next crisis.

TODAY THE BRITISH on the whole appear not to be listening and there is no longer an empire to represent the higher interest. The word 'loyalty' is still a part of the discourse, and it is still used to justify rebellion, but it has lost much of its former force, and mere assertions of Protestant 'loyalty' are less frequent, perhaps because they have been greeted with such scepticism by the British public. Routine references to Catholic 'disloyalty' are now rare and for one ultra editor 'loyalists' can even include Northern Ireland Roman Catholics (NL 19.4.82). Furthermore, and particularly since 1968, 'loyalty' has been subject to careful definition, debate and even questioning, lending some credence to the perception that today Protestant professions of loyalty 'are simply expressing an official emotion which no one any longer feels or believes in' (Paulin 1983:21). There is debate about what loyalty is or ought to be, about the correct ways to be loyal and about what the true objects of loyalty are. These additions to the discourse of loyalty are explained partly by the split in unionism, and the resulting competition between different unionist camps over, among other things, who is the most 'British' or 'loyal', and partly by changes in British political culture, where secularisation, indifference to Irish affairs and distaste for Northern Ireland Protestants seem to have spread throughout the country, even to the old allies of unionists, the Conservative Party. It was, after all, Conservative governments which had been responsible both for Sunningdale and the Anglo–Irish Agreement, so 'loyalty to the Tory Party' (OS Mar 1986) is no longer appropriate. The result of these changed conditions is a virtual end to the usurpation of loyalty.

Nevertheless Protestants do express loyalty to something, if not often to the parliament of the United Kingdom, and terms such as 'loyal Ulster' and 'loyalist British people in Ulster' are still found, though 'loyalty to the Motherland' soon disappeared. 'The emotional feelings of loyalty to the Crown ... inherent in most Protestants' (Chris Boston CDS 18.2.72) are often stated to be the true and abiding focus of loyalty, and 'no matter how intense has been the distaste for Her Majesty's Governments the Queen has retained the love, devotion and loyalty of her Ulster subjects' (OS Aug 1977). The 'Constitution' often referred to in conjunction with the Crown is defined more precisely as 'Ulster's constitutional position as an integral part of the UK' (Campbell McCormick CDS 31.10.69); and another local view involves even more wishful thinking: 'Ulster belongs to the Queen and therefore Thatcher has no right to sign deals on Northern Ireland with Garret FitzGerald' ('E.D.' BTimes 14.8.86). The usual attention is also paid to the symbols of loyalty: singing the national anthem and flying the Union flag, preferably one in good condition, without allowing the Irish Tricolour to be flown too.

Even the Crown, however, has lost the respect of earlier periods, and there is much more emphasis than previously on the conditional nature of loyalty to the Crown. Stated baldly, 'Ulster is loyal while the British Throne remains Protestant' (Beryl Holland CDS 19.12.80). Doubts about the Queen's commitment to the Protestant faith were raised by her visit to the Pope and her practice of attending Sunday race meetings, and an ingenious effort to prove that the Anglo–Irish Agreement is illegal involved the claim that she broke part of her Coronation oath by signing it. Another writer drew the moral that allegiance to the Crown is no longer appropriate:

> Ulster people must know by now, through bitter experience, how unstable are the kingdoms of this world. For with all their talk of democracy, such kingdoms do not hesitate to betray their people if it should become expedient to do so. Ulster's loyalty to the Crown has been rewarded with treachery by Her Majesty's government and parliament. How much safer then to seek citizenship in the Kingdom of Christ (Patricia Roberts IR 29.5.86).

Indeed a higher loyalty, to the Protestant faith, has long been advocated. Such assertions should not always, however, be taken at face value: the following illustrates the politicised nature of Protestantism in Derry as well as the implicit notion that Ulster loyalists are 'more loyal than the English' (Beryl Holland CDS 16.11.79) because loyalty is oppositional:

You have praised the people on The Fountain for their loyalism and steadfastness in the face of the republicans surrounding their area ... the man ... solely responsible for making The Fountain the most loyal area in Great Britain [sic] [is] Bobby Jackson ... who for over fifty years has upheld the Protestant tradition (Kenny Allen TLS 29.8.84).

Another alternative to the traditional loyalty to the British state is loyalty to Northern Ireland: 'the true loyalty of all of us should be to ourselves and our native Province' (NL 11.6.75), a view expressed in a preference for the Ulster flag over the Union Flag:

It is evident, too, these days, that the union Jack can be no longer regarded as the real symbol of Ulster Protestantism and Union- ism. With the present sell out to Westminster many Loyalists here in Belfast have realised this. True Unionists should fly the Ulster flag ... They are becoming very common at Paisley meet- ings, and I feel they are the most appropriate symbol of loyalty (Alan Armstrong IR 22.7.71).

Not only is the object of loyalty now questioned, but also the very nature of loyalty. Two interesting definitions illustrate different solu- tions to the problem of opposing state policy while retaining a claim to be loyal. The first, in the context of Sunningdale, claims that loyalty is absolute and unwavering, and that the principles to which loyalty is owed are those which underpin social order. The appeal then, like the old appeals to the empire, is to something higher than the state:

In the last analysis the object of loyalty is to some ultimate principle or set of principles, whether symbolised by a person or an institu- tion. Loyalty means unwavering fidelity to such principles 'even to the edge of doom'. Like love, loyalty is not loyalty 'Which alters when it alteration finds, Or bends with the remover to remove'. Loyalists are loyal in this unwavering sense to the principles of the Settlement on which British liberties and modern constitution rest – as stated in the statute book and as the law of the land. Further, they are loyal to the moral principles of truth-telling and promise- keeping, which Westminster has violated in relation to Ulster. Those who support such behaviour, even by a sovereign Parliament, are either morally blind or amoral. Yet these are the principles on which social order depends. Those who are disloyal to them are not merely opponents of Loyalists, they are enemies of civilisation and of the human race (Ernest Baird CDS 10.8.73).

The second definition, in the context of the Anglo–Irish Agreement, and possibly owing much to Miller's (1978) *Queen's Rebels*, is vague about the object of loyalty and even more vague about Protestants' 'duties and obligations' but clear that it is contractarian and hence conditional:

> the loyalty of Ulster has never been to what Sir Robin Day described as the 'here-today gone-tomorrow' politicians of Westminster but to the State itself; to the national concept of 'Britishness'. The embodiment of the State is in the person of HM the Queen, not Mrs Thatcher and her little friends. There are actually two kinds of loyalty. The first is the loyalty of a dog to its master ... The second, and commonly understood loyalty, is that of the two-part contract ... each party has certain duties and obligations to the other. No such contract can be changed unilaterally ... if one of the parties fails to meet its obligations, or deliberately reneges on the terms, the other need no longer be bound to it. When a contract is broken its terms are no longer valid, and this is precisely the case with Northern Ireland today ... WE didn't break the contract – YOU did. You dishonoured the contract by introducing a third party, against our firmly expressed wishes. Not even the mythical 'Bar of World Opinion' can hold up to this rewritten contract (Peter C Chambers CDS 13.2.86).

In this case then the disloyal act has been committed by the British government, a perception which has for some time had a certain propaganda value. This increased as Anglo–Irish talks became worrying: 'it is Britain who has shown a poor example of loyalty to this part of her United Kingdom, by denying Northern Ireland her democratic right to have her own Parliament' (Beryl Holland CDS 17.11.78).

Even before the usefulness of the contractarian argument was noticed, however, conditions for 'loyalty to Britain' (which in the context means willingness to obey British law) were spelled out. The British government should concentrate on 'understanding, not on crass arrogance, not on interference and certainly not on coercion, even in the mildest form' (NL 30.5.74); refrain from 'imposing on the good people of Northern Ireland laws which will greatly offend them', such as those on divorce and homosexuality (John McAuley BO 21.1.82); defeat the IRA; and 'fulfil its most important – some would say sole – duty, which is to protect the community from interference by an alien power' (OS Apr 1986). Since the government is patently failing in all these areas, it is not surprising that 'loyalist' has become almost synonymous with 'rebellious'.

It is not only the British government which offends ultra loyalty. Moderates who castigate ultras for their anti-Catholicism and sturdy defence of Protestant interests are equally unpopular, for this constitutes disloyalty to 'Ulster'. It is arguable that ultras' dislike of 'treacherous' Protestants who support the ecumenical movement, form political parties (such as the APNI) with Catholics, frown on violent demonstrations or agree to power-sharing with Catholics at any level, is even greater than their hatred of Catholics themselves. Thus moderate Protestants often earn the appellation 'Lundy' or traitor. For example, a letter complaining about loyalist bonfires on a mixed estate is answered with this typical (if inaccurate) historical analogy (Lundy died in a later campaign in mainland Europe):

> Has he ever read the history of Lundy?... he was a Protestant who betrayed his faith and his comrades, and was burned at the Siege of Derry in defence of the Protestant faith ('Steeple Protestant Association' BO 14.1.71).

The reason for Northern Ireland's current position is the attempt by some Protestants to 'placate and appease Republicanism' ('True Loyalist' IR 10.3.88).

Moderates are in fact as concerned about showing loyalty as ultras, but they interpret loyalty differently and in a way that can include Catholics. Whereas for ultras loyalty is ultimately to Protestant Ulster, irrespective of British opinion, for moderates it is loyalty to the Union:

> Twenty years ago ... it was taken for granted that the old loyalist common front ... meant that the best guarantee of Ulster's survival as a separate entity from the rest of Ireland depended on preserving the British link. That meant unquestioned loyalty to the Throne and to the Crown ... That there are strong elements within the loyalist community now committed to breaking the ties with the rest of the UK is nothing short of incredible ... The Union has always been the centre-piece of loyalist policy (PDN 14.7.78).

For moderates the Crown is British, and it is the symbol of the government, or 'the will of the people expressed through Parliament' (BT 4.10.72), and they respect what the Union flag symbolises for them, namely British parliamentary democracy, British law and the British armed forces. Catholics (or anyone else) are loyal if they join the British forces or obey British law:

> Catholics are just as loyal to the Crown as the Unionists and have the same right to live in peace ... To me a Loyalist is a person who is loyal to the Crown and British Empire. Look how many Catholics and Protestants died for their loyalty to the Crown and country of Britain (James R Sherlock CDS 7.1.72).

One feature of the split in unionism is the competition between the two groups over the correct way to show loyalty. For ultras loyalty is demonstrated by flying the Union flag continuously and singing the national anthem. The habit of leaving the Union flag hanging either upside-down or until it has been blown into tatters arouses some mockery from moderates, and loyalists' love for the national anthem and protestations of affection for the Queen are seen as insincere, given their behaviour: 'It was ludicrous to see the crowds muster under the British flag while showing their displeasure and opposition to the British Government. What hypocrisy!' (William Simpson BO 30.3.72). More seriously, when 'loyalist' intransigence and uncouth behaviour, including support for independence, appear to give Northern Ireland a bad name and threaten the Union, moderates deem it disloyal and unrepresentative: 'What the loyalists loyal to Northern Ireland Protestant rule only would think is becoming more and more academic, as they divorce themselves further from mainstream opinion by their behaviour' (IR 19.10.78) and 'extremists [who] beat their chests and talk about the sacrifices they make for Ulster, as if they have some monopoly on loyalty' appear to be 'heading down the road to Ulster Nationalism' (IR 2.4.87).

Thus the concept of loyalty is as important to moderates as to ultras, but their interpretations differ. For moderates, loyalty is shown by obeying British laws, even unpopular ones, and they include conforming Catholics among those who can be considered 'loyal'. Ultras, on the other hand, while attentive to the symbols of loyalty such as the British flag and the national anthem, are loyal primarily to Protestant Ulster. However, they attempt for the British audience to monopolise the concept of loyalty to Britain for themselves and exclude Catholics, whether those in Ulster or in the Irish state, from participating in such loyal feelings.

THE CLAIMS THAT Protestants, and in particular Ulster Protestants, hold the monopoly of the spirit of empire and of loyalty cannot be upheld. The Irish as a whole, Catholic and Protestant alike, played an important role in the British imperialising thrust, and Irish Catholics included colonisers as well as colonised, loyal subjects as well as dissidents. The usurpation of empire and loyalty is intended to rewrite this history in favour of Ulster Protestants. As noted in chapter 1, the rewriting of history in order to justify usurpation is normal in settler societies, as is the simultaneous disobedience and loyalty of settlers. That loyalty, however, was essentially to the metropolis which maintained the imperial spirit. If the metropolis betrayed its principles, in particular by deciding to give power to the 'natives', then settlers deemed disobedience itself a loyal act. This kind of legitimation is clearly demonstrated in the Ulster case.

6 The Legitimation of Violence and Illegality

THE TASK OF manipulating metropolitan opinion required more than merely contrasting sturdy settlers with incompetent 'natives'. During the third Home Rule crisis Ulster Protestants engaged in activities which were undoubtedly illegal, and the years 1912–14 in particular saw the elements of Protestant rebellion being set in place. In the 1939–49 period there was a demand for Dominion status accompanied by a veiled threat of violence, but with Stormont firmly in place and Westminster's refusal to intervene there was no actual clash between Northern Ireland and Great Britain. The modern period, however, has much in common with the earlier part of the century. There has been mass protest by Protestants, including extra-legal activities and physical attacks on the RUC; and violent Protestant military groups have been re-formed. Since a keynote of Protestant propaganda is the peaceful and law-abiding nature of Protestants compared with Catholics' propensity to violence and rebellion, it is necessary to persuade the audience, both in Britain and at home, as well as themselves, that such actions either fall within the parameters of law-abiding behaviour or can be justified or explained. Thus rebellion by self-professed loyalists is re-defined as acting on 'the right of conscience' (BO 30.8.12). Law-breaking is transformed into lawful and indeed necessary action taken in response to the dual threat from 'native' power-seeking and metropolitan untrustworthiness. So again the 'imaginary portrait' comes into play: Ulster Protestants are by nature law-abiding, so it follows that any action they decide to take must be justified.

Part of the process of legitimating Protestant law-breaking has already been surveyed, namely the definition of loyalty as the wish to retain the Union and thence the usurpation of loyalty, and the claim to understand and pursue the interests of the empire better than the British government. Here more direct attempts are examined.

ONE JUSTIFICATION OF the events of 1912–14 was the general condemnation of the British government as an 'oligarchy', a 'collection of minorities' and 'slave of the Irish party', without an electoral mandate, which has 'suspended the Constitution' (which merely means that it had limited the veto power of the House of Lords, which opposed Home Rule) and 'gagged' public opinion (which means that it refused Unionist calls for a general election). Counterpoised to the government are 'the people', more particularly the British people, since they are 'the "predominant partner" in the United Kingdom' (IR 26.10.16). Defiance was justified by portraying the people as solidly against Home Rule:

> Ulster is justified in proceeding to any lengths of resistance which circumstances may demand of her in order to bring her destiny to the judgment of the British people ... In that defence they are backed not by a collection of factions such as provided this Government with its only means of existence, but by a solid coherent majority of the British people – a majority which is growing and will grow (BO 25.8.12).

At first there were fears that they could not be relied on and needed educating in the rightness of the Protestant cause:

> The English and Scottish people, who have short memories, and are so immersed in their own affairs that they have not time to inform themselves about the history of the Nationalist Party and its leaders (NL 20.3.12).

However as Protestant rebellion gained force, the people of Great Britain were claimed for Ulster unionism. The evidence for this was largely those by-elections in Great Britain where Liberals either lost the seat or reduced their majority. In these cases, the main electoral issue was nearly always interpreted as Home Rule. By the end of 1913 there had been thirty-three by-elections in Great Britain since the introduction of the Home Rule Bill, in which seats had been re-distributed from ten Unionists, twenty Liberals and three Labour-Socialists to seventeen Unionists and sixteen Liberals. This record, according to Bonar Law, justifies rebellion (NL 2.1.13): 'sovereign power is vested not in the King but in the nation, from whom alone flows authority to Parliament' and if the government did not hold a general election on the Home Rule issue 'all loyal and law-abiding men would be bound to resist such a procedure' (IR 10.10.12). Hence Unionists are 'opposing themselves to the Government, but not to the nation' (CDS 27.9.12) and the passing of the second reading of the Home Rule Bill by a majority of 109 means that armed Protestants should carry on, 'not troubling further with questions relating to Parliamentary democracies' (LS 8.7.13).

Democratic idealism was evidently less than solid (not surprisingly in view of the fact that universal male suffrage in the United Kingdom was little more than twenty-five years old), as is evidenced by Protestants' opposition to the Bill to abolish plural voting. After all, the 'Parliamentary manoeuvres', which are the cause of the trouble in Ireland (PDN 25.5.12), were the result of representative democracy. When asked if he would accept Home Rule if the next election went against the Unionist Party:

> [Carson] pertinently asked ... why should Irish Unionists be bound by the results of a single election, into which all manner of confusing general issues may be introduced by the political gamblers now in power! Even if a dozen general elections were to go against the Unionist Party ... the wrong would not be any less a wrong even were the electors of Great Britain base enough to connive at it (LS 19.7.13).

Thus if 'the people' should fail them through formal procedures such as the ballot-box, there remain substantive justice, morality and natural law, which in the circumstances favour justifiable Protestant rebellion:

> Since Home Rule involves for Ulster, apart from the lesser things, the vital question of her birthright and her national allegiance, Ulster is justified in proceeding to any lengths of resistance which circumstances may demand of her in order to bring her destiny to the judgment of the British people (BO 23.8.12).

The ground was laid for illegal acts early in the crisis: if the Home Rule Bill becomes law it will have 'no moral force' (BT 10.5.12); but although higher law justifies illegal actions, the actual responsibility for them is the government's attempt to give Ireland Home Rule. Thus the actors simultaneously claim that they are acting rightly and that they are not responsible for these actions. A number of events illustrate these justifications.

In January 1912 Winston Churchill proposed to speak in favour of Home Rule in the Ulster Hall in Belfast. Despite the threat of troops to protect him, this was bitterly (and successfully, in that he eventually spoke in a Catholic area) opposed by the Ulster Unionist Council. Nationalists claimed that free speech was being muzzled, a charge which is not denied:

> an act of defiance and of suppression of free speech ... The Rotunda is not denied to the Orangemen in Dublin when they see fit to go there. None of these reasons seems sufficient to justify such a bold course ... in the eyes of outsiders or the English people (IR 25.1.12).

There was frank admission that preventing Churchill's speech would show the people of England Protestants were not bluffing (LS

20.1.12), but generally it is felt necessary to excuse the action. Hence 'the proposed Churchill invasion' (LS 27.1.12) is deliberately provocative and any trouble arising from Protestant opposition will be Churchill's fault. Churchill is, moreover, not even sincere in his beliefs, but merely committing 'apostasy for the sake of office' (BT 17.1.12). Thus any blame is cast in advance on the potential victim. Critics are also dealt with: since those who accuse unionists of muzzling free speech want to commit the far greater crime of forcing them under Home Rule, they have no right to accuse them of anything (LS 20.1.12). The contravention of the 'British' liberal virtue of free speech is met by claims that free speech in the abstract is different from free speech in practice, and is in any case less important than liberty: 'Is liberty to be trampled down, while its mere shadow – free speech – is to be regarded as sacred?' (BT 17.1.12). At the same time, free speech 'has been denied to Unionists in the House of Commons' (LS 27.1.12).

The attacks on Catholic workers which took place are justified by the *Londonderry Sentinel* editor by the attempt to force through Home Rule (LS 30.7.12); but a more sophisticated defence deplores the attacks while ascribing them to 'bands of irresponsible youths' whose 'outburst' is nevertheless 'not without provocation' being 'traceable to the wanton wickedness of the Ancient Order of Hibernians' outrage at Castledawson' (NL 31.7.12). Again there is a transferring of responsibility from the perpetrators either to the victims or to the perpetrators of previous offences, and the later attacks on 'the Sinn Fein workers in the shipyards', while not condoned, are excusable because 'the loyal and law-abiding allow[ed] themselves to be provoked by the disloyal and lawless in their midst' (NL 22.7.20). Subsequent Protestant rioting in Belfast, including attacks on Catholic churches and nuns as well as looting, although 'to be deeply regretted and generally deplored' are also explained away: some people 'lost their self-control' because of the murders in the South and West of Ireland, the perpetrators are merely 'the hooligan elements of the population' and Belfast Protestants are known for their volatility, unlike those in peaceful mid-Antrim and Portadown (BO 24.4.14, 30.7.20; PDN 4.9.20). The strife in Derry, on the other hand, was portrayed in simple terms: Catholics attack and Protestants defend themselves (LS 22.5.20).

To fight against Home Rule merely with words, however strong the unionist case was claimed to be, was not enough. The Solemn League and Covenant of September 1912 was therefore followed early in 1913 by the formation of the Ulster Volunteer Force. Since to have engaged in actual warfare with the British Army would have lost Ulster unionists public sympathy in Great Britain, it was necessary to assert that the threat of force was real while avoiding actually using it. The course through 'the dangerous and uncharted seas of armed resistance' was charted by the combination of Craig, Carson and Bonar Law (Boyce 1990:234). The latter, a Scot of Ulster origin, as the *Impartial Reporter* remembered, 'advised the people of Ulster to defend their birthright, by force of arms if necessary' (IR 24.3.21). Local newspapers did their part by justifying the existence and activities of this illegal force. Drilling had started before the UVF was formed, in order 'to give the best account of themselves that men basely deserted and left to the mercy of relentless enemies can give' (LS 13.7.12). The formation of the UVF is a matter for defiant pride: 'Ulster is not only drilling but organising and arming. Ulster knows that she is not only the unconquered colony, but that she is unconquerable' (IR 1.5.13). However, as Carson 'knows, as he says, he is acting illegally in ... publicly preaching armed opposition in a certain eventuality to constituted authority' (LS 18.9.13), such defiance required justification.

Hence the Home Rule Bill was re-defined as itself 'revolution': 'Mr Asquith planned revolution, and if he persists in his policy of force without consulting the people then he will be met by revolution' (IR 8.5.13). Ulster unionists are 'strictly on the defensive' (LS 1.8.14):

> They will not take the field against the army ... It will be for those responsible for the movement of the army to take the field against the drilled civilians ... The Government ... must either tolerate these or put them down (LS 29.7.13).

Illegality was also re-defined, such that the UVF exists to protect the liberties of all in Ireland, of whatever creed, and therefore its activities, though illegal, are not criminal (LS 16.12.13, 13.7.20). In any case it is:

> illegal only in the technical sense, for it has behind it the support of more than half the people of Great Britain, while in the moral sense it is the Government that is guilty of illegality, since it is engaged in a constitutional conspiracy to pass the Home Rule Bill against the will of the people (NL 18.9.13).

This support of the people of Great Britian, imaginary in that there was no way of measuring it, is extended to military support: the government will have to deal not only with '100,000 drilled men in Ulster but with probably an even larger force in Great Britain' (LS 3.3.14). Despite the fact that what actually made civil war likely was the formation of the UVF, responsibility was placed on the government, either indirectly, in that 'forcing upon Ireland a constitutional revolution ... must involve a civil war' (BO 4.10.12), or directly: 'on [Ministers] will rest the whole responsibility if blood is shed and peace overthrown in the land whose loyal population they have bargained to betray' (BO 3.1.13).

The prospect of war with Germany inspired the *Londonderry Sentinel* to remind its readers of an early speech by John Redmond in which he said he would secure the independence of Ireland by force if necessary. This enables the UVF to be cast in an even more heroic mould: 'The Ulster Volunteers ... will be kept at the highest possible pitch of efficiency and preparedness. The safety of Britain no less than that of Ulster demands this' (LS 4.8.14).

Armed resistance is judged in the light of the character and motivations of those resisting, rather than by recourse to legal definitions. The conduct of the UVF, 'a self-respecting disciplined body' (LS 24.2.14) which behaves with 'splendid self-restraint' (LS 4.12.13) and which can be proved to be law-abiding from the fact that there is little serious crime in Ulster (LS 19.3.14), is not that of an illegal body, especially since, unlike Nationalist Volunteers, it goes into action only under British colours in the 1914–18 war. Nationalists blamed the Easter Rising on the original armed resistance by Ulster Unionists, so any similarity between nationalist and unionist rebels must be dispelled:

> There is no analogy between the Ulster Volunteers and the Sinn Feiners. Ulster's Protestants were compelled to arm because of the transparent treachery and dishonesty of the Liberal Government in its political policy in regard to this country ... the Ulstermen were obliged to organise and arm in order to defend their rights and privileges as British citizens if an attempt was made to drive them out of their inheritance. On the other hand the Sinn Fein organisation was composed of men who were notorious rebels (PDN 27.5.16).

However, the Rising does act as proof that Ulster's armed opposition has been right all along.

The formation of the UVF was followed within a few months by the establishment of a Provisional Government based in Belfast. This idea had also emerged earlier in the period:

> There will be no attempt at marching to Cork, or even to Dublin, but Ulster will set about self-government on its own account, and will resist, by force if necessary, any interference with her lawful right to do so. There can be no rebellion in refusing to acknowledge the authority of a master to whom no allegiance has been sworn (PDN 25.5.12).

The plan was announced by Carson at an Orange parade with the disingenuous remark that if this was breaking the law 'let the law officers of the Crown prosecute him' (BT 14.7.13). Unusual for a lawyer, he 'said he knew nothing about legality or illegality; all he thought of was his Covenant' (NL 14.7.13). The law is not the issue: 'There is no law, Divine or human, which enforces men to submit to what the present Government proposes for Ulster' (BT 14.7.13). Some local editors do consider the matter of legality but conclude that:

> It is a statement of an intention to supersede the King's Government, but it is also an intention to supersede that Government only when that Government is engaged in an unconstitutional and, therefore, unlawful act (IR 17.7.13).

As for the charge of treason, just as the formation of the UVF is only 'technically' illegal, so the assertion that 'the Ulster Unionist Council ... had to resolve itself into a Provisional Government' is only technically treason, whereas the government is morally guilty of 'treason against our rights and liberties' (NL 25.9.13). Although 'the setting up of a Provisional Government is a step usually associated with revolution', this is not the case in Ulster as 'the Ulster Provisional Government will sit under the Union Jack' (LS 7.8.13) and hold Ulster 'against a Home Rule Parliament, in trust for the King and Constitution' (LS 11.7.14).

Carson and his reporters make no attempt to disguise the threat of force that backs up the Provisional Government:

> The resolute and resourceful Protestant community in the North East of Ulster has now practically completed its organisation ... It possesses a numerous, disciplined and well-armed army led by a distinguished British General, and officered by able soldiers who have done good service in the British Army. On Wednesday the Provisional Government was established at Belfast, and it is intended to protect that Government by force of arms (BO 26.9.13).

This is 'not an act of aggression' but the act of 'tens of thousands of the King's most loyal citizens ... determined at all costs to maintain their liberty' against 'the decrees of a Government whose soul is not its own, a Government whose every move is dictated by fear of the disloyal party in Ireland' (BT 24.9.13).

The 'Provisional Government' did nothing that the Ulster Unionist Council had not already done; more serious for the British political system was the implication of the British Army in the Ulster rebellion. It had been known or believed for some time that elements in the British Army were on the side of the Ulster Protestants and it was reported that the government dare not trust the army, large numbers of whose officers are in communication with the Ulster Unionist authorities (LS 31.1.14). The welcome possibility of a British Army mutiny was mentioned (LS 10.2.14), and the incident at the Curragh army camp confirmed these hopes.

The government's plan to dispatch troops to Ulster in order to prevent an outbreak of violence and make a show of strength was mishandled by the Commander-in-Chief in Ireland who, instead of tactfully allowing officers with Ulster connections to 'disappear' for a while, gave all officers the option of refusing to participate in operations. Led by Brigadier Gough, a number of officers did so, subsequently extorting a signed assurance from the War Office that the army would not be used to enforce Home Rule on Ulster. Something less than a mutiny, this was nevertheless a serious matter for the government and an occasion of joy for Ulster unionists. It is 'praiseworthy' since it harms the government 'tyrants who refuse the ballot to the nation and would give Ulster the bullet' and shows that 'the soldiers understand the Ulstermen and the Ulstermen understand them'. This is justifiable because the Army is commanded by 'the nation', which is, of course, 'decidedly opposed to' Home Rule (IR 16.3.14). The men are 'not rebels [as] they are prepared to shed the last drop of their blood in defence of the Empire [and] their judgment cannot be questioned'. Above the 'nation' and the 'Empire' stands a higher notion:

> [The government] forgot that in the Army there is a code of honour which rests upon conscience, and that the doctrine of moral right, though apparently discarded in Ministerial circles, has not gone out of fashion elsewhere (BT 22.3.14).

Had the Army's 'code of honour' dictated that it move into 'rebel-held' territory as directed by the government of a representative democracy, it is unlikely that it would have won such praise in Unionist Ulster – except of course where such territory was held by Catholics as in the 'no-go areas' of the 1970s.

Although the Curragh incident was held to have lessened the threat of civil war (which further justifies it), it was only shortly after this that large amounts of arms and ammunition were smuggled into Larne and North Down, an illegal act legitimated in part precisely by claims that the government is ready to 'force this country into civil war' (IR 25.6.14). The question of arms had long been a preoccupation. The UVF had started its drilling using wooden staves, occasioning both nationalist and British media mockery, and it was necessary at least to claim that the Northern Protestants had modern weapons in order to be taken seriously, even though a revival of the Crimes Act would make this illegal. In December 1913 there was a proclamation forbidding the import of arms and munitions into Ireland. This was treated by unionists in general with a mixture of ridicule, satisfaction that the government took them seriously and lofty determination to ignore it:

> it has come much too late to prevent the arming of the whole

population should that be the course decided upon by-and-by ... Let them make no mistake about it, we are in an armed camp and they know it (BT 6.12.13).

By now, confident in the support of the British Army and with a series of by-elections in Britain showing declining Liberal popularity, less need was felt to justify law-breaking. That 'the Government have obtained the King's signature to an illegal proclamation' is now irrelevant since Ulster will get all the arms it needed, with or without the proclamation (LS 23.12.13).

Nevertheless, despite praise for the feat of landing arms at Larne and Donaghadee and defiant claims that it is 'an evidence of the splendid organisation and the discipline of the Volunteers, and of the magnificent spirit which animates them' (NL 27.4.14), the fact that 'a breach of the law has indeed been committed' (CDS 1.5.14) had to be justified. Claims included the usual 'struggle for the preservation of civil and religious liberty in Ireland' (NL 27.4.14); the government's 'illegal' actions and 'constitutional outrage' beside which Protestant law-breaking is a mere 'technical infringement of the law ... actuated by the highest motives'; and the shifting of responsibility from those involved in gun-running to 'the real culprits [who] are Radical Ministers' (BT 28.4.14). Finally the essential character of the Protestant people, as defined by themselves, is proof that they are more acted upon than acting:

the King has no more peaceful subjects than the Unionists of Ulster. It is true that they have introduced an enormous number of guns against the provisions of a proclamation which a judge had declared to be illegal. But they have been compelled to do so for their own defence ... the hard-working, well-disposed people of Belfast (LS 28.4.14).

All the illegal activities, including the setting up of a provisional government, involved the threat of force, but the government 'plot' to use state force against the rebellion aroused extreme indignation:

The Government are specifically accused of having planned an organised blockade of the Northern Province by land and sea. An army of 25,000 men and a fleet consisting of a battle squadron and two flotillas of destroyers were to surround the Covenanters on all sides. The slayers then being ready, the peaceful victims were to be forced by the police into giving an occasion for their slaughter. It is no difficult task to stir up a riot in Belfast at any time, and during the present crisis the smallest spark would fire the tinder of political and religious hatred ... All the noble work of Sir Edward Carson and his fellow leaders in keeping their hot-headed followers in check would have been undone in an instant. Civil war would have commenced, and the Government would have pointed with smug complacency to the Ulster Army as the aggressors ... Thus did the Government propose to shatter the only argument against Home Rule the force of which they have appreciated, the stubborn preference of loyal Ulstermen for death, rather than the hated yoke of a Nationalist Parliament. The plot, as now revealed, is as revolting as any that has been hatched by the revolutionaries of Southern Europe or Mexico. It reeks of political cruelty worthy of a Borgia. No doubt the Government will indignantly deny the truth of the Ulster Council's statement, as Colonel Seely had already done. The people of Great Britain, however, will not be satisfied with empty words. They must have proof, and proof positive, that this crime has not even been contemplated by the Government (BO 24.4.14).

Aside from the impossibility of anyone proving they have not considered an action, it will be shown in chapter 8 that such force is considered justified against rebellious 'natives', for whose rebellion no excuses can be found.

THE 1939–49 PERIOD did not give rise to nearly the same degree of settler–metropolis conflict as the other two. A Protestant government was now legally in place, with control over the largely Protestant security forces. The potential for conflict was there, however, as the Dominion status campaigners recognised, for the nationalists' anti-partition campaign, supported by some Labour MPs and ministers at Westminster, highlighted the precariousness of Northern Ireland's existence, and a defiant attitude has already been noted in the claim that Ulster belonged to its Protestants rather than to the British state. Hence some self-justification is discernible in this period.

Part of this process was a new form of denial of responsibility, this time for partition, which was blamed partly on the British government, but mainly on nationalists. These protestations are rather spoilt by the assertion that there were 'very solid reasons for Ulster's historic stand' (LS 18.3.44). The veiled threat of militant opposition in the following is excused by the behaviour of:

officials across the water who know little of Ulster's special problems and perils and who seem to care less. Ulster Ministers must stand up to these people and the Ministers who back them. We consider that the Ulster Government should take a strong line in this matter and tell them 'Hands off' ... we have no doubt that if they took a resolute stand on that the Loyalists of Ulster would rally round them to a man (LS 20.6.44).

The same editor also threatened refusal to adopt the British Local Franchise Bill, first on the grounds of 'principle' (LS 12.1.46), but subsequently on more avowedly self-interested grounds:

> as long as Nationalists profess their desire to abolish the Northern Parliament and to place this State in subjection to another, then Unionists are entitled to use every device to defeat their Nationalist opponents (LS 17.1.46).

The same reason applies to accusations following the banning of an anti-partition demonstration in Derry:

> a characteristic outburst against the Government for the alleged forcible suppression of free speech. Free speech for what purpose? ... the free speech sought is the advocacy in Northern Ireland of the taking away of the rights of the Ulster people to remain part of the United Kingdom and Empire (LS 2.3.48).

It also serves as an excuse for discrimination against a Catholic ex-serviceman: 'every time the Unionists yield any concession it is a nail in the coffin of Unionism ... Every point of vantage yielded is a victory to the enemy' ('Ex-Serviceman' IR 7.9.44). In the event the principle of non-interference by Westminster was confirmed by the Labour government and the Ireland Act was a defeat for Catholics in Northern Ireland.

IN THE MODERN period, Protestant violence is once again seen to require justification and legitimation, but now it is only ultras who defend it. Such violence has taken two forms, confrontations with the security forces and the activities of Protestant paramilitaries in the assassination of Catholics (and indeed of fellow-Protestants). The latter are more easily ignored or explained away: after all, if Prime Minister Thatcher could publicly state that the IRA had killed 3,000 people in Northern Ireland since the outbreak of the current conflict (republican paramilitaries were responsible for around 60 per cent of fatalities, quite high enough to quote accurate figures), there is clearly little sense in ultras highlighting the fact that 'Protestant terrorist organisations ... have been responsible for just under half the civilian deaths during the present unrest in Ulster [and] have also brought down a government' (Bruce 1992:1). By 1989 they had also killed ten members of the security forces and two prison officers. This was far below the estimated 632 civilians killed by loyalist paramilitaries, compared to the republican toll of 574 and the security forces' 178 (ibid.:294), and yet it is confrontations between Protestants and the security forces which are most often selected for justification. In addition to involving very many more 'ordinary' Protestants than the loyalist paramilitary organisations and being recorded by television cameras for a world audience, these threaten the vital relationship with Great Britain which Protestants claim to wish to retain and upon which they depend.

The history of confrontation between loyalists and the security forces is almost as old as the current crisis. Paisley was proclaiming early in 1969 that Ulster might, as in 1912, have to oppose British troops in order to stay British (PT 11.1.69) and by September anti-Army slogans were appearing on Protestant barricades; soon Craig was reported to be threatening that the streets would run red with the blood of British soldiers (W J Wright BO 9.10.69). The publication of the 1969 Hunt Report saw the first serious confrontation and serious rioting resulted in the fatal shooting of a policeman on the Shankill, where several soldiers were also wounded. Loyalist attacks on the security forces continued throughout 1970, and in 1971 members of a banned Orange march at Dungiven attacked the security forces, who used CS gas and rubber bullets to quell the riot. In 1972 Craig's Vanguard movement was threatening to resist Westminster by force, and the suspension of the Northern Parliament led to more rioting, to a Vanguard-inspired strike which was accompanied by attacks on RUC homes and to the erection of Protestant barricades by, among others, the UDA. In October 1972 off-duty soldiers were attacked by Protestants in East Belfast and there was further trouble on the Shankill; the UDA, however, then relinquished their 'utterly foolhardy "declaration of war" on the British Army' (PDN 20.10.72). In February 1973 a loyalist strike was accompanied by violence and in 1974 soldiers were alleged to have attacked without provocation Protestants in Long Kesh convicted of terrorist crimes (W J Sloan, 'Loyalist Prisoner of War' PDN 4.1.74). The 1974 strike, however, was treated cautiously, not to say timorously, by the British government and the expected major confrontations between Protestants and the security forces did not materialise.

Minor attacks occurred throughout 1975 and there were fears in 1976 that the Protestant paramilitary groups might turn their attention from the murder campaign against Catholics to the security forces. This did not in fact happen until the 1977 loyalist strike, when extra troops were sent to Northern Ireland, but it was the RUC which bore the brunt of Protestant attacks. The following year, on the tenth anniversary of the first Civil Rights parade in Derry, there were further loyalist attacks on the RUC and the army, and the next major open confrontations also took place in Derry in early 1984, after the SDLP changed the name of the city council. In June 1985 loyalists trying to defy the ban on a march through the predominantly Catholic town of Castlewellan fought riot police, and further attacks on the RUC and their homes, apparently arising from the parades ban, culminated in a weekend of violence in Portadown during the Independent Orange

Order Twelfth of July celebrations. In total, 52 policemen and 26 civilians were injured. The RUC then became a major target for attack by Protestant extremists, both in direct conflicts and in being driven from their homes. This was exacerbated by Protestant reaction to the Anglo–Irish Agreement and the establishment of the secretariat at Maryfield, culminating in the violence of the Loyalist Day of Action in March 1986 during which the RUC was fired on in some loyalist areas. Attacks on the RUC continued into the following year. More recently, the Combined Loyalist Military Command, an umbrella group for loyalist paramilitaries, issued a statement pending its verdict on the Downing Street Declaration, in which it warned:

> Loyalist para-militaries have been in active existence for many years, with *mercurial* support from the general Unionist population. Therefore, we offer a word of caution to all those who are engaged in negotiative dialogue concerning Ulster's future. GET IT RIGHT or the nominal support we now have will very quickly become TOTAL (*Combat* Jan 1994).

Both outright condemnation and overt support and approval of loyalist violence against the security forces are rarely found among ultras. On the one hand they are prepared in the last resort to countenance any means to attain their end, namely the maintenance of Northern Ireland as a separate entity from the Republic of Ireland and as a place that is safe for Protestants to continue to live in, so they find it difficult to condemn outright actions which are in accordance with these ends. On the other hand they wish to present themselves as law-abiding in contrast to rebellious Catholics, and so cannot openly advocate violence. The horrified reaction of people who had always proclaimed themselves to be by nature law-abiding was no doubt to some extent genuine: the attack of the Dungiven Orangemen is 'tragic ... ironical and bewildering ... the official Government ban on the procession should never have been defied' (NL 14.6.71). It should be noted, however, that the government in question was Stormont, not Westminster, and attacks on the RUC were more unpopular than attacks on soldiers. Those who behave violently are not truly 'Protestant' but are 'so-called self-appointed "Protestant" gangsters who ... republican-style, deem it their duty to "take it out" on the RUC' (OS May 1986).

By contrast only one letter in the sample actively advocates militant Protestant action against the British. Comparing the situation with 1912, a Paisley supporter writes:

> It appears to be necessary to fight and win our civil and religious liberty. All that is required is for the UDA, the UVF and any paramilitary organisation to be given good leadership to enter the battle (Beryl Holland CDS 4.1.74).

Another supports the attacks on the RUC:

> RUC families have always lived under the protective arm of the
> loyalist communities and had it not been for this protection many
> more RUC men and women would have been dead at the hands
> of the IRA and INLA killers. The loyalist people are totally justi-
> fied in their actions against these turncoat RUC men and women.
> You cannot abuse the people who protect you and expect them to
> carry on protecting you ('Loyalist Prisoner' BTimes 1.5.86).

Much more common are condemnations accompanied by 'understanding' which serve as justification, and implicit condonation
where justification is unaccompanied by condemnation, but without
overt approval. First, there is the usual transfer of responsibility
away from the perpetrators, mainly to external agencies such as the
British and the Irish governments, or to republican provocation. This
began early in the period. The publication of the 1969 Hunt Report
and its acceptance by Stormont were initially welcomed by the
editors of the *News Letter* and the *Londonderry Sentinel*, but following
the major Protestant attack on the security forces, both papers failed
in their editorials to mention the death of a policeman and blamed
the Report and the government for the violence:

> Who do we blame ...? Stormont, Westminster, the Hunt Commit-
> tee's report, the ill-conceived timing of its publication on a
> Friday, or its official 'fait accompli' acceptance without opportu-
> nity for as much as a murmur of public debate or protest? ... The
> people in the streets ... feel that they are being bullied and
> betrayed (NL 13.10.69).

Continuing unrest was blamed on Catholic protests, whereby
'Unionists are now being diverted on to dangerous divergent routes'
(LS 19.8.70), and rioting and destruction by loyalists in Portadown
(which started as attacks on Catholic commercial property but
extended to Protestant shops) were excused on the grounds that the
courts are too lenient (PDN 31.3.72). Although some ultras were
against the 1974 strike beforehand because it will be 'detrimental to
Ulster's cause' (NL 25.4.74), responsibility is transferred to 'Messrs
Faulkner and Fitt' (NL 16.5.74) and the British government's 'over-
lording resolve to bludgeon the Province into subjection' (NL
24.5.74). There is no choice: 'What else were they to do, what else
were we all to do when deaf ears at Westminster were being turned
consistently on democratic cries from the country?' (NL 25.5.74).
The republican 'no-go areas' and the failure of British security policy
to halt the IRA campaign also excuse loyalist violence. The 1977
strike was viewed sympathetically by the *News Letter*, which made

advance excuses for any violence that might occur, warning the government to 'avoid indulging the reputed English penchant for reversing popular opinion by ham-handed moves likely to cause surges of emotion' (NL 3.5.77).

The conflicts with the RUC in the wake of the ban or re-routing of some loyalist parades (especially where republican ones were permitted by the RUC to go ahead) were also blamed on the executive:

> a matter of deep regret ... it must be viewed against the background of events that caused distress and disappointment to many thousands of people ... the postponement of the only legal march on Sunday – that organised by the Londonderry branch of the DUP (LS 11.10.78).

It was in 1985 that matters came to a head, for the policy on parades was viewed in the light of the Anglo–Irish talks. After the violence in Portadown:

> the real culprits, the real villains yesterday were snug and safe well away from the scenes of violence in Dublin and London. The man who must bear the main responsibility for attacks on the police and on innocent civilians is ... Douglas Hurd (NL 13.7.85).

The Anglo–Irish Agreement justifies violence, even when it includes attacks on the RUC. An editorial headed 'No Justification for Violence' concludes that 'the Agreement and those who signed it have many sins to answer for' (OS Aug 1986), and one writer concludes that the way forward is through violence:

> There is no point in denying that there was violence in Portadown, but as loyalists know it was sparked off by the police presence in the area ... Hermon banned the wrong parade – it should have been the Nationalist parade, in Londonderry. It is clear that at this stage violence will be the ultimate solution for a Republic-free land in Ulster (D Ballantine PDT 11.4.86).

Secondly, it is by and large Catholics who commit violence – Protestants, who are essentially law-abiding, merely protest. Hence reports of loyalist violence, unlike those of republican violence, are exaggerated or constitute merely legitimate protest. Loyalist violence against the security forces has certainly not matched that of republicans. (It would be surprising if it did, considering that Protestants have commonly perceived the British Army and the RUC to be on their side.) One method of legitimating Protestant violence, therefore, is to point out that it is minor, especially compared with the IRA campaign. Protestant violence is re-defined as loyalty, as when Paisley and some of his supporters were sentenced to a short spell in prison after their attempts to stop a PD demonstration in Armagh: 'The only crime that the Loyalists have been guilty of is loyalty to the Crown and to the Constitution' (PT 8.2.69). Similarly, violent persons are portrayed as concerned individuals: 'The chaps manning the barricades are ordinary citizens who are greatly disturbed at the state our province is in at this time. They have a great love for their country' ('UDA Supporter' IR 13.7.72). These perceptions fit the old contrast between violent Catholics and peaceful law-abiding Protestants. The latter are painted in a pathetic light:

> Back in 1969 there was no UK community more strictly disciplined, more in tune with authority – authority, right or wrong – than the majority in Ulster. It did not, therefore, come easily or naturally for them to question or kick or revolt. But in the past few years it dawned on the people that they were slowly but surely being herded towards the edge of a cliff. They did not understand, but, albeit in frequent bewilderment, they went along with authority and the dictum of the Government. It is only at the point at which Parliament would decree that they should jump over the edge of that cliff that they are saying 'No' (NL 27.5.74).

Even after more than a decade of growing loyalist street violence, Protestants are still basically peaceable and only 'considering' violence:

> the Government can also derive little comfort from the finding [in a Mori poll] that ten per cent of the Protestant section of the community would favour armed revolt. It is a measure of the anger and sense of betrayal apparent in Ulster today that a significant percentage of a normally law-abiding section of the community is prepared to consider a resort to violence (NL 25.11.85).

One explanation for this apparent change in character is that republican violence has been seen to pay off and therefore has set an example to loyalists. Loyalists, however, unlike nationalists, use violence to express protest:

> Anyone who expresses shock and disbelief at the violence which marked the Loyalist Day of Action must be very naive ... What did they expect? ... Eighteen years of violence may not have brought Sinn Fein and the IRA a day closer to their peculiar version of a workers' paradise ... but those years of violence have created, in the eyes of some Loyalists at least, the atmosphere for the most significant advance in Irish Nationalism since the declaration of the Irish Republic. Is it so astounding, therefore, that

some Loyalists should take what they see as a leaf out of the
green book and seek to express their protest through violence?
('Amazed' LS 12.3.86).

Thirdly, loyalists have been deliberately provoked into violence by the
British or Irish government. The majority of such claims are found
from 1985 onwards: 'The Dublin strategy ... was to provoke loyalists
into violent reaction which would set them on a path of confrontation
with the security forces' (NL 31.12.85). The security forces themselves
are accused of provocation, and the violence at the banned Portadown
parade was inspired by a last-minute police ban and a big police and
military presence, followed by the 'discharge of a vast quantity of
plastic bullets in such an indiscriminate fashion resulting in one death
and serious injury' (Wilfred Breen OS May 1986). This was the occasion of the first Protestant death from a plastic bullet. Ultras either
ignore the previous such deaths of Catholics (which included children), deny that they were actually caused by plastic bullets or claim
that the victims deserved their fate. A Protestant cannot be put into
the same category as riotous Catholics.

Finally there is recourse to denial – the security forces attacked
without provocation. This is the most comfortable way to deal with
violent loyalist confrontations with the security forces, and it has a
much longer history than claims that such violence was provoked. It
consists of giving the impression that Protestants have suffered attack without having done anything to deserve it and without retali-
ating. In the early days the culprits are the British Army: 'Can we be
loyal to a flag whose so-called Army shot Protestants in the Shankill
Road?' (Mervyn Woods PDN 9.1.70). The RUC soon came under
attack, however, and the violence at the banned Orange parade in
Dungiven was described thus:

> If the Queen's loyal citizens wish to parade their loyalty in the
> streets, then they are beaten down with batons, rubber bullets
> and tear gas by mercenary troops (George Tottenham IR 17.6.71).

This is a frequent explanation of the nature of the violence following the Anglo-Irish Agreement:

> The RUC said that many of the crowd at Craigavon Bridge were
> only 'unruly mobsters'. As a peace loving law abiding loyalist I
> greatly resent that tag; I was there, as were hundreds of others, to
> show my opposition to the undemocratic Anglo–Irish Agreement in
> a peaceful orderly fashion. I am no unruly mobster ('Waterside
> Loyalist' LS 12.3.86).

The existence of Protestant paramilitaries and Catholic deaths is more often ignored than defended, but it cannot always be excluded from the Protestant discourse; so in some of the unionist literature current loyalist violence is excused as 'secondary' while republican violence, categorised as 'primary', can have no excuse:

> Protestant organisations such as the UDA can be termed 'secondary' terrorist groups; that is, groups whose military activity depends upon the strategy and tactics of the 'primary' terrorists ... For [the UDA] paramilitary action does not constitute a case of putting violence before the law, but of carrying out the violence needed in order to enforce deep-felt wishes of the law-abiding citizenry (Aughey & McIlheney 1984:59, 74).

The modern UVF, however, was formed in 1965, before NICRA and the current revival of the IRA, and killed its first Catholics in 1966, when the IRA was moribund; and the first explosions of the current conflict were set in 1969 by Ulster Protestant Volunteers (UPV) and UVF men who intended that the IRA should be blamed. This has been explained as 'getting your retaliation in first', on the grounds that for most of their history, and especially since 1912, Protestants have felt threatened by Irish nationalists and in loyalist eyes 'even extended periods of peace could never be anything other than a ploy to lull loyalists into a false sense of security' (Bruce 1992:31). Some form of justificatory legitimation for loyalist terrorism against Catholics is nevertheless necessary and such actions need to be defended not only in the court of world opinion but also to many Northern Ireland Protestants who prefer violence to remain a state monopoly.

One way of dealing with loyalist violence against Catholics is silence. A casual reading of some newspapers, in particular the editorials of the *News Letter*, gives the impression that only Catholics carry out shootings and bombings and only Protestants suffer. IRA bombs in Belfast bring the comment that there have now been 1,151 deaths, but without any hint that some of these were perpetrated by Protestants (NL 6.2.75). On occasion violence is hinted at as the work of loyalists but the impression is given that it is not (NL 7.4.75); and the Miami Showband killings, condemned before UVF involvement was known, did not lead to condemnation of the UVF (NL 7.4.75). Bruce (1992:169) has noted an attempt to deceive the readership of the *News Letter* into assuming that a particular gun-running scheme involved republicans when in fact it was carried out by loyalists.

In a similar way some editorials and letters concern themselves only with Protestant deaths, as if there were no others: 'Protestant homes [are] plunged into lifelong grief' ('Regular Reader' BO 11.11.82) and 'the majority of Protestants [are] murdered in their thousands for wanting to remain part of the UK' ('An Independent Unionist' IR

12.11.81). The campaign in the Border counties, characterised as 'the relentless slaughter of Border Protestants' (OS Apr 1983), is genocide. A common theme is that of Protestants driven from their homes or fearing for their personal safety, particularly in Fermanagh, South Armagh and Derry. Protestant memories of civilians killed in major bombing and shooting attacks are confined to IRA and INLA actions such as those of the Abercorn, the La Mon Hotel, the killing of ten Protestant workers at Bessbrook, the Droppin Well bombing, Enniskillen and the Shankill, particularly when the victims were Protestants rather than Catholics or members of the British Army.

Ultras' approach to the incidence and distribution of violence is also notably selective. The largest category of deaths in the current conflict is that of Catholic civilians (that is, Catholics who are not paramilitaries). From 1969 up to 30 June 1989 the 896 Catholic civilians killed by all parties (security forces, republican and loyalist paramilitaries) constituted 32.5 percent of all deaths in the conflict, compared with 575 Protestant civilians killed, or 20.8 per cent of all deaths. The burden on Catholics is the higher in that Catholics constitute about 40 per cent of the population. Security force deaths, at 862, were slightly lower. Furthermore it is not the case that the main killing fields are in the Border counties. Over half the fatalities in the same period were in Belfast, with only 7.8 per cent in South Armagh and 2.8 per cent in Fermanagh. Obviously the population of Belfast as a whole is also much greater; but the most dangerous area in Northern Ireland is the relatively small one which includes Catholic North Belfast. This area alone accounted for 19 per cent of all deaths, 219 people being killed by loyalist paramilitaries, 176 by nationalist paramilitaries and 60 by the security forces (Irish Information Partnership 1989). In most cases Catholic deaths (and Catholics who have fled or been driven from their homes) are simply ignored by ultras. Killings which have not become part of the Protestant history of violence include the loyalist bombing of McGurk's bar which killed fifteen Catholics, the Miami Showband murders, and the murder of five Catholics following the Bessbrook murders.

Where loyalist violence is hard to ignore or excuse, a justificatory device used is to underplay it, for example, using republican violence to 'cancel out' loyalist violence (OS May 1974). At other times, the blame is transferred to other agents. The *Londonderry Sentinel*, for example, had previously supported Prime Minister Heath for 'admonishing the extremists at both ends of the political spectrum for maintaining the tension and the steady stream of shootings and explosions' (LS 22.11.72) and yet in the following these actions have become 'protests':

Extreme elements of the majority of the Ulster people have become more active in their protests against developments and conditions since the introduction of direct rule, largely because they were left without democratic representation when the Northern Ireland Parliament was closed down (LS 28.12.72).

The *News Letter* seems more forthright shortly afterwards, but condemnation swiftly turns away from the actual perpetrators:

the rampaging, the burning, the intimidation and the shooting that were an outcrop of Wednesday's 24-hour loyalist strike can only be condemned in the strongest possible terms. But last to stand in judgment on those responsible for the latest wave of violence should be the Ministers who have allowed our country to sink into such an appalling condition. Theirs is the ultimate guilt, for where else have they been heading us but for such disaster since the dark day they took over Stormont? ... We cry to-day for those on the Catholic side who have suffered mindless 'Protestant' threat and intimidation. And we have contempt for men in power in London who should have seen it all coming and who could have done so much more to prevent it (NL 9.2.73).

The same newspaper also claimed that official rejection of local proposals for a 'Third Force' 'it can almost certainly be said, brought about the raising of up to half a dozen private armies' (NL 16.7.74), 'private armies' being a euphemism reserved for loyalist killers rather than republican ones; and loyalist killings of Catholic civilians are blamed on the Secretary of State for Northern Ireland (NL 7.1.76).

Another legitimating device is to re-define criminality as patriotism. For example the setting up of UDA barricades in 1972 was applauded with only a hint of warning against violence:

It is a sombre hour and heavy responsibility devolves on the UDA and all citizens, who can exert influence to ensure that every step taken in the weeks that lie ahead is measured solely against authentic needs for the protection of the country, its people and their homes (NL 29.6.72).

When the British government treats loyalists as criminals, there is outrage. Detention without trial was long used in Northern Ireland but it was virtually only Catholics who were detained. Under British government direction loyalists are now also detained, to the fury of some ultras, and this fury is not abated when loyalists, like republicans, are imprisoned under the Diplock system of non-jury courts with a single judge. One described the measure as 'the insensitive, insane detention of Loyalists who dared to take measures to protect their families and province against terrorism and treachery' (Bill Bailie OS Sep 1973). Respectability is conferred on loyalist paramilitaries in an editorial approving the healing of the rift between them and the Unionist Party (NL 14.2.75, 2.12.76), and one writer claimed that 'these men form the vast majority of grass roots opinion and are entitled to votes in elections. If the crunch comes ... it is these men who will save Ulster' (Beryl Holland CDS 5.3.76). The same writer seems to suggest that loyalist criminal actions should be ignored when she voices the complaint that when, following the killing at Warrenpoint of eighteen soldiers, 'Protestant para-militaries ... took a little action, as a warning for the security forces to step up their action on the IRA ... the Loyalist areas were searched and several questioned' (Beryl Holland CDS 26.10.79). Some of the prisoners themselves not unnaturally legitimate the activities which had led to their incarceration in similar fashion, and those who are 'really responsible for the bombings, the shootings, etc ... are the so-called sensible, reasonable and peace-loving leaders in the community [who] are not sensible or reasonable or peace-loving enough to talk things over and find a real solution' (Mark Trotter HMP Maze IR 25.6.87).

The commonest response to loyalist terror, however, is to label it as a reaction to republican violence. Loyalists are not acting but reacting. This can be combined with blaming loyalist violence on the British government:

Some Protestants have retaliated against republicans ... not surprising ... aggression has come constantly, and well nigh completely from the R.C. community ... This is not to say that Loyalist people of Northern Ireland have not equipped themselves for defence ... But they were driven to do so because of abysmal failure by Whitehall to defend them, and by their strictures that if the people did not behave, the troops would withdraw (OS Apr 1973).

In 1975 an IRA ceasefire was announced. By this time loyalist para-militaries had killed 298 people, that is, a quarter of all killed up to that point, which was only half the total killed by the IRA but well ahead of the security force killings (Irish Information Partnership 1989). The *News Letter*, however, hails the IRA truce as:

acceptance of the case we have made here consistently since 1969 that the root of the violence has been essentially on one side. On the other side there have been simply the reactions, albeit, at times, crude and criminal in their manifestations (NL 2.1.75).

The ceasefire was broken so often that the number of killings by nationalists, 100, was to be the fourth highest figure between 1969 and 1989. What was not pointed out by ultras was that in that same year loyalists killed 113 people, mainly Catholic civilians (Irish Information Partnership 1989). More recently, the resurgence in loyalist violence that led to their carrying out more killings than republicans from the beginning of 1992 until their ceasefire (a fact widely reported in Northern Ireland) was still described as following 'the IRA's well-tested tactic of trying to usurp the political process by violence' (BT 13.10.93) and 'playing the IRA game, inflicting terror on whole communities' (BT 14.10.93), with the Shankill bombing giving loyalists more 'motivation' (BT 15.4.94). Thereafter the same paper decided that loyalist paramilitary actions were 'no longer reactive' (BT 29.4.94).

Finally, there is the device of blaming the victim, in this case claiming that the Catholic victims deserved to die. As pointed out earlier, some ultras have chosen to assume that all Catholic victims are members of republican terrorist organisations, thus legitimating loyalist killings. For example, in what appears to be a reference to the activities of the 'Shankill Butchers', whose methods provoked virtually universal horror and outrage among the general public in Northern Ireland, one writer stated:

> cutting throats is not part of our heritage, but if it is necessary to cut the throats of the men who wish to force us by the bomb and bullet into a United Ireland, then so be it ('Londonderry Unionist' BO 29.3.84).

This is, however, unusual. The 'Shankill Butchers' aroused such shame that the *Orange Standard* took the unusual course of stating that even the IRA had shown remorse after the La Mon killings (OS Mar 1979), and the murder of 76-year-old Roseanne Mallon caused even the *News Letter* to admit: 'No one community has a monopoly of suffering' (NL 10.5.94).

THE GREAT MAJORITY of those who unequivocally condemn loyalist violence against the security forces are moderates. Protest strikes are generally unpopular, not least because they provide an opportunity for violence and the intimidation of Protestants who are unwilling to join in by paramilitaries, who are no longer seen as defenders of their people but as 'crooks, murderers, thieves and gangsters' (IR 4.3.76). Occasionally blame is shifted from the perpetrators of violence. A dissident asks if the Shankill Protestants are 'just people of low intelligence, living in appalling conditions, nurtured politically by cunning politicians of the Official Unionist Party, on a diet of bigotry and intolerance for sixty years' (James Thompson CDS 24.10.69). The Portadown papers and the *Impartial Reporter* sometimes join ultras in blaming the British and/or Irish government for sparking off Protestant reaction, for example, because of Britain's 'foolish acquiescence to blackmail by burning, bombing and murder' (IR 6.7.72). On the whole, however, moderates along the whole spectrum seek to dissuade Protestants from defying the British government and reject double standards:

> Those who condemn violence cannot credibly qualify their attitude to suit the occasion. Nor is it enough to be a supporter of law and order and the police only when they are doing what you want them to do (BT 15.7.85).

There are, however, other reasons for condemnation. First, it is behaviour of the kind associated with nationalists and republicans:

> In a week when the SDLP has engaged in a contemptible attack on respected institutions such as the flying of the Union Jack ... it is distressing that such disloyal steps should share headlines with the attacks on police families in Portadown (PDT 23.8.85).

Secondly, it is dangerous for the Union. For one thing, the war against the real enemy is in danger of being forgotten:

> How can the police and the army devote all their energy to beating the terrorists when they are too busy trying to reason with people who stand for the National Anthem one minute and stone the Crown forces the next? (PDT 8.9.72).

More important, Northern Ireland might lose British support:

> Hard-line Protestants ... are jeopardising Ulster's existence by turning against their British heritage and traditional loyalty to the Crown ... they should heed Carson's words: 'When Ulstermen fight the Army, then the country is lost' (IR 19.10.72).

Moderates are ever mindful of the British audience, for loyalist rioting and clashes with British forces 'must add to the feelings of frustration and alienation which the name of Ulster conjures up among many in Britain' (BT 28.6.85).

Violence against Catholics is also strongly condemned, especially by the *Belfast Telegraph*; but it is often seen as self-defence, retaliation, part of a 'Protestant backlash' or 'counter-violence' (BT 9.8.77), and it is dangerous for the Union, as it is only when 'loyalist paramilitaries ... commit crimes which are horrifying to the international community, as well as Britain, that the danger of outside intervention arises' (BT 26.10.93). It also helps 'to enhance republican claims to be defenders of an oppressed minority' (BT 25.1.94). The UVF are, however, 'callous sectarian killers' (BT 27.12.93).

THERE IS CLEARLY a tendency throughout the three periods of this study to legitimate violence and law-breaking when it is carried out by Protestants. A few ultras do condemn it (for a rare example see Desmond G R Green CDS 21.2.75), and even the *News Letter*, which has been extensively cited in this context, initially accepted the 1969 Cameron Report's 'strictures on the extremists [and] the dreadful affair at Burntollet' (NL 12.9.69). After a long period when its condemnation of loyalist violence against Catholics was markedly mild, it came again to condemn such violence as criminal, morally wrong and likely to make matters much worse for all in Northern Ireland (NL 23.1.81, 30.5.85), and called the Ulster Freedom Fighters (UFF) as callous as the IRA (NL 16.11.85). There is certainly a sensitivity to nationalist accusations that unionist politicians support loyalist paramilitaries:

> Those who condemn the Protestant paramilitary groups and accuse them of having the support of various Protestant Loyalist organisations had their theories dispelled on Saturday [by] Mr James Molyneaux, the Sovereign Grand Master of the Royal Black Institution ... [he] made one of the most vital pronouncements by a loyalist leader for some time, when he declared: 'The Royal Black Institution is a Christian organisation and ... all those who protest – and call themselves Christians ... have a heavy responsibility to distance themselves from those who perform, or even advocate, criminal acts. No so-called loyalist gunmen need look to us for sympathy or support' (LS 2.9.81).

Mr Molyneaux's regret that similar pronouncements by the leaders of other Protestant groups had been disbelieved is, however, disingenuous in view of the history of Protestant politics. The major unionist parties may have failed to support the Protestant paramilitaries, but their condemnations of loyalist violence have rarely been as forthright as that of Mr Molyneaux, and major unionist newspapers such as the *News Letter* have been, to say the least, ambivalent about their role.

The imaginary portrait is once more drawn on to point the moral that Catholic violence is of a different nature from Protestant violence. The former is 'primary', a kind of original sin, the latter 'secondary', that is, a mere reaction to Catholic violence. Catholic mobs are rebels, Protestant mobs are angry protesters. Catholics have no good reason for violent actions (which therefore are inexcusable), whereas Protestants act under the duress of circumstances, on high moral principles, goaded by British ministers and provoked by the security forces. Protestant killings which cannot be excused in these terms are better ignored.

The Legitimation of Violence and Illegality

VIOLENCE IN SETTLER societies, on the part both of settlers and 'natives', is normal. Colonies were won and maintained by violence or the threat of violence. 'Native rebellion', however, is painted as arising out of the primitive nature of the people rather than out of legitimate complaints. Settler violence, on the other hand, is often part of the structure of coercive domination, carried out by legally-constituted authorities, and is characterised merely as the upholding of 'law and order' which is necessary in any civilised society. Illegal acts of violence by settlers are, however, more difficult to legitimise, because legal coercive forces exist, and because settlers are supposed by nature to be more 'civilised' than 'natives'. In the case of Ulster, with the extensive coercive powers available, which from 1921 to 1972 were largely in Protestant hands, it is clearly a problem when Protestants carry out illegal acts of violence against Catholics. Where possible, such acts are ignored by ultras, or excused by the claim that Catholic victims were themselves terrorists, or, since 1972, that this is inevitable in view of the incompetence of British security policy. What is never conceded by ultras is the long history of violence in Ulster. Violence must be portrayed as an aberration, or, particularly in the case of violence against the security forces, as justifiable response to republican violence and British government policy; otherwise the continued existence of Northern Ireland requires even more strenuous exercises in legitimation. These might still, however, fail to convince public opinion of the rightness of the Protestant determination to keep the six counties within the United Kingdom.

7 Colonial Rule and Protestant Alienation

NORTHERN IRELAND has been reduced since 1972 from the proud position of a 'self-governing state' to the frustrations of being a 'direct rule colony', one whose fate, moreover, is in British hands. Ultras and moderates alike are exasperated by this 'colonial rule', perceived as such even before the dissolution of Stormont. Some moderates use it as a warning that the people of Northern Ireland should settle their differences peacefully, but ultras use this perception of 'colonial rule' to warn Protestants to distance themselves from Britain and British solutions. They are suspicious of British intentions. One warned that 'the four leading Whitehall lackies [sic] in Northern Ireland' had all served in colonies that are now independent (PT 25.4.70); another that, lacking 'a few copper mines, tin mines or such-like ... we are expendable' (H E Browne PDT 16.6.72).

More common, however, is dislike of the treatment of Northern Ireland as an administrative colony, that is, one where metropolitan officials rule powerless 'natives', which now include Protestants. Such references multiplied from all parts of the political spectrum as direct rule wore on, but also preceded the dissolution of Stormont. 'Mr Callaghan thought that Northern Ireland was a Crown Colony inhabited, perhaps, by peoples inferior to those who inhabit the other parts of the UK' (John Kerr IR 16.9.71); and the *Orange Standard* complained that the imposition of Sunningdale was 'the first western example of Iron Curtain treatment of a satellite' (OS Feb 1974). British calls to bring the British Army back from Ulster brought ultra reminders that Ulster is not 'an outpost of the former Empire such as India or Palestine' ('Disgusted Loyalist' PDN 17.11.72) or 'some sort of colony owing some sort of allegiance to England or to Great Britain' (PT 23.3.74). Apparent British indifference to the conflict led a moderate to declare that Westminster thinks 'The natives are simply being restless and as long as the shooting, bombings and arson can be restricted to that remote island, then it's all very acceptable' (PDT 28.8.74). Such complaints increase after the fall of the Executive and the failure of subsequent attempts at devolved government.

In the absence of agreement on a local administration, Northern Ireland has been governed by a system of 'direct rule' which consists largely of legislation being promulgated by Orders in Council. The highest officer of state is the Secretary-of-State for Northern Ireland representing the Westminster government. The system of government by Orders in Council was described by Enoch Powell as 'semi-colonial ... being treated as a race apart, a sort of caste of untouch-ables' (OS Mar 1977). Even the pro-government *County Down Spectator* complained that Northern Ireland is used as a guinea-pig for legislation, commenting that '"We can't get it past the home crowd but it's good enough for the colonials" is an attitude which lost Britain an empire' (CDS 14.10.77). Direct rule is frequently com-pared to or referred to as colonial rule, 'not to be tolerated by a people who have the competence to govern themselves' (OS Nov 1977); and Northern Ireland is 'now being governed in much the same way as a 19th century British colony' (Wilfred Breen OS Apr 1979). One pro-independence campaigner urged: 'We are a people in bondage, but we shall yet be free, if we are given determined leader-ship' (Rev Hugh Ross IR 24.9.87).

'Protestant alienation' is a relatively recent term. If Catholics have long felt alienated from a state perceived as colonial, then once it came to be perceived in a similar way by Protestants it was not illogical to borrow the term. Alienation in this context can be inter-preted in a number of ways. It can describe the feelings of power-lessness and frustration engendered by 'colonial rule'; a feeling of loss of autonomy and of confidence in the future; and a feeling of separateness from something that should be close. In this third meaning there is little that is new. Protestants have often demon-strated alienation from those elements in Britain which oppose them. A feeling of 'togetherness' exists on the Protestant side in the main when they are fighting side-by-side with the mainland British in some major war, or when the royal family is behaving as it should. Otherwise 'English' (and even in some contexts 'British') are sometimes terms of abuse and often terms denoting an alien way of thinking and behaving.

What is new is that from 1972, for the first time since 1921, Northern Ireland has been directly ruled by the metropolis. The British people can no longer be counted as Protestants' natural allies. British power in the world has declined to the extent that governments have to listen to 'world' opinion, in practice, that of Europe and the USA; and the media, ever seen as hostile, have a new weapon, television. If Protestants have often felt 'under siege' by Catholics in Ireland, some now feel that much of the world is against them. These changes have affected the tone of many editorials and letters. Determination, moral certainty, optimism and even the sense of taking part in an exciting, if serious, adventure are the hallmarks of the 1912–21 period. The moral certainty and grim determination remain but pessimism, frustration and hopelessness lie behind much of the angry rhetoric of the modern period. Furthermore, whereas it appears, particularly in the 1912–21 period, that the audience editors address is the British public as much as the local populace, modern ultras appear more inward-looking and isolated from mainstream British opinion and political culture than do their predecessors. 'Protestant alienation' therefore seems an apt description.

A letter listing ten reasons for 'Protestant alienation' gives the Irish government, the IRA, and nationalist claims that the Orange Order is sectarian one place each, another two to the Roman Catholic Church for its position on education and mixed marriage, and the other five to British influence: the lack of democratic government; the breakdown of law and order; discrimination against Protestants; the imposition of proportional representation; and British radio and TV's 'pro-Republican publicity campaign ... since the start of the present Troubles' (Wilfred Breen OS May 1985). Although not included in Mr Breen's list, the attitudes of the people of Great Britain are also an element in Protestant alienation: 'There is a feeling that British affection for Ulster is, at best, lukewarm' (BT 24.2.94). How new though is this sense of alienation?

The modern emphasis on the nefarious influence of the British government is certainly not new. Since at least 1912 British governments have been 'proving' that they do not understand the Irish problem: that is, they do not know how to govern Irish Catholics. It is almost axiomatic that any British initiative in Ireland is ill-fated: 'It is a puzzle to us ... how what is popularly believed to be the common sense Englishman fails to grasp ordinary everyday things in Ireland. John Bull is often stupid' (IR 1.8.18). The British fail to understand the importance of unionists and their advice:

> The Chief Secretary ... happens to suffer from the disadvantage of both a plentiful lack of knowledge of Irish affairs and a constant desire to regard the Nationalists as the only people in Ireland worth troubling about (LS 7.6.17).

This led to feebleness and appeasement when faced with nationalist 'sedition', showing 'no real sense of justice, but only a contemptible disposition to pander to the forces of lawlessness, and a quite ridiculous fear of offending the Nationalists' (LS 12.12.14). Furthermore, English ministers tend to pursue their self-interest and this interest is frequently party political rather than national, especially since the Liberal government's reliance on Irish Nationalist MPs' support means that 'control of the destinies of the country has passed into the hands of the Celtic fringe' (LS 27.5.13). English untrustworthiness is well known: 'Ulster may be betrayed ... may afford another example of "Perfidious Albion" ... Ulster may invoke curses on British Statesmen who violate pledges and betray loyal men' (IR 9.5.18).

Doubts and fears about the British government re-emerged during the 1939–49 war, particularly since the Labour Party formed part of the wartime coalition and the USA, with its many citizens of Catholic Irish descent, exercised a growing influence on the British state. It was feared that Irish unity might be granted in exchange for the use of Irish ports. Unionist leaders, however, were confident that they could retain sufficient autonomy while still constitutionally a part of the United Kingdom, and so it proved until 1969. Despite the Labour Party's historic antipathy to unionism, Attlee's personal friendship with Stormont Prime Minister Brooke, to whom he made a private visit in Fermanagh in 1948 (IR 19.8.48), may have been a factor in the Protestant victory over the Anti-Partition League.

The essential mistrust of British governments re-surfaced with a vengeance, however, with a Labour government's intervention in 1969 and a Conservative government's suspension of Stormont in 1972. Although the majority of Protestants in the 1912–21 period had wanted a continuation of the full Union rather than a parliament of their own, the experiment had proved successful enough for sufficient numbers to wish to continue it. Even reform arising from some of NICRA's demands was acceptable as long as it was carried out by a Unionist government, and many whose views later hardened initially approved of O'Neill's programme (NL 10.12.68; LS 11.12.68; PDN 7.2.69). Some, however, had long been convinced that O'Neill and his supporters were 'tools of ecumenism' and their ranks were soon swelled by those who thought them weak puppets responsible, along with Catholics, for the outbreak of the conflict and the 'interference' of the British, and hence unfit to bear the mantle of leaders of Stormont. Nevertheless, despite O'Neillite 'appeasement of the enemies of Ulster' and consequent 'discrimination' against Protestants, Stormont with its Unionist majority making executive decisions was still a vital safeguard for Protestants:

I think that while some form of Unionist Government remains in Stormont we will have nothing to fear, but should the Unionist Government be suspended or abolished, then I would fear for our future (James Elliott BO 16.10.69).

This is what lies behind some of the hostile reaction to 'the most calculated insult ever offered to a free people' (PDN 14.4.72), the never-to-be-forgiven suspension of Stormont in March 1972:

Betrayal is a bitter, dangerous word that is not used carelessly except in anger [but is] the only word apposite ... In one stroke Mr Heath has succeeded in piling further torture, danger and disaster on a loyal public that has known little else for a period of more than three years (NL 25.3.72).

Martin Smyth later described the reaction of 'a large proportion of our people in Ulster' as 'rather like that of the people of Prague when they wakened one morning to find Russian tanks in their streets' (OS Dec 1976). Even before its abolition Stormont rule was contrasted favourably with British rule, and in memory it was transformed into a fifty-year golden age of peace, democracy, progress and prosperity for all, in which the Union was perfectly safe. More to the point is what it meant for Protestants:

> while Stormont was often weak on policy and in personnel it was at hand, always approachable and it was our own. It was the perpetual safeguard against Ulster's absorption into a united Ireland (OS Jan 1973).

Protestant fears were soon realised in the establishment of the 1973 Executive and the Council of Ireland, which combined the Catholic threat in two dimensions: local Catholics were given participation in government, and the Republic of Ireland was formally accorded a role, albeit advisory, in Northern Ireland. Such fears have been sustained by continued British refusal to countenance any replacement for Stormont which does not involve power-sharing with Catholics and insistence on engaging in inter-governmental talks on Northern Ireland with the Republic. Ultra refusal to accept such a 'solution' to the conflict has remained constant and they see it as the prime example of British political ineptitude and lack of principle. This wilful insistence on power-sharing arises from a secret wish to get rid of Northern Ireland: 'Under Direct Rule Westminster is seeking to destroy the Union and to implement Mr Harold Wilson's policy for a United Ireland' (A T Jackson CDS 19.1.79).

The electorate does have a vote in Westminster elections but Northern Ireland MPs form a tiny minority in the House of Commons and have little influence on legislation except when the government has a slim majority. Even the new Select Committee for Northern Ireland has only a minority of Unionist MPs. Many ultras therefore no longer desire integration: 'When the DUP was formed in 1971 our Policy was total integration, but when we saw Direct Rule was working against the Unionists, the DUP Leader supported the Devolution line' (Beryl Holland CDS 22.1.82). British rule was early seen to be 'working against the Unionists', in that any Catholic gains are Protestant losses rather than an attempt to remedy injustices. Protestants are ill-used and discriminated against, whereas Catholics always get what they want. Hence Catholic claims of discrimination are matched by a chorus of claims that, whether in jobs or housing, education or local government, security or the treatment of loyalist prisoners, or in plans for any assembly short of one with majority rule, 'the Government is now discriminating against the Protestant' (Beryl Holland CDS 12.5.72).

Given all the evidence it is clear that: 'There are two forces the Protestants are up against, the English politicians and the Republicans' (Beryl Holland CDS 13.8.76). The classic dilemma of settlers *vis-à-vis* their metropolis, as put by one of the most inveterate letter-writers, could hardly be better articulated.

There are also continuities with the past, and the workings of the 'imaginary portraits' of Catholics and Protestants described in chapter 3 can be discerned. A picture emerges of 'Ulsterpeople who have remained peaceful' gaining much less than 'those who have created most trouble in this country' (LS 7.6.72). Since the reason for this strange but consistent British behaviour cannot be anything to do with justice (since Catholics are merely troublemakers without legitimate grievances), and no other reasonable explanation can be found, it clearly has to do with the character of the British. In addition to the imaginary portraits of Catholic and Protestants, therefore, can be added a third, that of the British, or more specifically in some cases, the English.

What is the nature of British/English ignorance and misunderstanding? Fundamentally, they do not understand Catholics. They do not see that it is no solution to give in to Catholic demands, for these are always followed by even stronger demands (PDN 14.4.72), as Catholics are incapable of gratitude, seeing kindness as weakness: 'The panic legislation that was introduced ... was interpreted not as an earnest of goodwill towards "the minority" who were so critical of the administration, but as an admission of weakness' (LS 26.8.81). Attempts to 'appease' or 'placate' the 'insatiable minority' (W Breen IR 16.3.72) are therefore ill-conceived. The acceptance by some ultras of the necessity for O'Neill's reforms is now forgotten; on the contrary, Catholics have had no wrongs to complain of, and the British credulity in the face of Catholic 'lies' about their treatment under Stormont is a large part of the problem. Even good behaviour in Catholics is suspect, but it deceives the gullible British:

> Republican prisoners who are presently outwardly conforming, are non-conformist rebels at heart, yet they receive full privileges, whereas Loyalist prisoners, who are the real conforming prisoners, are classified as being non-conforming and subjected to the loss of many privileges ('Loyalist Prisoner' BO 17.2.83).

As always when the 'natives' are restless, the British fail to take the appropriate coercive action, persisting in conciliation attempts:

> The Minority only had to march, attack the police, overturn their vehicles and destroy property – which went on for several years without prosecution – and were given all they demanded ... Seditious speeches were made from platforms and no action was

taken ... Is it any wonder the True Loyalists of Ulster ... feel discriminated against and frustrated? (Beryl Holland BO 14.1.82).

The British understand nothing about Northern Ireland, seem incapable of learning and therefore can produce only unrealistic solutions:

> Northern Ireland affairs are complex and beyond the comprehension of any armed only with the honest desire to hold what to them appears to be a fair balance. Elsewhere they would succeed. Here, alas, failure is inevitable. John Bull, for all his skill in handling different brands of nationalism, has still a rudimentary idea of what lies beneath the surface in his other island (NL 3.4.70).

They do not understand the sterling character of 'the majority': 'The antipathy, of all English political leaders, to Ulster majority politicians is one of the incredible features of the Ulster situation' (OS Oct 1974). Nor do they understand how deeply they feel:

> The slide towards anarchy really began when the power concentrated in Stormont was lifted and placed in the control of a handful of men who were strangers to this country. They arrived as overlords, however well meaning, benevolent and legitimately appointed, with no fundamental understanding of the will of the majority of the people of Ulster to retain their British citizenship come what may (PDN 30.6.72).

This is, however, an unusually benign view of British intentions, not shared by those who complain of 'the usual abysmal ignorance of the Ulster problem and the typical high handed haughtiness of some English politicians' (OS Apr 1973).

British attitudes and actions are not always inexplicable: British political life has been corrupted by Irish immigrants who, inexplicably, can vote in Great Britain (OS Nov 1976; PT 21.1.67; NL 4.10.72); and the English usually follow their own interests: 'many English politicians ... only seem to want us when they need our men and territory for their wars' (Sammy Wilson CDS 3.4.81). Along with perceptions of ignorance and self-interest are the old notions of 'perfidious Albion'. When one editor declaims 'Gone forever is that trust which loyalist people had in the British Government' (NL 30.11.85), he is hardly stating anything new. There was very little trust to lose in 'English politicians who have continually sold us out, used us as a political shuttlecock and who have shown that they can in no way be trusted' (D G R Green CDS 30.6.72). Kipling's poem *Ulster* was resuscitated: '"Rebellion, rapine, hate, Oppression, wrong and greed Are loosed to rule our fate, By England's act and deed"' (LS 4.4.73), and in a speech Martin Smyth claimed:

Soon the British Ulsterman may find himself as persecuted as the German Jew in the early days of Hitler, through the existence of offensive legislation such as the Exclusion Order and constant reference to the amount of money that Ulster's war damage costs the taxpayer (OS Jul 1976).

Another example of 'persecution' is British interference in the electoral system. Proportional representation (PR) had been abolished by the Stormont government in 1922, not only to ensure that Catholic representation was minimised but also to keep the unionist vote from fragmenting into class parties (Patterson 1982:28). By the time the British government restored PR for all except Westminster elections, serious unionist divisions had already appeared. Paisley's Protestant Unionist Party had won no seats in the 1969 Stormont general election, but Paisley obtained only 1,414 fewer votes than O'Neill and in the 1970 by-election took the Bannside seat; and four days later the nucleus of the APNI was launched. Hence in the first modern election under PR, the May 1973 local government elections, there was a great range of unionist party labels rather than the monolithic Unionist Party of past times.

This destruction of the unionist unity always considered so important to Northern Ireland's survival has been deliberately engineered by the British (OS Mar 1973). It is a sign of British discrimination against Protestants: 'Northern Ireland became the only part of the UK ... where the voting system was changed apparently in the hope that control would be wrested from the majority of the population' (LS 8.7.81). Although one editor recognised that the O'Neill government had collapsed without the benefit of PR (NL 4.2.75), few others are so charitable. Despite the judgement that PR is a ploy which has failed (LS 10.3.76) there are constant complaints about it. These frequently focus on the fact that PR is not used in Britain: 'As British citizens in an integral part of the UK, we are entitled to retain the same Parliamentary voting system as adopted by Westminster' (Beryl Holland CDS 10.9.71). It is 'alien to centuries of Westminster tradition' (Knox-Cunningham OS Aug 1973), and not only is it not used in Britain but it is used in 'a foreign country, Eire' (Bruce Milligan CDS 9.6.72). As well as being un-British it is also undemocratic: 'the system that gives the elector more than one vote' (LS 21.5.80), and it is also undemocratic to employ different voting systems in different parts of the country (LS 11.7.77).

Direct rule is another example of the lack of democracy. Ultras (like moderates) deplore the reduction of local government powers and the subsequent lack of respect for the views of ratepayers but dislike most the lack of a local parliament and want 'the control to a much greater degree of the affairs of their own country' (LS 28.10.81). Such a parliament would be run on majoritarian lines: 'almost the entire

Protestant population [is] more determined than ever to adhere to its demands for a form of Government that reflects the wishes and the will of the majority of the people' (LS 13.4.77). The loss of local power means there is no check on 'the excesses and aberrations of the NIO' (NL 26.1.84). The lack of accountability and refusal to listen to local opinion by 'the English dictators' (Beryl Holland CDS 8.7.77) make direct rule a 'tyrannical seizure of powers by the NIO ... in Northern Ireland where there is no peace and no democracy' (Neil C Oliver IR 10.2.77). Elections seem pointless:

> Alas, what are we voting for? Are we in Northern Ireland not simply ruled by the NIO and a bunch of English civil servants? Does our vote matter a whit? Are we not being fooled into believing that we have a democratic system when we well know that the majority of people in Northern Ireland have no say? Another election is but a political gimmick to delude us ('Political Realist' BTimes 2.5.85).

Being on the receiving end of British imperial policy even in its kinder aspects is a bitter experience:

> No country has suffered more, and recently, from the interventions of those who are certain that they know better than the citizens do what is needed to make for us a better, peaceful and prosperous Province. The paternalism of the NIO, which disregards the democratically expressed views of the people by the ballot box, and ignores their elected representatives on the premise that it knows best is hard for any democrat to swallow (OS Nov 1986).

Although moderates have much in common with ultras in their views of direct rule, they are far less attached to the old Stormont and more willing to accept the necessity for reform. Stormont had been undemocratic, unfair to Catholics, a police state ruled by a selfish clique which cared little for the working class, lived in the past and blamed Catholics and nationalists for its failings (see *inter alia* H Malcolm M'Kee CDS 24.1.69; J E Hamilton CDS 5.3.82). It was Stormont rule which was responsible for poor relations between the British government and the people of Northern Ireland: 'We spent fifty years distancing ourselves from our mainland compatriots. We have reaped the harvest of alienation' (CDS 17.7.81). Much of the criticism of Stormont comes from Labour supporters, but others too welcomed early British reform policies, and the suspension of Stormont aroused a relatively muted reaction, though none as insouciant as the editor who asks what can be so terrible about direct rule for a people which cherishes its link with Britain (CDS 31.3.72).

A few moderates praise 'benevolent direct rule' (BT 1.7.77), and by and large place more trust in the government's promises and in the sincerity and good intentions of British ministers:

> At the outset James Prior showed a clearer understanding of the Ulster situation than most of his predecessors and introduced the Government proposals with cautious sensitivity, avoiding any suggestions that pressure was being applied on anyone to accept what was being put forward, but rather left the field clear for our local politicians to express their views freely ... Before the debate concluded, Mr Prior tactfully placed the onus on the Ulster leaders by advising them it was better that they should find a common ground to discuss their differences instead of the British government forcing something on them. At the same time the Secretary of State did not let anyone lose sight of the fact that there must be a degree of constitutional cooperation between North and South ... It could well be that at the conclusion of his sojourn in Ulster, James Prior leaves behind one worthwhile achievement: he has engaged our politicians in debate with a willingness to further dialogue – and he has left them the ball to play with (IR 5.7.84).

Some moderates feel that Northern Ireland is 'an embarrassment and a liability' (CDS 31.8.73) and is lucky to be treated so well:

> We should be very thankful to Westminster. Our political status is guaranteed; no change can be made unless with the agreement of the majority. We have massive injections of cash to keep our ailing economy operating. We have the defence of the British Army, involving, as it has done, the deaths and serious injuries of many soldiers. What has Britain got in return from Paisley? – nothing but abuse and insult ('True Loyalist' BO 28.1.82).

Nevertheless they are generally anxious to see devolved government returned, so direct rule was welcomed as long as it appeared temporary. As successive power-sharing experiments failed, it became as irksome to moderates as to ultras. Although only Westminster can help Northern Ireland, 'the English may not have a great reputation for healing Irish wounds' (BT 4.1.72). The *Impartial Reporter* in particular is angered at the 'complete alienation' of 'the once fiercely pro-British population' (IR 16.9.76, 10.1.80), and even the most moderate editor noted that ignorance and lack of realism have led to misconceived policies:

> Over the last eleven years Westminster has expended quantities of time, patience, money, tolerance and good will on this bad-tem-

pered little province; but there's no more real understanding of the Northern Ireland situation now than there was before. For how could a government truly cognisant of the Ulster mind and way of life publish a document as important as these proposals [Atkins' power-sharing proposals] in the run-up to the Twelfth? No-one in Northern Ireland is at his most lucid during the holiday period ... given the Ulster trait of sticking religiously to statements, however daft, made in the heat of the moment, the timing of the paper is little short of tragic (CDS 11.7.80).

The British Labour Party's hostility to unionists during the third Home Rule crisis was not forgotten and this made it particularly disliked and distrusted, particularly under Harold Wilson's leadership:

> Although it was not his Party that ended, whether temporarily or for good, the Government at Stormont, he obviously still hates the majority Party in Ulster. Probably because of the large number of Irish Labour voters in several constituencies in England (IR 5.10.72).

It soon became apparent that neither of the big parties at Westminster can be trusted:

> Behind the scenes, Mr William Whitelaw ... appears to be running a competition with Mr Harold Wilson ... to see who can give away most to the Republicans ... steadily building up resentment among more than two-thirds of the population (IR 20.7.72).

What lies behind British policy is its hostility to and contempt for Northern Ireland, as evidenced by the 'unfriendly, downright antagonistic administrators in Whitehall' (IR 11.2.71) and the fact that Heath spoke to the people 'like naughty children' (IR 23.11.72). The English style of governing is typified by 'insensitive English politicians' (PDN 1.10.82).

As time went on, most British politicians of either party simply are not interested or concerned:

> A complete lack of interest in Northern Ireland is apparent among the great majority of MPs at Westminster. This is evident from the way MPs abandoned the House when the Order was being considered, showing clearly that they were not interested in the fate of direct rule ... highlighted when the Rev Ian Paisley MP forced a vote on the Order. There was a hurried scramble to find sufficient MPs in the chamber to make a quorum to get the measure through (IR 6.7.78).

The British government is more interested in foreign reactions than in what the people of Northern Ireland think or want (PDN 31.8.79), and the result is remote impersonal rule:

> London-based Direct Rule, dealing with decisions affecting the welfare of Northern Ireland, is a totally unsatisfactory substitute for a local Stormont administration ... Direct Rule is far too remote, with vital decisions being made in London by people apparently out of touch with feelings on the ground in the province ... Few Englishmen in the past have shown the qualities to understand the Irish in such matters, whether as Lord Lieutenants in pre-border days in Dublin, or as Secretaries of State since the early 1970s (PDT 28.6.85).

It is carried out moreover by an uncaring government (IR 13.6.74; PDT 16.10.74); but direct rule is the fault of intransigent local politicians rather than of some sinister design orchestrated from Dublin.

There is also the basic English flaw – the doubt that they will keep their promises or tell the truth. Moderates tend to report rather than affirm loyalist distrust, but a similar message comes over:

> When both sides totally mistrust the Government of the day, it shows what a mess we are in – and the Government leaders have only themselves to blame ... We have reached the stage where many, if not most, of the statements uttered by the NIO, the Secretary of State, the PM even, are immediately disbelieved. A major factor for that must be the way those in authority have been less than frank in their dealings with the people here (IR 18.7.85).

The well-known English/British vices of incompetence, muddle and hypocrisy, long noted in Northern Ireland, are evidence of the inability to learn from experience:

> The British Government's history of limping from crisis to crisis and then hoping things will work themselves out – only to realise too late that they won't – is again evident ... Ministers say they will never sit down with Sinn Fein ... Yet they gave the party the ... go ahead to fight the local government elections, thus expecting the Unionists to do what the Government would not. Government ministers cannot really be surprised when their hypocrisy is thrown back in their face, and Craigavon's Unionist councillors are exploiting the situation to the full ... Perhaps the Government – not renowned for correctly gauging the feelings of any section of the Ulster mentality – felt that Sinn Fein would fare badly at the polls ... It did not happen and ... proscribing the party at this stage would

create another monster the Government probably – going on its previous track record – could not handle (PDT 9.8.85).

Finally, the Anglo–Irish Agreement and the talks which preceded it aroused almost as much ire among moderates as among ultras. It was accepted by the APNI (though they later said that they wanted it modified) and a few other moderates: 'there are plenty of moderate unionists who want to give the agreement a chance and who happen to think that Mrs Thatcher has no intention of selling out the loyalist population to the South' ('Moderate' BTimes 30.1.86). Others rejected it:

> The British Government has made an historic decision in signing the Anglo–Irish accord with Dublin, and will not have to live with the consequences – the reality that the vast majority of the million strong Protestant and Unionist people in Northern Ireland find themselves alienated from the Westminster Government over the deal which will give Dublin a say in the running of the Province. Ulster is thus plunged into the turmoil and uncertainty of a future fraught with danger and difficulty. Unionist anger and sense of betrayal and treachery is understandable ... the presentation of the 'package' ... revealed an appalling lack of sensitivity. How could they possibly have imagined that an agreement fraught with suspicion and more than a sniff of betrayal could be presented to the Ulster public without bitterness and resentment, especially as no Ulster Unionist leader had been consulted about the contents? ... details were with-held from the Ulster people, while Dublin newspapers were reporting many of the main facts in their editions last week ... nothing is likely to be the same again ... No one in London or Dublin should be under any illusions about the depth of feeling in Northern Ireland or the very real fears on the part of Unionists that it contains the potential for pushing them, against their will, into an all-Ireland republic. These fears may very well be unfounded, but it is easy to be philosophical and enthusiastic about the agreement in the quietness and tranquillity of suburban London and Dublin, well away from the streets of Portadown, or any other large Ulster town (PDT 22.11.85).

A similar complaint was made when instead of pledging unqualified support to its 'natural friends here' (BT 8.11.93), it was the Irish government that was the first to see the Mayhew plan for the future of Northern Ireland (BT 8.2.94).

Whereas ultras react with anger and violent protest, however, moderates often react with hurt feelings:

The Press and the TV neglect the thousands upon thousands of good, decent people ... We do not shout and rage, nor are we bigots. We are frightened in a way that you could hardly imagine in the relative peace you thankfully enjoy. We feel more frightened because our best friend, as it were, has let us down ... What the Houses of Parliament fail to understand is not the merits or defects of the Anglo–Irish Agreement, but the unfairness of its implementation. It is this which galls us and makes us think we have no defender (Rev B A Hunt IR 13.3.86).

It is clear that, although there are differences between ultras and moderates in their perceptions of the British government, notably on the issue of whether the government is biased in favour of Catholics, as ultras believe, or is impartial, as many moderates believe, their antipathy to the experience of direct rule is remarkably similar. Being British may involve British standards and democratic practices but it does not involve being ruled by mainland ministers and officials. Full integration into the United Kingdom on the lines of Scotland or Wales is an option favoured by few. Both moderates and ultras want a local parliament, the main differences being that moderates accept that powers would be limited and shared with Catholics, whereas ultras demand powers at least equivalent to those of the old Stormont and without power-sharing. Since the former is rejected by ultras and the latter by the British government, direct rule with all its frustrations and inadequacies is a compromise that both sides in the unionist camp hope will be temporary.

ULTRAS AND MODERATES have much in common too in their attitudes to the British media. There is a number of studies of the media in the context of Northern Ireland (see Elliott 1976; Cathcart 1984; Curtis 1984; Schlesinger 1987; Butler 1991; Moloney 1991; Miller 1994), which are particularly critical of the BBC for its unionist bias. Despite its self-censorship, the BBC was reviled by unionists long before the current crisis, and for all the Protestant mockery of the Irish state, a few make complimentary references to the Irish state broadcasting service because of the even greater censorship exercised within it; and the *Belfast Telegraph*, having called the British broadcasting ban 'emotional' and 'illogical' (BT 3.11.93), criticised the Irish state for dropping its broadcasting ban on Sinn Féin (BT 12.1.94). Ulster Television (UTV), started in 1959, has been exempt from the kind of hatred the BBC has aroused, perhaps because it is unionist-owned, but the BBC and the British media in general have continued to be very unpopular with Protestants, especially ultras.

Protestant contempt for the British media goes back long before the institution of broadcasting, to the Home Rule crises:

There is nothing more amusing to the Ulsterman than to read the efforts of English writers in English papers ... on Ireland and Home Rule: for with the exception of the *Morning Post* no English paper seems to understand it (IR 28.12.16).

This editor later accused such papers of 'assisting sedition indirectly', explaining this partly by the presence of Irish journalists on these papers giving out 'foul exudation and effluvia' (IR 22.1.20). This dislike was also expressed in the 1939–49 period, particularly when Northern Ireland was referred to as being in 'Eire' and when doubts about special powers and discrimination and the activities of the Anti-Partition League were given sympathetic coverage.

From 1968, however, sections of the British media, now including radio and television, have been accused not merely of ignorance and misjudgement but of deliberate lies and distortion. The long media silence on Northern Ireland had first been deliberately broken by the *Sunday Times* in 1966, which described it as a 'political slum'. Hence even before the advent of NICRA Paisley declared: 'the *Sunday Times* has launched a campaign of lies in order to smear Ulster' (PT 16.1.68). Once trouble erupted, the British media were accused of deliberately fostering negative images of Northern Ireland, the Stormont government, the RUC and Protestants. Indeed, the *Orange Standard* was set up in 1973 explicitly to counteract the influences of 'minority persuaders and an often unbalanced media coverage of the Ulster crisis' (OS Jan 1973). The British media are positively pro-nationalist and pro-Catholic ('Realist' IR 28.10.71), and they are more concerned about the British Army and bombs in Britain than about the RUC and bombs in Northern Ireland (PDN 29.9.72).

Those which have supported the Protestant view of events, such as the *Daily Telegraph* and *Sunday Telegraph*, the *Sunday Express*, the *Daily Mail* and on one occasion, when it 'admitted' there was a case for the Union, the *Sunday Times* (OS Jun 1983), have of course won praise, and the *Londonderry Sentinel* is quick to discern that its colleagues in Fleet Street are beginning to take the Protestant view of the situation (LS 28.7.71). More typical among ultras is Paisley's claim that Fleet Street has 'been busy for years deceiving the public on the vital question of Rome's conspiracy to take over Northern Ireland' (PT 11.1.69), and the assertion that the RUC's every move is 'monitored by left-wing, pro-republican journalists' ('Law and Order Supporter' TLS 29.8.84). The *Daily Mirror* in particular is a 'pro-Republican rag' (John McAuley BO 20.5.82) and the *Sunday Express* lost its popularity when it described Northern Ireland as 'an Irish bog' (OS Jul 1983).

It is television, however, that has the greatest opportunity to bring images into British viewers' homes, and the dictum that the camera cannot lie was very quickly refuted by ultras. Independent

Television (ITV) and the unionist-owned UTV were occasionally listed as co-offenders in the 'pro-Republican publicity campaign ... since the start of the present Troubles' (Wilfred Breen OS May 1985), especially when they broadcast allegations of RUC brutality and programmes such as 'The Troubles' which are less fair than the BBC equivalent (OS Dec 1977). Most of the odium, however, is reserved for the BBC, which casts even Radio Telefis Eireann (RTE) in a very favourable light (OS Aug 1975). Ultras habitually criticise almost anything the BBC produces about Northern Ireland, including 'Songs of Praise', especially on the occasion when the BBC used the name 'Derry' throughout, demonstrating 'what now seems to be BBC policy of mis-naming Londonderry to pander to one section of the community' ('Licence-paid viewer' TLS 7.1.76). This was mocked by moderates, one of whom pointed out that the *Londonderry Sentinel* gives the services for 'Derry Cathedral' every week (B M Story TLS 17.12.75).

Even programmes such as that which 'exposed' Martin Galvin of Noraid (OS Sep 1983) did not restore its reputation, and a programme about Orangeism won Orange approval, but qualified by a complaint that Andrew Boyd's anti-Orange contribution 'was an example of the BBC's constant concern to give two opposing views of a subject' (OS Dec 1983). In fact the main complaints arise whenever views are expressed (or are immanent in the material) that show unionism and loyalism as anything less than admirable and righteous. There are no two sides to the question of Northern Ireland; and the timidity and effective censorship of the BBC noted by commentators are insufficient. Of the programmes which roused ultra ire, only two had been subject to British government interference, and reactions were relatively mild to the first of these, namely 'The Question of Ulster', although the 'Tonight' programme on allegations of RUC brutality was ill-received (OS Apr 1977).

There was a particularly furious response to a 'Panorama' programme on Northern Ireland which pointed out how much Britain spent on it:

If the BBC wished to arouse public opinion in Britain against the continuance of Northern Ireland as part of the UK, and whip up opposition to the presence of the Army here, it could scarcely have done better than through the presentation of Monday night's Panorama programme. Ulster was portrayed ... as a turbulent, subsidised, irreconcilable area into which British blood and British money are being poured to no purpose except to the detriment of the British public. And this national broadcasting and television organisation, forbidden by its charter to have a political opinion, circumvented the restriction by commissioning a public opinion poll to prove – at least to its own satisfaction – that the majority of people in Britain now believe that the Army should pull out ... figures based on interviews with 505 persons purporting to speak for the entire nation was an act of gross irresponsibility giving comfort to the enemy of the State and a new stimulus to its murderous activity ... That ... it provided a platform opening the way for British citizens to declare themselves in favour of deserting other British citizens in time of war in a different part of the UK does not seem to have occurred to those responsible for the programme as bordering on treachery (NL 27.9.72).

In view of the ingrained hostility to the BBC it is perhaps not surprising that one letter-writer called the new Radio Ulster 'a new attack on the intelligence, credibility and mentality of the people of Northern Ireland', and asked: 'Is this the British Government's secret weapon to drive the people of Northern Ireland out of the UK?' ('Disbeliever' TLS 5.2.75). Radio Foyle, however, is much more unpopular, principally because it includes items about Donegal.

Why should the 'British Bias Corporation' launch such 'a long series of prejudice against the loyalist and Protestant community' (PT 23.3.74)? Further:

> Why must the Northern Ireland image always be projected on the national network exactly as the enemies of Ulster want it? ... Is it not because there are so few people within the BBC set-up either in Belfast or London who are sympathetic to the cause of Ulster? (W Breen IR 2.12.71).

Various explanations are advanced. The staff are disproportionately Catholic, evidenced by the 'monopoly of broadcasting time' given to Roman Catholic services (Wm Henry Stothers PDN 10.1.75); the habit of saying 'Catholic' instead of 'Roman Catholic'; the over-extensive coverage of papal visits; and generally propagating 'the existence and influence of Roman Catholicism in these islands and elsewhere' (OS Jun 1979). They report what the British government tells them to. The BBC perpetrates 'the use of current affairs programmes to give favourable coverage to left-wing and subversive movements' ('Another WASP' OS Mar 1980). At the same time it is on the side of the far-from-left-wing Republic of Ireland; but perhaps the most satisfying explanation is that of 'those IRA sympathisers still in employment at the BBC' (Alex Scott OS Apr 1980).

The censorship of the programme in which interviews with both loyalist and republican advocates of violence (Gregory Campbell of the DUP and Martin McGuinness of Sinn Féin) were to be screened won a more ambivalent response. It would be free publicity for the IRA, but given that the programme had actually been made, 'it was stupidity and moral cowardice of a uniquely peculiar kind to ban it ... But banning it has given it even more helpful publicity' (NL 1.8.85). There is no doubt, however, that ultras approve of the reluctance of the broadcast media to make controversial programmes in the first place.

MODERATES ATTEMPT TO take a balanced view of the media and are more aware of liberal ideas of freedom from government interference and censorship and of the general responsibilities of journalists to report events, however unpleasant, as they 'cannot hide their heads in the sand and not see what goes on around them' (IR 23.1.69). The *Belfast Telegraph* shows both an appreciation of the problems and a warning that the BBC should heed local feelings (which ones is not clear nor how opposing views should be dealt with):

> Other letters – about which churches should be on 'Thought for Today' and whether 'Ulster' is nine counties or six – show that the service could get sucked into the usual politico-religious morass, but that is not its fault. It would be unfair to pass judgement after only two weeks and the most important thing is that the BBC should be receptive to the listeners' ideas and have an open mind on future development (BT 16.1.75).

The ITV programme on the RUC's ill-treatment of suspects is necessary:

> for the good of the community in general and the police in particular ... Broadcasting companies and newspapers – including this one – can have the highest regard for the contribution that the security forces are making in the war against terrorism, but this does not mean they regard them as being above criticism (BT 12.3.79).

The government ban on the Campbell/McGuinness programme is also misconceived:

> it is a credit of people in Northern Ireland, few of whom wanted to hear from Sinn Fein, that the basic untenability of the position was recognised ... the incalculable benefit to the nation of a free Press is defended almost nowhere except in the industry itself. Outside, lip-service is paid by politicians who in reality hedge the whole business round with so many restrictions that the quality and impartiality of British reporting, which is respected throughout the world, is achieved more despite Government intentions than because of them ... A programme comparing the lunatic fringe politics of Northern Ireland's far right and far left might have told us little we did not already know, but would have been clear evidence to mainland viewers of why the problem here is proving so difficult to solve (CDS 8.8.85).

Moderates also recognise the value of courting the media:

> One aspect on which few would disagree is that the Loyal Orders fell down badly on public relations and communications ... there were valid claims by media people ... that official comments were not available ... That some television personnel were forced by 'loyalists' to beat a hasty retreat behind police lines in order to do their job was deplorable and certainly very bad for the Orange cause (PDT 18.10.85).

When the results of the bombing of Belfast on 'Bloody Friday' were shown on colour television, this benefited the unionist cause because it 'brought home to the people of England what the people of Ulster have had to endure over the past four years' (IR 27.7.72). Even controversial programmes have their value for:

> residents in those high-risk areas of South Fermanagh, whose plight was fully highlighted in the BBC TV 'Spotlight' on Friday evening. Generally the presenters of the programme have been credited with giving a balanced picture of the tragic situation and the fears and life-and-death problems of those immediately concerned ... unlike some previous TV 'in-depth' surveys of the Fermanagh situation, when a very biased impression was spread abroad. This time the viewers were given the facts ... and people were left to form their own opinions. The great pity is that this programme was not shown throughout the UK ... At the same time both the BBC and ITV have been screening their versions of 'The Troubles' in Ireland ... Undoubtedly Robert Key's [sic] carefully researched series has enlightened many viewers ... revealing just how ruthlessly the newly-established Government in Dublin went about capturing and executing the anti-Treaty IRA forces ... in a manner far more vicious and without a shred of mercy than either the notorious Black-and-Tans or the British Army (IR 5.2.81).

Television sometimes, if inadvertently, shows the positive side of Northern Ireland:

> Portadown has been rarely out of the national headlines this past week and has figured in television programmes such as ITV's Weekend World and World in Action. Unfortunately, the publicity is not the sort which the town or its people would welcome ... Yet, coming through was another picture of Portadown ... quite a few [scenes] showed Portadown looking prosperous, bustling and with attractive housing.
> One correspondent in a national Sunday newspaper spoke of

the vivid contrasts in so much of Ulster life ... there was the beautiful countryside, the friendly people and the prosperous appearance of Belfast and provincial towns like Portadown, Bally-mena and Newtownards (PDT 11.4.86).

Nevertheless, the *Impartial Reporter* and the Portadown papers are frequently critical of the British media and incline on occasion to ultra views. The *Impartial Reporter's* favourite mainland newspaper is the *Daily Telegraph,* 'which appears to understand the Ulster situation better than most' (IR 12.1.81). The mass media in general become interested in the conflict only when there are bombings and shoot-ings in Britain, and the continuing violence in Northern Ireland is the more depressing because of:

> the apparent indifference of so many people and of sections of the media on the mainland to the plight of the embattled natives of the Province. On Sunday night the television news carried only scanty details of the Lurgan bombings – a sharp contrast to the saturation coverage which minor events in London often receive (PDT 15.10.75).

It is as if Northern Ireland does not exist. A commentator at the Cenotaph ceremony says he hopes young children watching will come no closer to war than this, yet: 'Even as the viewers were looking in, murder and violence were stalking the streets of British territory only a few hundred miles from the Cenotaph' (PDT 12.11.75). On the other hand, when the media do focus on the violence in Northern Ireland, the attention is usually as unwelcome as is being ignored:

> How difficult is the task of convincing people overseas, and even in mainland Britain, that 90 per cent of Northern Ireland is peace-ful most of the time and that the streets of Portadown and other large towns, are probably a great deal safer than comparable urban areas in England. The positive side of Northern Ireland rarely makes the headlines in cross-channel papers, yet despite 15 years of violence, tens of thousands of Protestants and Roman Catholics live and work alongside one another in the province and respect one another's traditions. The overwhelming majority of both communities abhor violence ... If many of the people who criticise the province from armchairs in England and Scotland were to take the trouble to cross the sea and observe the province at close hand, they might be surprised to find just how normal most of the country is. Instead they are all too ready to accept the view of Ulster as portrayed by some television companies (PDT 17.8.84).

So it is problematical whether things are worse when the media are ignoring Northern Ireland or when they are giving it their attention. Part of the problem of media attention is the deleterious effect on the local image, notably of Fermanagh and Craigavon and the plight of 'the Protestant masses, abused by the cross-channel media for so long' (IR 12.1.81) but the major concern is defence of Northern Ireland as a whole. Allegations that local methods of keeping law and order are unduly heavy-handed and discriminatory are resented, as indeed are media reports which seem to suggest that the people of Northern Ireland are collectively guilty and should be abandoned, an attitude which 'intrude[s] on the suffering and agony endured by the innocent people here' (PDN 18.5.79, 28.9.79). The news media concentrate on the trouble-making, unrepresentative minority, estimated at between 10,000 people and 30,000 of the population (IR 28.8.69; PDT 15.1.75). By giving republicans free propaganda in 'publicising forces working for anarchy', the media deny an airing to 'the orthodox views of the majority' (IR 1.2.73). When the British media criticised the BBC TV programme in which an interviewee claimed to have murdered Airey Neave, this is years too late:

> It is ironic to citizens of Ireland that a fuss should be made in this case and the newspapers and television screens full of accusations of 'biased' reporting after ten years during which Irish people have seen so many programmes and news reports glorifying the murderers and criminals. Even the very word 'terrorist' is a journalistic invention which gives a cloak of respectability to the 'freedom fighters' (IR 19.7.79).

Allegations that the security forces used torture on suspects in Northern Ireland are given disproportionate cover compared to that given to republican violence, or are 'selective reporting' which in any case fails to acknowledge that 'when dealing with violent criminals, police forces have to reply with violence, and the limits are hard to define' (IR 15.3.79, 22.3.79). The media also thrive on trouble and even cause it:

> how can London-based editors justify the kind of reporting we had on Sunday, when Mr Whitelaw was said to be negotiating with the Provisional IRA ... All proved to be speculation, but how damaging to the Whitehall initiative. It plays on the fears and mistrust of the ordinary, not very imaginative, mass of people in the province, who react by putting up barricades and retreating into their own groups for mutual reassurance – the opposite of what is wanted if any form of confidence is to be created (IR 8.6.72).

As in the 1912–21 period, however, the *Impartial Reporter* is ever-optimistic that realism is just around the corner. The early claim that the English media has been 'hoodwinked by a false campaign of vilification and propaganda' but is 'belatedly changing its tune' (IR 11.9.69) is repeated throughout the period:

> of late there has been some realisation of the way newspapers and visiting news reporters were hoodwinked. While they have never apologised for their mistakes, they now tend to give a better-balanced picture, though there are still some propagandists about (IR 19.7.79).

Moderates on the whole take a much calmer view than ultras, and subscribe to the values of a free press even when they do not find reports on Northern Ireland very palatable. Among both groups, however, there is much bitterness at what is seen as anti-Protestant bias, whether perceived by ultras as caused by pro-republican sympathies or by moderates as a slur on what is (or could be) a basically peaceful and progressive part of the United Kingdom. Such reactions are not surprising, for it is through the output of the British media that the people of Great Britain are thought to form their opinions.

DISCOVERING WHAT the people did think was difficult in the earlier periods. Guesswork was based primarily on the results of general and by-elections, and in 1912–21 the customary reverses of parties in power gave hope that the people were swinging to the Conservative and Unionist Party and were therefore against Home Rule. Only one editor (a Scotsman) told his readers that there was principled British support for Home Rule:

> There are in Britain probably tens of thousands of persons who support Home Rule in order to bring about a reconciliation between the Irish and the British people. That is a high object. To attain it would be worth almost any price (CDS 28.2.13).

This is a result, however, of misconceptions about the effect of the Bill, which would not attain this object.

From the non-conformist point of view the church of the majority of English people is an object of suspicion:

> the Church of England that deplores the Reformation, that abhors the word Protestant, that crawled some years ago to the feet of the Pope, begging to be acknowledged as a branch of 'the true Church' (PDN 2.3.12).

The ignorance, gullibility, passivity or cupidity of the British and the dangerous presence of socialists were more widely remarked, and despite their supposed support it is still necessary to educate them, and long after it has been asserted that it wholeheartedly supports the Ulster cause British public opinion frequently 'is beginning' to see the matter correctly. Either unionist propaganda (a word then used without pejorative connotations) is still in the process of 'awakening the English mind to the dangers of the Home Rule Bill' (IR 11.12.13) or such awakening lies in the future:

> The conspiracy will be defeated by the commonsense and patriotism of the British people, who, we cannot but believe, will rouse themselves at long last to a great effort, too long delayed, to wrest the destinies of the country from the hands of its enemies and theirs ... How exactly this will be cannot be known at the moment (LS 14.12.12).

Exasperation occasionally smeared the portrait of the British as allies. They do not take seriously unionist warnings of civil war, and while Ulster Volunteers are drilling, hospitals being organised and businessmen taking out insurance against war risks, things that 'have become part of the ordinary life of Ulstermen', Great Britain is sleeping:

> people in Great Britain, and the Government ..., are just as indifferent as though the Empire was only faced with some petty tribal raid in India or Africa, and not with a conflagration that will convulse the Empire and rapidly spread across the Channel (LS 11.6.14).

They are still capable of being swayed by nationalist propaganda, and even though the outbreak of war and Protestant volunteering gave more confidence in English support, the people still refuse to see things correctly. The nationalist refusal to have conscription for Ireland should have been 'a large political mistake' – were it not for 'the short memories of the British public' (LS 20.1.16). Even at the time the English reaction is unaccountable:

> And strange to say the English people seem quite content with this inequitable and unjust distribution of the burden of citizenship. The fact is that the Nationalist Party's profession of loyalty to Britain is merely a game of bluff designed to befool the electorate of England and Scotland with the view of furthering their Home Rule propaganda (PDN 8.1.16).

Another lost opportunity is the Easter Rising which 'should open the eyes of the English and Scotch electorate' (PDN 29.4.16) and make Englishmen begin (still beginning) to see the dangers of Home

Rule; but the Rising has adverse effects on some 'good folk across the Channel who are feeling weary of the Irish question and desire to get it out of the way, no matter how' (LS 27.5.16).

By the time of Lloyd George's proposal for the partition of Ireland, it no longer matters what the British electorate think, as they are tired of the matter and ignorant of Ireland, and still capable of believing nationalist propaganda; but since Ulster's cause has been won, their opinions are no longer important and assertions of their support ceased. There is no doubt that the main value of imaginings about the British people is as a legitimation for Protestant rebellion; and uncertainty about their opinions and descriptions of them as different (and inferior) in outlook from Ulster people show a sense of separation from Great Britain and its people rather than the 'kinship' that lies at the base of the later claim to be 'British'.

THE IMPORTANCE OF British public opinion is also evident in the 1939–49 period. The ban on anti-Northern Ireland speeches at Queen's University Belfast is welcome because the speakers might have conveyed 'to the British public and others the false impression that they reflected the outlook of the educated classes in Ulster' (LS 16.3.39). Northern Ireland's war effort will win British sympathy, and conscription in Northern Ireland 'would have ... removed the stigma that attaches to us in the eyes of many British people' (CDS 31.5.41). In the run-up to the Ireland Act the Ulster Unionist Council requested details of friends and relatives in England and Scotland to whom leaflets could be sent and thanked the thousands who supplied them (Ulster Unionist Council BO 22.10.48).

Some calls for Protestants to be aware of British opinion were perhaps intended merely to pull into line those who had failed to join up, voted against Sunday entertainments for troops, engaged in strikes or complained about rationing; others to show nationalists the hopelessness of their cause since the great mass of British people are for Ulster and against (or worse, 'blandly unconcerned' about) the Republic (LS 10.5.49). Nevertheless the British, and in particular the English, are not whole-hearted about Northern Ireland:

> While Ulster has always found and we believe always will find, staunch friends in Britain ready to stand by her at all costs, we also know that there have been those who have been ever ready to placate her foes, and the foes of Britain. The British people succumb too readily to Southern Irish blandishments and promises (LS 28.10.44).

As always, the English people are ignorant of Ireland, meaning that they did not understand why Protestants wanted nothing to do with a united Ireland. There are those whose 'base ingratitude' is such that they have forgotten Northern Ireland's war record and think they know enough to express anti-unionist opinions: 'Britain always seems to be able to produce people like these (British meddlers ... who called themselves the Council for Civil Liberties), and Ulster's enemies invariably count upon aid from such types' (LS 1.1.46). This is why it is necessary to publicise Northern Ireland's case:

> The English people know little about Ireland but what little they know is from Nationalist sources. In the matter of propaganda, the anti-Partitionists are alive, the Ulster Unionists are dead ... If Ulster has lost her friends in England it is her own fault (IR 24.4.47).

In the last resort, however, it again does not matter what the British people think. When the prime minister of Northern Ireland warned that people in England would react to the demand for Dominion status by telling the North to join the South, a supporter of Dominion status commented:

> But if that were said by Britain, is that all there is to be said? What would Carson and his men of 1912 have replied if they were spoken to like that? Are the leaders and rank-and-file of to-day so decadent that they would be deterred by such an answer, and forced into silent submission? We do not believe it (LS 29.11.47).

In any case there is evidence that the British people are not what they had been. Despite their courage in adversity, strikes both during and after the war prove that 'The British working man in the past had a great reputation for hard work: he is no longer a "working" man' (IR 23.1.47). England has become like a pagan country, a 'fruitful field for missionary endeavour' (IR 6.2.47). Even alleged English qualities have their disadvantages. Their 'modesty' about their war effort, in which 'the part played by England's sons and daughters ... completely overshadows that of the United Kingdom and Empire [is] commendable up to a point, but ... a wily enemy seeks to work the most harm out of it [and] the Ministry should tell more of England's proud and inspiring story' (LS 9.7.42). British tolerance is useful as an argument against the Irish, who do not have this virtue (IR 10.3.49), but the British are 'criminally tolerant' when people are allowed to protest against the bombing of German civilians (IR 4.5.44), when Germans are rescued from sunken U-boats (IR 25.5.44), and when 'the filthy Italian scum' and 'Nazi prisoners' are 'pampered' in prisoner-of-war camps (IR 5.10.44); and they are 'the biggest fools in Christendom' for sending wheat to Germany (IR 31.7.47).

For some this British decline began with the election of the Labour government in 1945, 'an administration which [the English] elected in a moment of post-war hysterics' (Ralph Stone IR 12.8.48). Nevertheless there are dangers in alienation from the English:

> We say we did not want or ask for our Parliament. Yet we accepted it. It was the surrender value of our No Home Rule policy ... our Parliament makes England think we are separate in some way now ... It is madness to imagine England will stick to us because we are loyal. They place their own valuation on our loyalty. And no matter what that is they think the ports and food [from 'Eire'] for sterling better value (H Malcolm M'Kee CDS 16.10.48).

PROTESTANT PERCEPTIONS of the people of Great Britain came to the fore again from 1969. Although the attitude of the British people is not listed by Mr Breen as a cause of alienation it is increasingly difficult for ultras to feel much kinship with them. There are disturbing signs that they are sympathetic to NICRA's claims and against the Stormont system ('Fed-up' IR 1.5.69), although happily 'Protestant Unionists are undoubtedly spreading disgust throughout Britain by their persistence in effectively nailing the despicable falsehoods broadcast by the offshoots of dissension' (Harry C Higginson CDS 16.10.70). The *Londonderry Sentinel*, among others, reveals striking continuities with the past, with its assertions that the British people are on the Protestant side, while always 'beginning' to see the truth:

> more and more people throughout Britain are now regarding the present unrest as a continuation of the campaign of the marching men of the civil rights movement – and as part of a mass operation to overthrow the State of Northern Ireland (LS 13.5.70).

Their opinion is important when they support Protestants, for example, when a private letter from the English editor of a monthly magazine praises Ulster and Paisley ('An editor's room mate' PDN 4.9.70), and it is still necessary to counteract anti-unionist propaganda on the mainland:

> Parliamentarians and not least those who teach in the schools must get down to the business of instructing our friends across the Irish Sea just what the real Ulster is like and what it thinks, not what destructive minds are conjuring up to destroy not only Northern Ireland but the very heart of Britain itself (PDN 26.11.71).

A special approach is required:

Modern communications ensure that the speech in the Ulster Hall is heard just as clearly in the Surrey living room, and all who speak in Ulster's name have a duty to remember that they are addressing both audiences. The Ulster audience must realise that the leader who shuns colourful oratory and presents himself as a statesman will convince Britishers as well as locals, who shouldn't need convincing anyway (OS Jul 1974).

British support is valuable not only for its practical help but also for its effect on Protestant morale:

> The loneliness of the Unionist Britisher which he/she felt when the Anglo–Irish Agreement was ratified has been lessened by the support we are receiving from England and Scotland, from among others 'The Friends of the Union' and the Loyal Orange Institutions of Scotland and England (OS Nov 1986).

The age of the opinion poll has brought Protestants little comfort. Disturbing evidence was early explained away as 'several new devices in psychological warfare such as the rigged opinion poll' (Kennedy Lindsay OS Aug 1973). It is only a 'relatively small but highly vocal section who from time to time have clamoured for a withdrawal from Ulster' (NL 3.2.75); but sometimes doubt sets in:

> The fact must be faced that for the vast majority of the people of England, Scotland and Wales, the financial state of the country and its industrial problems are of much more moment across the Channel than Northern Ireland's concern to remain part of the UK and be saved from the possibility of being landed into an all-Ireland republic. Northern Ireland is on the fringe of the General Election in so far as it affects the rest of the UK and, alas, it seems to be increasingly clear that Northern Ireland is, herself, on the fringe of the other UK countries (LS 27.2.74).

The paper reverted, however, to the position that the British were on their side (LS 17.4.74).

Others were less sanguine. The television coverage means that 'we have no friends in England now' (Jack Redmond PDN 31.10.69) and some oscillated between claiming British support and complaining of a lack of sympathy among the majority of British people and the '[unfair] verbal attacks of our compatriots in Britain' (OS Jan 1973). British people (like the government and the media) do not care about Ulster people, but only about themselves:

> the most emotive reaction was caused by IRA bombing in England, ... the killing of Army men in Northern Ireland was less

unendurable, and ... the murder of Ulster people came in a bad
third place (NL 11.5.77).

Hence even sympathetic reactions to the IRA campaign in Britain are
often tempered with the comment that the British now know what
it is like in Northern Ireland.

The English as ever have short memories and Ulster support in
the great wars seems to have been forgotten, judging from:

> the abusive attitude of some ill-informed English people in recent
> months ... especially galling to find that many English people
> nowadays appear to have greater sympathy towards Eire than they
> do to the Ulster which stood shoulder to shoulder against the foe
> in 1939–45 ('British and Irish' PDN 14.3.69).

There are grounds for hope:

> The British Government has a short memory, but let us hope that
> the fair-minded British public has not. Surely they must prefer the
> loyalty of a people which has given so much for the mother
> country in two world wars to an evil terrorist group ... Surely
> Britain's honour will triumph in the end ('Fair Minded Loyalist'
> PDN 14.4.72).

British public support for the Anglo–Irish Agreement, however, shows
that it is best to ignore what they think: 'our citizenship, our Britishness, is a fact sealed in blood: it is not in the gift of mainland opinion'
(David Z Crookes BTimes 20.3.86). A letter from Leeds saying the
English people think of Protestants as 'the parasites of Ulster ... bigots
and cranks' brought an equally embittered response:

> what on earth has an Ulster 'loyalist' in common with an Eng-
> lishman? They barely speak the same language and certainly don't
> have too many common cultural links ... Do 'Loyalists' want to
> continue to ally themselves with a country where one's status is
> determined by one's school, one's father's occupation, one's abil-
> ity to speak 'the Queen's English'? ('Disillusioned' LS 22.1.86).

The Downing Street Declaration prompted an Orangeman to declare:

> there has never been a more pertinent time to ask, when will the
> majority of people in Northern Ireland realise that while they
> wish to be British, that the Queen, the Government, and the
> entire opposition in Parliament don't want them as part of Brit-
> ain; add to this the predominant view of ordinary people on the
> street in England, Scotland and Wales that they too want rid of

Northern Ireland, and the picture is very clear, those who are in the majority in Great Britain don't want Northern Ireland to be part of the Union. We can now see what the Downing Street accord really means to the majority in Ulster. In reality it is saying, 'Goodbye Northern Ireland, we are rewarding your loyalty to our Queen and our country by giving you to Albert Reynolds and the terrorists' (Bro Melvin McKendry OS Feb 1994).

Along with the growing sense of alienation from the British people, a variety of explanations was advanced. They are 'deceived by their political leaders' (NL 19.11.85). It is in their character arrogantly to assume that the English know best: 'a typical Englishman ... just cannot bear to let people manage their own affairs without English interference' (Mary I L Thornberry CDS 9.5.69). The Protestant message has failed to get across because 'there is a mental block when Englishmen think about Ulster which prevents them from ever really understanding what is happening there' (OS Dec 1977).

These are hardly new claims; but there is a new emphasis on moral decline in Britain and a 'loss of national character' (OS Mar 1978) which has erased patriotism and a serious attitude to life: 'The minds of the British people are occupied with trivia, thus diverting their attention from the really serious national problems' ('Another WASP' OS Mar 1980). Moral decline includes trade unionism which 'governs down-at-heel Britain with its teeming hordes of pseudo communists' (R H Atkinson IR 29.4.76), a perceived breakdown in law and order, and the legalisation of homosexuality: 'What have the good people of Ulster in common with these perverts? The English used to be a great nation but they have gone bad' (Gerald Hardy IR 12.3.81).

Reasons for this decline are not hard to find. There are too many Irish people in Britain, and many of the pro-IRA English are of Irish extraction (OS Nov 1976). As claimed in 1912, there is the growing influence of Roman Catholicism: 'Britain's downfall began when the Church of England started to bow the knee to Rome, and kiss the Pope's ring' ('Keep Ulster Free' IR 14.1.82); but simultaneously 'In England, one sees a whole generation of young atheists' (Carola Peck LS 6.12.78). Britain has then declined from a mighty imperial power to a semi-pagan state not unlike those she had colonised: 'religiously, Britain is a mission field which needs Christian evangelism' (OS Jul 1982).

MODERATES ARE MORE prone to attribute importance to British thinking, and advocate courting mainland opinion, whether to keep up the level of troops in Northern Ireland or to show them how attached Protestants are to the Union, for politicians 'reflect to a large degree the feelings of the people who returned them' (PDN

16.1.76). The people of Great Britain are not fond of Northern Ireland, so if 'Ulstermen and women [are] rapidly becoming the lepers of Western Europe' then they need to refurbish their image (IR 4.7.74), and Paisley's call for a mainland referendum is simply too dangerous an exercise in democracy to pursue (PDN 19.12.80). Yet the British are not the only people with short memories. When a *Guardian* opinion poll found that only 18 per cent of the 'ordinary people of Britain [saw] the province remaining part of the United Kingdom in the long term', the *Belfast Telegraph* seemed to think this was a change in British opinion, 'which has always gone along with government support for the union' (BT 10.11.93).

When considering why the mainland British are so ill-disposed, some reasons are shared with ultras. There is their ignorance, their propensity to believe republican lies and their gullibility:

> The foolish English cannot believe that they are disliked and reviled behind their backs: they come over on holiday and believe they are accepted on their own merits; when they get a slap in the face they dutifully turn the other cheek. When they are murdered they don't understand (IR 30.8.79).

They are excused to some extent because 'the Ulster Government did not indulge in any form of public relations and had its head firmly in political bunkers dug 50 and 75 years ago' (IR 19.2.70). One solution to mainland incomprehension, advanced by the editor of the *County Down Spectator* from 1970, and supported by some readers, is to have British parties (particularly the Conservative Party) organise in Northern Ireland, to normalise political life and make Northern Ireland like the rest of the UK. That the Conservative Party finally organised in North Down was predictable.

What is inexcusable to moderates as well as ultras is that the British people react against violence only when it happens in Britain or involves British soldiers. The British reaction to the Birmingham bombings evoked a disgusted response from the *Impartial Reporter*:

> the people in England are not as patient, as tolerant nor as law-abiding as the people of Ulster, who endured for more than three years without retaliation intolerable injury from bombs and murders, and were deprived of government, reputation and representation. It took just a few months and two or three killer bombs in Britain to produce a violent backlash in factories and against Irish property. The British public was not going to stand for any nonsense, although they had been content for five years to let the bombers and gunmen run rampant in Northern Ireland ... In the light of what has happened since Birmingham, a lot of hypocritical whitewash has gone down the drain ... In Britain, fortunately,

a hard line against traitors cannot be described as bigotry and repression. It is known as 'the will of the people', ignored at their peril by politicians and free-thinkers and anarchists (IR 28.11.74).

The *Impartial Reporter* and the Portadown papers are again similar to ultras in seeing the British people as having lost their greatness. Under the headline 'The secret of Britain's greatness seems to be lost', the catalogue of complaints includes the 'trendy' legalisation of abortion and homosexuality, the 'steady erosion of former standards and values', attacks on the monarchy, religion and the police, and the claim that '"liberal" attitudes' have led to soaring crime rates, broken marriages, promiscuity, illegitimate births, full prisons, cities unsafe to walk in even in the hours of daylight and vandalism rife everywhere. It is no wonder the 'hardy and industrious Scots' want independence and even regions of England itself want more self-government. Society has become corrupted and weak as well 'and this is reflected in the timid and half-hearted – at best – approach to dealing with terrorism in NI ... the UK is truly a sick society by any accepted standard today'. It would help reverse the trend to return to 'old-fashioned but well tried standards'. Finally Britain needs a Churchill or de Gaulle to restore pride and dignity (PDN 13.8.76). Only one editorial offered an excuse for this decline, that 'Britain, by the expenditure of her energies, wealth and blood' in two terrible world wars, has 'reduced herself to her present struggling status as a world power' (CT 30.6.76).

The British people have their defenders and admirers too:

As one who resided in and has been connected with North Down for over three score years, I advise Mr Preston not to underestimate the intelligence of the average Englishman. To those who aver to be full blooded Unionists but who call Englishmen 'collaborators', 'quislings' and 'foreigners' I say you are not Unionists at all who destroy the Unionist cause (E Devine CDS 26.6.86).

They are reasonable, peace-loving people who are alienated by extremist politicians on both sides in Northern Ireland; but this characterisation is not so much an expression of faith in their good-will as an argument against extremism and for the kind of bridge-building policies favoured by moderates:

how many [here]... would be aware that in England the 'Troops Out' movement is daily gathering weight? And how many would believe that the reputation of 'Unionist' politicians stinks across the water, and that the constant drain of casualties among the forces of the Crown are blamed not only directly upon the Provisional IRA and INLA, but also indirectly upon the moronic intransigence of

'Unionist' politicians? The first step towards reconciliation with British public opinion must be the acceptance of power-sharing and a genuine attempt by all who have influence to build the bridges between moderate Protestant and moderate Catholic (W P Barbour IR 17.11.83).

DESPITE CLAIMS OF kinship with the people of Great Britain, for ultras they are a different and in many ways inferior people, too many of whom do not share ultra values. This is typical of settler ideologies, which, while claiming to draw their virtue from their metropolitan origins, fear and denigrate changes in that metropolis, particularly when they are seen to threaten the existence or position of the settlers. Moderates, however, tend to see themselves as reasonable, genuinely tolerant people, similar in this to the people of Great Britain but with the added element of understanding their local situation in a way that those outside can never do. The prime divergence between moderates and the British lies not so much in political values as in the determination of the former to preserve the Union.

8 An Acceptable Level of Violence or Peace at any Price?

FOR MANY YEARS, a major feature of the situation in the north of Ireland has been the rationale behind retaining the draconian powers of the Civil Authorities (Special Powers) Act, when from 1922 onwards there was no revolt, and even the IRA's 1956–62 resurgence failed for lack of Catholic support. In other words, Catholic pressure was insufficient to explain the excessive concentration on internal security. Boyce (1979:40) explains this in part by the fact that the Royal Irish Constabulary (RIC) had always been an instrument of government policy, a role inherited by the RUC, and in part by the preference of the Unionist government for the 'security' response to the 'due process of law' response, a stance supported by Protestants generally. Farrell (1983:280) explains it by the desire of the rank and file, and of leaders like Dawson Bates, to preserve Protestant domination. Many other observers have contrasted the political values of Northern Ireland with the more liberal ones of Britain, without stating the obvious: that the very existence (whether active or passive) of Catholics and the Republic of Ireland in itself posed a threat to the six counties that did not affect Britain.

This contrast between the preference for quick effective action against those defined as the enemies of the state over the neutral concept of the rule of law has been described in chapter 1 as typical of settler societies; so particularly relevant to this study is Weitzer's (1990) comparison of Northern Ireland and Rhodesia. He conceptualises both territories as repressive internal security settler states, that is, where security was oriented towards internal rather than external foes. Repression in both involved not only coercion but the serious and systematic violation of civil and political rights; in Northern Ireland this was so far-reaching that the South African prime minister in 1963 expressed envy of the legislation that made this possible. When settlers lost control, however, Northern Ireland alone was 're-colonised' by the metropolis, and according to Weitzer, security policy under direct rule has been much more benign than under Stormont, being subject to checks and balances previously absent.

Certainly the British began by claiming that the role of the security forces was neutral between contending parties; but this perception is not one that many Catholics would accept today. The IRA, better armed and organised than before, is a greater threat than in the past, both in Northern Ireland and in Great Britain. Security legislation has not become any less draconian and the abolition of trial by jury for offences against the state (plus non-political armed robbery) has made the system even more illiberal. It is true that the Diplock Report had implied that the violence was a manifestation of deep-seated political grievances; but the Gardner Report, which recommended ending both internment and special category status for those convicted of politically-motivated offences, implied that the violence was to be treated instead as a wave of serious crime. This criminalisation of the conflict did not, however, lead to the restoration of 'normal' legislation or policing. Nor did it isolate the 'criminals' from their community, as the success of Sinn Féin has shown.

On the other hand, as a member of an international community in the age of television, the British state has to be seen to observe certain limits on its military action. Furthermore, whatever Catholics in republican and nationalist areas might perceive, from the ultra perspective British security policy has been just the same as it has been in previous conflicts against nationalist insurgency in Ireland: inept and half-hearted, typified more by words than by action. There are then considerable continuities observable between the 1919–21 period and 1969 to the present, and the 1939–45 period is also relevant.

The 1912–21 period is particularly interesting in its foreshadowing of later arguments about security policy and their implications. There is clearly a correct way to deal with Protestants and a different one for Catholics, each arising out of their assumed 'characters'. In particular the imaginary portrait of Catholics as violent and requiring firm treatment lies behind the 'reluctant' acceptance of the most extreme measures, including the suspension of the civil liberties which Protestants claimed to cherish. Hence government policy was consistently criticised when it was humane and praised when it was 'firm'. There is also the matter of defining the situation: was this a war or merely a campaign against criminal 'outrages'? If it was a war, extreme measures were justified because wars are customarily all-out affairs; but at the same time this definition gives the enemy a certain status and a right to negotiate a peace settlement. Whether it was war or not, however, it is Catholics who are responsible for everything that happens, including things that happen to them, in contrast with Protestants' views of their own illegal actions.

Clearly the view of the British Army's role in Ireland varied according to circumstances. It is being used correctly when putting down Catholic riots in Falls and Cullingtree in 1907 but not when protecting Winston Churchill speaking for Home Rule or intervening when Harland and Wolff workers drove out Catholics in 1912, and certainly not when liable to be used by a Liberal government against Protestant rebellion:

> the country must now have a correct appreciation of what the claim to use the Army to enforce Home Rule would mean. It would mean, under the Parliament Act, bureaucratic rule resting upon militarism – the worst form of governmental tyranny known to civilisation. It would destroy all freedom; it would wreck the United Kingdom; it would disintegrate the Empire (NL 25.3.14).

On the other hand, militarism was acceptable when putting down Catholic rebellion and executing the rebels: 'Fortunately for the friends of lasting peace in Ireland the Irish government is no longer in charge ... The military have possession, quite a different matter' (LS 6.5.16). Once the government was back in charge, however, it commits the faults it was accused of again later, such as releasing prisoners against Irish Unionist advice, giving those still in prison good food and refusing to deal with 'mobs' and 'spouters'. Its proper role is again fulfilled from 1919, when its deployment was euphemistically called 'Lord French's determination to change the conditions in Ireland for the better ... [with] tanks ... field-guns and gun-carriages' (LS 5.6.19). 'Militarism' and the destruction of 'all freedom' were now considered right and necessary, as is shown by unionist editors' support or advocacy of the 'proclaiming' of Sinn Féin, that is, the banning of a political party and suspension of the freedom of speech which has been partly responsible for all the trouble; a refusal to release detainees on hunger strike; internment, that is, imprisonment without trial, and setting aside the law; and the establishment of concentration camps. A 'regime of firmness' (LS 27.11.19), in contrast to the previous 'years of weak government and perpetual concessions' (BT 14.4.20) which have led to similar problems in India (PDN 4.9.20), is the entire answer to the problems in Ireland and 'if order cannot be restored by ordinary means, then extraordinary means are not only necessary but essential' (BT 14.4.20).

Once again, however, the British wrongly place political considerations above military ones. In a foreshadowing of the modern argument that the security forces' 'hands are tied', it is regretted that the Commission which condemned General Dyer's action in shooting dead unarmed Indian civilians has had the result that, in dealing with riots:

> military men, and sometimes police officers, have to think of their official future. They realise that so long as it is possible to be court-martialled or sat upon by a Commission for any action of which the politicians may happen to disapprove, there is greater

safety in following the line of least resistance than in showing outstanding activity (LS 1.6.20).

English MPs were criticised for complaining about detention without trial (BT 14.4.20), and government proposals in which 'there is to be no martial law and nothing in the shape of military coercion' (LS 20.5.20) are wholly inadequate. Having advocated such 'firmness' as the only means of stopping the violence, the *Londonderry Sentinel*, however, no doubt unintentionally, contradicted itself when, reporting on the hanging of Kevin Barry, it commented that 'the firmer attitude of the authorities ... is responsible, no doubt, for the fresh outburst of criminality reported to-day from various parts of the country' (LS 2.11.20).

The course of events involved much more, however, than such policy decisions. The behaviour of some of the British troops was criticised both in Ireland and in Great Britain. In the unionist newspapers, on the other hand, such behaviour was deemed deplorable, perhaps, but understandable, as when Shropshire soldiers wrecked shops (LS 11.9.19). An early defence that killings by the army do not constitute murder because 'soldiers do not shoot down any person except when they are first attacked' (LS 10.6.20) was not repeated once British army reprisals, at first unofficial but later ordered by military authorities, became known. When Protestants in Derry 'took revenge' for the IRA killing of two policemen the *Londonderry Sentinel* disapproved, in part because 'the burden eventually falls on the ratepayers' (LS 9.11.20), but its consequent statement that it had always condemned reprisals is demonstrably false: rather, the editor saw them as regrettable but justified when they attained the proper ends. This editorial following the official (though as it turned out temporary) banning of reprisals is typical:

> Reprisals are exceedingly unpleasant things. They savour of warfare in savage or half-civilised countries. It is not infrequently the lot of British officers to have to order the destruction of villages which are known to be concealing malefactors. The method is the only one possible. It does not always bring the malefactors to light, but it shows the community that crime cannot be carried on or connived at with impunity. It is deplorable that the sort of warfare suitable to untutored populations should be thought necessary in Ireland ... If reprisals are to be condemned, as they undoubtedly are, however easily they are to be understood, at all events it can fairly be claimed that they have proved effective in many instances (LS 19.10.20).

Hence killings by the IRA are 'cowardly assassinations' but reprisals are 'regrettable but perfectly understandable in the circumstances' (LS 2.11.20); and deeds which are too much even for the *Londonderry Senti-*

nel to countenance are 'the few misdeeds of some frenzied policemen' (LS 21.10.20). Another editor did not even pay lip-service to the notion that reprisals are regrettable:

> There is an active section of opposition Radicals who think they can make political capital by denouncing what they regard as the errors of the Crown forces in the suppressing of outrage in Ireland. It is true that, when their attention is called to it, they disclaim all sympathy with assassination and incendiarism as political weapons; but it is only when they think that the soldiers or police have made a mistake that they show any real gusto ... [They] do not seem to realise how many homes in their own constituencies have been bereaved in the process of putting down outrage, and how hot is the indignation against not merely the perpetrators of crime, but against all who seek to make the task of dealing with it more difficult (BO 10.6.21).

This raises the question of the status of the conflict – war, rebellion or 'outrage'? – and of the IRA – soldiers, rebels or criminals? It is not usual in a democracy legally to take reprisals against the family or neighbours of 'the perpetrators of crime' or to burn down the houses of their supporters, and in defence of reprisals the terms 'war' and 'warfare' are appropriate. Yet the claim by Sinn Féin and the IRA to be at war with the British government was disputed, since they used this claim to justify murder, and (as in the above quotation) they were defined not even as 'rebels' but as 'criminals'. Perhaps Protestants' own rebellion 1912–14 glorified the term 'rebel' too much to apply to Catholics; equally, since Home Rule was still thought an evil to be averted, it could be claimed that one should not negotiate with 'criminals', as Lloyd George did: 'It is the gunmen who have made the opportunity, and therefore any terms made could only be regarded as concessions to that cruel gang' (LS 7.12.20). The term 'criminal' also implies a lack of motive, for crime merely arises out of criminality and does not have to be explained. Coercion then is no more than a legitimate response and the responsibility both for the 'crimes' and the British 'repressive measures' (LS 20.4.20) lies with the 'criminals': 'the plain truth [is] that the criminals themselves and those who shield them are responsible for the military and police action' (LS 3.7.19). When six 'criminals' were executed under martial law in Cork, it was feared that this would make peace more difficult and it is 'very deplorable that young Irishmen should have to be shot' but 'if there were no murders there would be no executions' (LS 1.3.21).

Thus the ritual pattern of Catholic criminality as well as the legitimate Protestant 'reaction' described in chapter 6 was laid down for the coming century, as was the advice to be tendered to British governments who do not fully share these perceptions.

BRITISH MILITARY ACTIVITY in Northern Ireland in the 1939–49 period was limited to the use of the ports and the stationing and training of troops there during the 1939–45 war. Nevertheless the resurgence of the IRA and its 1939 bombing campaign in England brought Ireland to British attention. The English reaction to this was carefully monitored, and it was noted that sections of the press proposed kid-glove solutions for dealing with the IRA. There were also lessons to be learned from Britain's handling of the conflict in Palestine in 1946–47, and the later claim that 'the British Government is dealing with these Jewish terrorist organisations with kid glove methods' (IR 27.6.46) was an unconscious precursor of complaints about the British military involvement in Northern Ireland from 1969. Another British response to the IRA bombs was the July 1939 Prevention of Violence (Special Provisions) Bill, providing for the registration of all Irish people in Britain and the power to deport suspects, which was 'rushed through' Westminster (LS 29.7.39), and formed another precursor of modern complaints that Westminster takes most seriously attacks on the mainland.

One editor, however, tried to understand why seventeen MPs voted against it on the second reading:

> It may be said that this legislation is not entirely free from the danger of excluding or expelling from the country some person or persons, who might thereby have a grievance, though we may be quite sure that it will be administered with every desire to prevent this happening. The danger, however, cannot be regarded as in any way commensurate with the peril we should incur if we did not take the necessary steps to see not only that these acts of terrorism receive condign punishment, as they have in the past, but that we are armed with the means of preventing them (BO 28.7.39).

The special security measures available to the Northern Ireland government had frequently been criticised as discriminatory by nationalists and the Irish government. Hence the IRA bombing campaign in England in 1939 was undoubtedly useful to the Stormont government as 'vindication before the world of the action it felt compelled to make recently in the internment of a group of Irish Republican Army leaders' (BT 17.1.39).

The *Londonderry Sentinel's* editorials on the IRA reveal many of the contradictions observable in the modern period too. A constantly recurring theme is the retention of the emergency or 'special' powers which Northern Ireland, despite the claim that it 'successfully crushed the Republican criminals' nineteen years ago (LS 7.2.39), is 'forced by circumstances beyond her control' to keep ready to use against the IRA (LS 21.5.46). The old adage that 'England's difficulty was Ireland's opportunity' still held as far as the IRA was concerned, and as the war in Europe drew nearer it was perceived that in addition to 'the rather minor powers of the Special Powers Act' (LS 18.7.40) an adequate garrison against the IRA threat must remain as it always had. The IRA campaign did indeed move back to Ireland and continued during the war, lending support to Mr Justice Megaw's suggestion that 'it is well worth considering whether the law of treason and treason felony should not be regarded as applying to that body' (LS 18.7.40).

The IRA was seen as such a threat to the state (however defined) that legislation which was far from 'minor' remained in force, permanently backed up by a resident British Army garrison. It might be thought therefore that the IRA constituted a rebel movement or an opponent in war. Unionist propaganda certainly raised the possibility of an Irish war:

> If Britain is ever tempted to weaken her garrison here, then the menace from the South may take actual shape in the invasion of the North ... the Ulster people ... must be organised not merely in Belfast and its environs, but throughout the province and along the border (LS 14.12.39).

Such a characterisation of the situation, however, confers a degree of legitimacy. After all, the quoted IRA defence of their actions was that '"every shot fired in the war of independence was legitimate warfare to drive the enemy out of Ireland"' (LS 11.4.39). This Protestants were always at pains to deny, preferring to denigrate IRA members as 'criminals'. The difficulty of this position is apparent in the following:

> The soldiers of the Irish Republican Army belong to an illegal body and are not really soldiers at all. They wear no uniform and do all their criminal work secretly and by subterranean methods, using bombs and bullets and high explosives under cover of darkness ... The Ulster Government is up against ... nothing less than a rebellion staged on the lines of the 1916 revolt, in which, no doubt, many 'innocent' people in Northern Ireland would participate. To cope with such a menace no steps can be too extreme, and the peace-loving people of Northern Ireland can rest assured that the Government is ... prepared to deal with any and all eventualities (LS 17.1.39).

On this reading IRA activity is a complicated mixture: a rebellion, carried out by criminals, supported by much of the civilian population and properly subject to the most extreme measures (which are not, however, specified but certainly were meant to go beyond the sanctions of criminal law). The *Londonderry Sentinel* often repeated its allegation that IRA members were not really soldiers on the grounds specified above, thus affording a nice comparison with later admiration for resistance movements in Europe who 'strike in the dark for the cause of liberty' (BO 19.6.42). It is also pointed out that 'the alternative to the present Government is not a different party, but a different Constitution' (BT 12.6.47), which argues against the 'criminal' label for anti-state activities. These contradictions in the discourse about the IRA were neither new nor destined to disappear.

Another continuity with the present lay in reactions to an attack on Stormont's security policy by some Westminster MPs in 1947–48, which reawakened suspicions of the metropolis. Northern Ireland might have won plaudits for its role on the Allied side, but the debate on the Northern Ireland (Extension of Powers) Bill gave Labour MPs hostile to the Special Powers legislation an opportunity to attack it. Prominent among its critics was the Labour MP Geoffrey Bing, a native of County Down, but it was still claimed that those against it have 'little or no knowledge of Northern Ireland' (NL 14.6.47). The British government's colonial troubles proved useful again in this argument: 'What Britain is doing to-day in Palestine, is what the Ulster Government had to do in the Six Counties' (IR 12.6.47). The Special Powers Act is 'an Act which nobody likes' (BT 14.6.47), but it was made clear, at least to readers in Northern Ireland, that its ending would be solely the decision of Stormont:

> when ... the country is set in peaceful ways the Northern Ireland Government will give, of its own volition, those reliefs which its Westminster mentors would have it give under pressure and before the area is finally safe from anarchy (BT 28.6.47).

It was unclear, however, when or how it would be achieved. Ultimately it is Britain's responsibility, for it is Westminster which was responsible for partition (Unionists having carefully disassociated themselves from the decision) and it is therefore Westminster which must safeguard Northern Ireland from attack:

> Northern Ireland cannot be expected to remain indefinitely, as it were, a besieged area, subject to periodic attacks which, calling as they do for defensive measures, cause serious interference with her political and industrial economy (NL 6.1.49).

The blame for the necessity for special powers then was laid firmly at Britain's door, as well as at that of Northern Ireland's 'anarchic' elements. It should be noted, however, that the IRA at that time was based in the Irish state – the internal threat was from Catholic nationalists, whether armed or not.

MANY OF THE KINDS of criticism of British security policy shown in the earlier periods – and the contradictions in the conceptualisations of conflict – are also evident in the modern period. The deployment of the British Army in 1969 was at first, it was hoped, a reprise of its historic role in times of strife when, having helped Stormont to restore order, the Army would withdraw, leaving Ulster 'largely, but not entirely, in charge of her own peace keeping' (PDN 22.8.69), a view which lingered on as the 'temporary' emergency continued. The circumstances of this intervention were, however, recognisably different, in that the British government claimed that the Army was to play a neutral role. One aspect of this 'neutrality' was that violent confrontations with the security forces involved not only Catholics but also Protestants. It is not surprising, therefore, that British security policy attracted criticism, from ultras in particular, almost from the first. Considerable alienation from the British state was expressed, in the modern as in earlier periods, long before the term 'Protestant alienation' became popular. Even before the suspension of Stormont, 'it is the many groups of Protestants who are now the second class citizens while the minority – aided and abetted by Major Clark and the Army – rule the majority!' (Campbell McCormick CDS 22.1.71). Traditional British help had become unwelcome British interference: 'Mr Callaghan sent the British Army to inflict upon Northern Ireland certain reforms, at gunpoint' (John Kerr IR 15.4.71).

Since the conflict was not quickly ended, critics can justly claim that British security policy failed. Of interest here, however, are the ideological elements of ultra criticisms. Underlying some of the criticisms are the ancient perceptions that Catholics have no genuine grievances, that they respond only to 'firm' treatment, and that they see government concessions merely as signs of weakness. One long-held perception is that 'it would have been possible to bring the disturbances and the political unrest here to an abrupt end by firmness' (NL 17.3.76). This specifically means firmness towards Catholics: 'If the British Government had shown a firm hand to the rioters in Belfast and Londonderry in 1969 maybe Northern Ireland would not be in the position it is now' ('Londonderry Loyalist' BO 15.3.84). Another perception is that by simply removing certain people 'the enemies of Ulster would soon be routed out and our province could live in peace again' ('Anti-English' BO 31.12.81). Instead British policy has been weak, timid, nervous and vacillating, wholly inappropriate given the nature of the enemy, and characterised by 'inadequate measures, trammelled by inertia and timidity, [which] are no match for armed and resolute wickedness' (NL 23.11.74). This kind of attitude merely gives 'encouragement to terrorists and, without a doubt, that outlook has encouraged the men of violence and the bombers to keep the campaign going' (LS 26.5.76). Even during the 1993–94 'peace process' the government was warned (by the *Belfast Telegraph*, now much less moderate than earlier in the current period) that 'any signs of weakness will be ruthlessly exploited [by the IRA]' (BT 22.12.93).

Some have accused the British government of giving more direct encouragement:

> The chief factor in keeping the campaign of violence going has been the hope given by the Government to the Provisional IRA that their aims may be achieved. This impression has been conveyed ... by a succession of hints from the 15-year Irish reunification proposal by Mr Harold Wilson, to the latest reference ... by Mr Merlyn Rees to closer integration of Northern Ireland with the rest of the UK being 'not on' because of '800 years of Irish history' (NL 7.1.76).

The only Secretary of State popular with ultras is Roy Mason, whose policy is 'resolute and uncompromising' (NL 31.3.79) and whom the *Orange Standard*, in an editorial favouring a Labour government, remembered with affection as 'the only popular Northern Ireland Secretary [who] understood the emotions of Ulster Unionists where the others misunderstood them' (OS Jul 1994); and the most popular prime minister was Margaret Thatcher during the 1981 Maze hunger strike. Otherwise, instead of 'action' the government offers words. Promises are so often broken that new ones are quickly dismissed as hollow.

So the British governments in the current crisis, like those in the 1912–21 period, fail to understand the true nature of Catholics; but not only do they display timidity towards the enemy and fail to 'protect the loyal Protestants' (Beryl Holland CDS 17.11.72), they also display arrogance towards Protestants who do understand Catholics, by refusing to listen to local opinion. Above all, they fail to listen to 'the Ulster Unionist Party, a body whose advice he [Whitelaw] has sedulously refused to accept but whose experience in dealing with irreconcilable terrorists is greater than that of any Government agency under his command' (NL 11.7.72).

The failure is not, however, due only to inefficiency: rather, the reason for British failure to end the conflict is 'the obvious lack of will on behalf of our Government to defeat the terrorist in our midst' (Ulster Service Corps, Portadown Branch CT 23.6.76), whereas, according to DUP MP the Rev William McCrea, 'if the IRA was taken with determination and the will to win, they would be destroyed' (IR 3.3.88). For some the hated Foreign Office is behind this lack of will:

> The government has played around on the margins with a number of short-term 'get tough' measures, but its general 'softly, softly' policies are largely dictated by a Foreign Office desire to placate international opinion, especially in the United States (NL 19.2.94).

Instead of acting, the government is indifferent to the fate of the people of Northern Ireland, leaving them to suffer 'without any aid or succour from the Westminster Government' (Robert Rainey BO 29.6.72). It reserves genuine outrage and decisive action against republican violence in Great Britain. One piece of evidence for this indifference is the aim expressed by Maudling as keeping the conflict down to 'an acceptable level of violence'. Any level of violence is not unnaturally unacceptable and the phrase became notorious, commonly resurrected to explain lack of security action. Nevertheless, it is significant that one of the unionist slogans following the Downing Street Declaration declared that 'the people of Northern Ireland earnestly want peace but not a peace at any price' (BT 22.12.93), which implies that a level of violence is preferable to a united Ireland.

Further evidence of British indifference comes from a comparison with government reaction and rapid security force action following violence in Britain:

The horrified reaction at Westminster, and generally in London ... proves yet again that outrages in the metropolis, or other cities on the mainland, are regarded there in a far graver light than any carried out by the Provisional IRA or INLA in Northern Ireland ... It has been truly said that one bomb explosion in London, or in any other city in England, is worth more to the IRA or INLA than many such blasts in Northern Ireland (NL 21.7.82).

It is clear that there is no 'acceptable level of violence' on the mainland. Of course, IRA activity in Britain can be useful. One editor saw the bright side of the Old Bailey bombing:

We are not, surely, to be regarded as selfish or heartless if we are heard to pray that, out of yet another day of death and devastation, the people of Ulster, as well as the people of Great Britain, may expect to draw benefit from the introduction of more resolute Government action (NL 9.3.73).

There was suspicion that the 1975 IRA ceasefire might not be, as claimed, unconditional, and some wondered about 'the pressure there might have been from Whitehall to get the bombing of London stopped at all costs' (NL 10.2.75), as if life were 'cheaper across the Irish Sea' (PT 23.3.74).

A few advanced more sinister reasons than mere English arrogance and incompetence: the failure in security policy is deliberate, because the British government is pro-Catholic and secretly working towards a united Ireland. There has been a 'deliberate failure over several years to enforce the rule of law in Ulster and to afford protection from murderous attack' (Ernest Baird CDS 4.1.74).

For some ultras this 'deliberate failure' is part of a secret design:

> As I write I just feel heart-broken at the way the British Government is dealing with the situation in Northern Ireland ... a warning ... to all my fellow Protestants ... they are on the edge of a united Ireland ... do not be brain-washed that the British Army is over in Northern Ireland to protect the Protestants from the so-called IRA, because they are not. Everyone should know what lies under the carpet between Mr Heath and Mr Jack Lynch ('Fermanagh Protestant' IR 10.8.72).

That the IRA and republican areas generally obtain favourable treatment in security matters is a recurrent theme:

> It is quite evident that two laws are in operation in the United Kingdom against the Irish Republican Army. Across the water the authorities are out to defeat, disarm and destroy the IRA, hence the arrests of many IRA suspects over the holiday period and the deportation of two others to Northern Ireland ... The Government have decided to defeat the terrorists and have evidently the will and purpose to achieve their defeat. A different law operates in Northern Ireland. The Secretary of State here has no intention whatsoever of either rejecting the objectives of the IRA, a United Ireland, or of destroying them as a terrorist force ... Now he has further demonstrated his policy of peace at any price by refusing to detain those who have been deported from England as IRA terrorists. He has thus established the principle and precedent that deported terrorist suspects from England can be dumped in Northern Ireland without any fear of police action being taken against them (PT 4–17.1.75).

Other ultras have seen evidence of a British pro-Catholic bias in security matters, beginning in 'that disastrous Wilson period, in which blatantly sectarian policies ... were inflicted upon this Province by Westminster at the expense of the security of the whole community' (NL 22.9.72). 'Ulsterisation' and the arming of Protestants in the UDR and RUC has not changed this view. The comment on a speech by Secretary-of-State Whitelaw, in which he told an American audience that if British troops were withdrawn, Protestants would massacre the Catholics, contained no denial of Whitelaw's assertion but simply declared:

> The fact that since 1969 British troops have been so engaged in defending Republican strongholds and R.C. Churches is a basic reason for the stalemate and mounting deaths and destruction. If they had been used to seek out and destroy terrorism they would have won long since (OS Apr 1973).

One example of a biased security policy was the continued existence of Catholic 'no-go' areas, where the army and RUC did not penetrate. That these were allowed to exist from 1969–72 and again in 1975 aroused high indignation. The Army should 'go into all areas of the Queen's realm and restore law and order' (Campbell McCormick CDS 10.4.70).

Catholics then receive gentle treatment despite being the cause of the conflict. The needs of Protestants, on the other hand, are neglected:

> What a commentary that, after the months of demands for greater security and more troops had fallen on deaf ears, the Government was able to rush upwards of 1,200 more soldiers to the Province at the week-end because of the possibility of the strike! (LS 4.5.77).

Criticisms also bring to light certain significant contradictions rarely, if ever, addressed by ultras. The first four are directly linked, in that they raise questions about the role of the British state in Northern Ireland. First, to what extent is the British Army seen to have an integral, as opposed to an occasional *'deus ex machina'* role, in policing Northern Ireland? Units were always stationed there, but were deployed only at the request of the nominally subordinate Stormont government. Secondly, can the insistence that Northern Ireland is an integral part of the United Kingdom be reconciled with the protests against the Hunt Report, which was perceived to be both inappropriate to Northern Ireland's particular situation and a usurpation of local decision-making? Thirdly, how, in a constitutionally unitary state, could calls for the Army to be directed by Stormont be justified? Fourthly, what is the British Army supposed to be doing in Northern Ireland? It was sent in ostensibly as a peacekeeping force, but ultras perceive its role solely in terms of defeating the IRA and other republican para-militaries and protecting Protestants, not of protecting Catholics or controlling crowd behaviour in general. So how does this fit with stated aspirations for future peace in Northern Ireland? Fifthly, is the conflict a war or merely a police action against criminals (who happen to espouse republican politics)? Ultras often contrive to hold both views at once.

The first of the contradictions outlined above involves the status of the British Army in Northern Ireland. Despite the perception that the Army's role in Northern Ireland was (initially, at least) temporary and therefore by implication an external force, republican hostility and British public and media doubts necessitated a strong insistence that the Army belongs as much to the people of Northern Ireland as to Great Britain: 'it was not some foreign body who was coming to help nor was it simply the officers and men of the British Army – it was our army for we are part and parcel of Britain and what is hers is ours'

('Loyalist' BO 21.8.69). However, within a few months of its arrival on the city streets and for some years thereafter, the competence and behaviour of the British Army was questioned. Some of these criticisms were relatively sympathetic towards British soldiers, but one writer suggested it is 'naive to think that there are no soldiers with Fenian sympathy in the British Army' (Beryl Holland PDN 16.4.71) and later declared that 'the once great British Army is incapable of defeating the IRA' (Beryl Holland CDS 6.9.74). The Army has clearly failed in its historic role in Northern Ireland. The general perception seems to be that the Army's proper role is that of swift, decisive and successful reaction in situations that are beyond the local security forces' control, followed by withdrawal.

Secondly there is the matter of the 1969 Hunt Report. Having 'our army' merely as an adjunct to the Stormont government was clearly the preferred option, but the Hunt Report recommended a wholesale reorganisation of Northern Ireland's own security forces, on lines closer to the British model, with an unarmed police force. It was the Stormont government which accepted the Report, and this no doubt explains why it received a mixed reception from the unionist press rather than wholesale condemnation. In some quarters there was qualified support, but this was quickly transmuted to criticism after the loyalist riots which followed. After that, it was held to be ill-timed and should not have been accepted by Stormont without public debate, for elements in the Report aroused 'fears and suspicions and apprehensions' (LS 15.10.69). These negative feelings, which, it was claimed, had led to loyalist violence against the security forces, were the ones that became typical and within a few months the criticisms of the Report in general mounted, ranging from claims that it was due to 'the stupidity of well-meaning fools' ('Disillusioned Moderate' IR 11.11.71) to the declaration that 'it was only when our defences were deliberately smashed by Westminster that the floodgate was opened for the terrorist, the anarchist and the criminals' (NL 25.3.72). Criticisms of the Hunt Report's recommendations can still be found over a decade later ('An Independent Unionist' IR 12.11.81). The UDR, intended as a non-sectarian replacement for the all-Protestant USC and forming a regiment within the British Army, did not at first attract much ultra support, being criticised on the grounds that it was controlled by Westminster and that it refused entry to certain loyal Protestants while failing to exclude members of the IRA. This evoked the comment that 'the name of the regiment should be changed to "The Regiment for the distruction [sic] of Ulster"' (Beryl Holland CDS 6.2.70). The disarming and reorganisation of the RUC, whose Chief Constable was now to have served previously in Great Britain, attracted less criticism (and in any case it was later re-armed). One editor reported that in the train of the disarming of the RUC 'has come a stronger link than ever between Northern Ireland and Britain'

(LS 15.4.70), but this was not a typical reaction from those ultras who commented on this aspect of the Hunt Report. One editor, for example, claimed that 'the stripping of the RUC of its teeth ... was an act of folly which is equalled only by the surrender of the Irish ports with World War II staring England in the face' (PDN 3.7.70).

The main cause of grief was the disbanding of the USC. The section of the USC which was mourned long after its demise was that of 'our gallant and indefatigable "B" Specials' (John S Davidson CDS 3.5.74) who 'worked unselfishly to secure the country free from terrorism without fear or favour' (The Portadown branch of the Ulster Service Corps CT 23.6.76) and who (unlike the British Army) 'never once shot dead or killed an innocent woman or child, either by accident or otherwise' (Quintin Y Lawson IR 27.4.72). The British Army, 'many of them mere youngsters' (PDN 3.4.70), was no substitute for the 'B' men:

> The IRA are running rings round the security forces. The poor soldiers just do not know the proper way to deal with these thugs, whereas the 'B' Specials had the remedy and everyone could live in peace ('Hopeful' IR 17.6.71).

Whatever the justice in these complaints, the criticisms of the re-organisation of security sit uneasily with claims that Northern Ireland is as British as Birmingham and should be treated in the same way.

A third contradiction involves the political control of the Army. If the United Kingdom is a unitary state, it is logical that its army should be directed by its executive. If, on the other hand, it is correct for the Army to be directed by a subordinate parliament in a delimited region, what kind of state does that make the United Kingdom, and what kind of region does it make Northern Ireland? These problems were not, however, addressed. Instead there were early calls for the restoration of security policy to Stormont's hands:

> The majority of the True Blue Unionists at the grassroots are disgusted with the Government handing over the security of Northern Ireland to Westminster, with Englishmen at the head who know nothing about the problems here (Beryl Holland CDS 27.2.70).

As the military learned efficiency and the level of violence fell, criticisms of Army competence also decreased; but since the conflict was not resolved, it became more apparent to ultras that the real problem was not the British Army itself but its political direction. Hence resentment that the British Army, UDR and RUC are under Westminster, not local, direction continued to be expressed long after the abolition of the old Stormont:

If, as Mr Mason promises, the UDR, RUC and Army strengths are to be increased, this will make little difference to the present ghastly situation. Properly used, the UDR and RUC would be sufficient to obliterate terrorism and restore order. However, while England continues to blunder, this desirable object will never be achieved. We must have again a Parliament of our own, with responsibility for this Province securely in the hands of men who know the situation, and who know how to deal with it, and who can be trusted – Ulstermen (W A Norris LS 11.5.77).

The reason for this dissatisfaction is plain: 'Ulstermen' would have solved the problem, whereas Westminster has clearly failed, and this failure is no accident: 'The Government will find it impossible to convince the people that the Army is not virtually operating with one hand tied behind its back – because of political directives' (LS 11.8.76). The implication is that the military should direct the elected political leaders of a unitary state, and not vice versa. Furthermore, the military should be allowed to fulfil the wishes of a minority in that unitary state over the heads of the majority and the elected parliament.

The fourth contradiction is inherent in complaints concerning the nature of the Army's role in the conflict. Unleashing an army on a population sits uneasily with the notion of an army as a peacekeeping force, and with general protestations that the ultimate aim was to return lasting peace to Northern Ireland. So there was little doubt in some minds as to the Army's role. It was not there to keep the peace and help effect a long-term solution to the problem by reconciling Catholics to Northern Ireland's existence, but to support Protestant determination to retain the status quo, that is, their power as a majority over Catholics. On the Army shooting three Protestants, Paisley's paper commented:

add to them the other incidents involving the Army, deaths caused by British Army vehicles, and the activities of undercover operations ... Add up the Protestant deaths and you will get more than the 'Bloody Sunday' score. Why can't the Army own up to its incompetence and face the consequences? Failure to do so will make worse the dwindling respect the loyalists have for the British Army ('Battlefront Witness' PT 9.2.74).

The Army's job is perhaps then to shoot Catholics, but certainly not Protestants.

This interpretation of the ultra position is supported by their almost exclusive emphasis on Protestant deaths and suffering, giving the impression that only Protestants were affected by the violence. Security force deaths including those of British soldiers were sometimes highlighted and less frequently Catholics are included in the general suffering; but most ultras express concern only about 'Protestant homes plunged into lifelong grief' ('Regular Reader' BO 11.11.82) or other adverse social effects such as Protestants being driven from their homes. The following writer may appear an extreme example, angrily mourning 'the majority of Protestants murdered in their thousands for wanting to remain part of the UK' ('An Independent Unionist' IR 12.11.81). This is not the only example, however, of a skewed perspective. In particular there was a focus on 'the relentless slaughter of Border Protestants' (OS Apr 1983), characterised as 'genocide' (K Loan CDS 11.12.81). Numbers of Protestant deaths were enhanced by including those in the UDR and RUC Reserve as Protestants rather than members of the security forces.

Sidney Buchanan's last editorial for the *Londonderry Sentinel* focuses entirely on the suffering of local Protestants:

> In my early days in journalism there were 'differences' between the Orange and the Green, but there were no occasions when Protestants had so much reason to fear for their personal safety that they were reluctant to visit parts of the city-side of Londonderry ... Nor were there occasions in those days when teenagers carried out concerted efforts to intimidate their victims with fire and paint bombs, tar and stoning attacks on First Derry Presbyterian Church, the oldest Presbyterian congregation in the city, and the Apprentice Boys of Derry Memorial Hall (LS 2.11.83).

In view of this perspective that suffering was a Protestant monopoly, it is not surprising that the Army's role should be seen as support for Protestants; but such a role augurs ill for a lasting peace.

Linked to the issue of the Army's role is a fifth contradiction: the status of the conflict. To the IRA and its supporters the conflict was a war. Judging by some of their recommendations and by the kind of Army action that was most appreciated, ultras agree with this conceptualisation. Internment, typical of war situations, was popular in principle, and the ending of detention was much more unpopular than its beginning. Martial law and a curfew have also been advocated. 'Bloody Sunday', described at the time as not only 'a sad day for Derry [but] also one of the grimmest and most trying experiences the Army has had since it moved in as a peace-keeping force in 1969' (NL 31.1.72), was viewed retrospectively as the right way to deal with the enemy: 'Those 14 people had it coming. They were not murdered. They were rioting – and knew what the consequences would be. They killed themselves – they were not innocent' ('No Surrender' LS 13.2.85). RUC interrogation methods, involving mental torture and physical abuse, were also defended, on the grounds that Northern Ireland's abnormal circumstances dictate abnormal remedies, although one editor attempted to have it both ways by claiming that in any case the injuries were self-inflicted (NL 16.3.79). Certainly government insistence on 'working within the rule of law' was unpopular, unless the law were changed (LS 16.4.80), and the UUP warning that people should not break the law has not stopped 'the murder of innocent Protestants' ('Awake' IR 22.1.87). The Amnesty International Report provided further support:

> it should be studied with care ... precisely because it looks critically at the actions of the paramilitaries ... Those who are so careless of the human rights of the ordinary inhabitants of this province, on a daily basis, cannot be combated without adopting tactics that run close to the legal limits. Occasionally the mark is overstepped by the security forces – as when suspects are shot in the heat of the moment (BT 9.2.94).

What exactly was meant by 'untying the army's hands' was not often explained but where it was, it is clear that it meant launching an all-out offensive on anyone suspected of being a republican paramilitary and treating certain areas as enemy territory: 'the time has gone for a "low profile approach", the time has come to stamp out the violence, to corral those places in which it finds succour and shelter' (NL 22.7.72). The sight of 'known' terrorists walking freely in public with no legal evidence against them has long enraged Protestants:

> Noted IRA men have, at times, been seen openly walking about in extremist Republican areas ... Republican gunmen have paraded here, wearing hoods and carrying weapons ... without hindrance or apprehension by security forces ... Rather than have a ruthless manhunt in known extremist enclaves ... the ordinary Ulster public has been put through the ordeal ... of body searches and other harassments (NL 21.7.82).

The claim that 'extremist enclaves' are not in fact subjected to 'ruthless manhunts' would ring strangely in such areas, which are routinely subjected to these.

Much more extreme measures than capture, however, were called for, and despite Lord Brookeborough's denial that the Ulster people either want or have called for 'savage measures' (LS 16.4.80), there is evidence that measures at least appropriate to a war were popular in some quarters. One man asked: 'why aren't the stone-throwers shot on sight instead of fined? It has been claimed by the IRA that to-day's stoners are to-morrow's bombers. Stones are lethal, the same as bullets' ('Ex-Serviceman' LS 13.6.79). Another reader recommended 'shipping out rebel communities' (William Gerald Hardy BO 2.7.81); and the alleged 'shoot-to-kill' policy raised no eyebrows among ultras. For example, the press officer of the Bangor DUP wrote:

We trust that Mrs Thatcher sees to it either that the death penalty is re-introduced to keep the murderers out of circulation or the men of the security forces are allowed to shoot the enemy on sight (Beryl Holland CDS 16.10.81).

Hence evidence of such a policy being followed, for example, the shooting of two IRA men in the Gransha Hospital grounds, brought acclaim:

Yes, of course the Army undercover unit shot to kill. The two terrorists they shot set forth that morning to kill. It was the Provisional IRA who described the current insurrection as 'a war' and in such circumstances, all is fair. Why shouldn't the Army shoot to kill terrorists? The two Provos killed on Thursday were armed and the IRA admitted they were 'on active service' ... soldiers on active service know what the risks are ... The reason for the latest outcry (not from Sinn Fein, note) is that no-one expects the Army to clamp down on terrorists ... The IRA has been shooting to kill for years. On Thursday the Army beat two of them at their own game. So let's not have any more nonsense about minimum force and so on. It's too much to hope for, of course, but it would be nice to think that this latest episode might discourage the odd Provo from taking to the streets with a rifle ... If they are [shot], it will be as a result of their own evil deeds ('Not Surprised' LS 12.12.84).

An Alliance (APNI) supporter reported that 'more and more ordinary Protestant folk are saying that the only answer is selective counter-killing; the taking and execution of hostages; even "getting one's own retaliation in first"' (W P Barbour IR 22.3.84); and a moderate unionist wrote: 'I could hardly believe my eyes when I read your report of the Bangor DUP calling on Maggie to bomb Dundalk, West Belfast, the Bogside and Dublin' (W J Houston CDS 15.5.86).

Apart from such recommendations there are other signs that the situation is defined as war by ultras as well as by the IRA. One editor was greatly encouraged by 'the disclosure that [Rees] had that day instructed the Army authorities to move on to a military victory over the IRA' (LS 5.2.75). The same editor held that 'the present warfare in Northern Ireland against its people, the guardians of its peace and its property, has been allowed to drag on longer than Britain's last two major conflicts' (LS 18.11.81). It has also been compared with the war in the Lebanon; but most telling are the parallels drawn with the Falklands War. This was the best proof that Britain could defeat an enemy if it really wanted to, and 'similar measures' were advocated in Northern Ireland:

> Pledges of protection that were given to Northern Ireland long before the Falklands landings were never activated yet, within ten or eleven weeks, the intruders in the Falklands have been sub-dued and the threat to the British people has been virtually removed. What a contrast to Northern Ireland where hardly a week passes without a member of the Security Forces ... being gunned down in full view of the public ... The Falklands campaign has proved that the UK has the ability and expertise to deal with plunderers, but why has there been so much reluctance in exercis-ing similar measures to save the lives and homes of 1,500,000 people about 50 miles from the mainland of the UK, compared with about 2,000 people, 10,000 miles away (LS 23.6.82).

The reference to '1,500,000 people', that is, the whole population of Northern Ireland, raises the question of who the enemy was in this war. Apart from the small number in the IRA and their misguided supporters, the government of the Irish Republic is ultimately responsible for the conflict, as well as providing a safe haven for republican paramilitaries, and all agreed that something should be done about the Border. Some held that it should be rigorously policed, with extra troops including the Special Air Service; others that it should as far as possible be sealed, such as the DUP's suggestion of an electronic fence. Again such recommendations fit the idea of a war.

If the conflict was a war, however, then the soldiers were on only one side: republican paramilitaries are 'criminals' and 'evil men', not soldiers; and whereas the measures suggested for catching them are appropriate to a war situation, those suggested for dealing with them when caught involve no more than criminalisation. There were some calls, though not unanimous, for capital punishment, but more commonly the call was for convicted men to be treated like any other criminals and not 'given food which would do credit to the Cuisine of a 4-Star hotel and ... assured that a remission of sentence will mean an early release' (OS Nov 1983). Prison issues loom large at times. The suspicion that the mass break-out from the Maze prison in September 1983 was part of a covert decolonisation attempt by the British government was cited in chapter 2. Appar-ently smaller issues, such as the offer in October 1980 of civilian clothes for prisoners, also raised ultra hackles:

> An act of madness ... taken under pressure from a group of men ... convicted of some of the most dreadful crimes imaginable ... a supreme example of Government weakness in face of criminal

violence, of appeasement to force ... the irresponsibility and crass stupidity of the Government's decision ... the path to peace has been immeasurably made more difficult and the restoration of normal living in the Province has been indefinitely postponed (NL 24.10.80).

Whatever merits there had been in the government's hard-line handling of the 1981 republican hunger strike were negated for ultras by the concessions granted after the campaign ended:

Last weekend Mr Prior flew back to Northern Ireland to see what concessions he could grant the murderers this week and Mrs Thatcher is visiting the wounded and the sick and the families of the deaths created by the supporters of the hunger-strikers on their vicious attack on the Irish Guards (Beryl Holland CDS 16.10.81).

What lies behind this double approach? It is not, of course, unusual to label enemies as 'criminals' or to threaten to try them as 'war criminals' (as in the Gulf War, for example). Nevertheless, war involves an armed contest between opposing states, rulers or parties within a state. The term 'war' implies that the enemy has some kind of political status, and hence there is a possibility of negotiation. It is principally on this point that ultras refuse to accept the logical conclusion of their demands that warlike methods be used: negotiation with the enemy, for whatever purpose, is anathema, and republican militants are therefore 'criminals'. It is no coincidence perhaps that ultras used the term 'war' to define the situation largely when the government was not treating with the IRA. Then the rhetorical advantages need not be missed:

In no other country in the world, stained by the blood of its martyrs and strained by the exigencies of civil war, would a government, whatever its party complexion, be permitted to prevaricate and exercise such a sterile attitude in place of a firm determination to win the battle and the war (OS Nov 1983).

It is, therefore, British government relations with the IRA that arouse the greatest bitterness and indignation. First Wilson and then Whitelaw talked to the IRA. The headline 'Whitelaw's Blackest Hour' introduces an editorial stating that it is 'disquieting ... that Mr Whitelaw should still have to assimilate the elementary understanding that you cannot place trust or confidence in hardened criminals' (NL 11.7.72). Rees made another attempt early in 1975, resulting in an official though temporary ceasefire, because Rees has 'given comfortable assurances to the Provisional IRA' ('Zarah' PDN

4.7.75). There were also rumours of further talks in 1976 and most recently in 1993–94, characteristically denied by the British government and then admitted. It was not the lack of success of these talks, however, but the very fact of talking to the IRA which attracted condemnation at the time and was frequently referred to later. William Ross, MP for Londonderry, summed up the general feeling when he regretted in the House of Commons that 'the Government had not decided "to fight the IRA instead of talking to it"' (LS 28.12.78).

IN SOME RESPECTS there is no clear dividing line between moderates and ultras as regards security policy. Some of the fiercest criticisms come from the Border newspapers of Fermanagh and Armagh, which Protestants perceive as the most dangerous areas in Northern Ireland. Ending the conflict was, not unnaturally, held to be equally important by both ultras and moderates and it was widely held among moderates throughout the period that no lasting political settlement within Northern Ireland, including power-sharing, could be made before it ended. This is hardly surprising in view of the fact that the only political solution the IRA would accept is a united or at best federal Ireland.

Like ultras, most moderates saw no danger in the initial handing over of responsibility for security to the Army, which had been 'suggested by Ulster' and was 'a temporary handing over of responsibility to Whitehall, without any loss of its own constitutional rights' (IR 21.8.69). The *Impartial Reporter*, however, although agreeing with the necessity for reform in Northern Ireland, joined with ultras in judging that this should have been like the old days, when the Army would do its work at Stormont's bidding and then retire to barracks:

> Did the Governments at Whitehall and Stormont make their mistake by bargaining with rebels instead of at once restoring law and order to the few trouble-making square miles of Northern Ireland? The Army should have been placed at Ulster's disposal; law and order restored, and then, reforms discussed (IR 2.10.69).

The corollary, however, of Westminster's take-over of security is that it has borne the main responsibility for restoring peace, which it has patently failed to do. The only paper in my sample which did not criticise British security policy is the *County Down Spectator*. Even the *Belfast Telegraph*, while maintaining its moderate stance, occasionally offered stern advice to the government to improve its performance; but the border counties of Armagh and Fermanagh produced the greatest barrage of criticism. Moderates rarely advocated extreme measures, but some shared the ultra distrust of political considerations and when the *Belfast Telegraph* asserted that 'tighter laws ... should not automatically be ruled out on civil libertarian or, worse, political grounds' (BT 18.3.94) it is clear that the old Protestant monopolisation of a love of civil liberty is in abeyance. Some moderates certainly felt that the political direction of security policy was impeding an end to the conflict, and they reiterated ultra complaints that the government was lacking in firmness and decisiveness, and that action when taken often came too late to be effective. From the Border too came criticisms of the disbanding of the USC and of talks with the IRA. The 'no-go' areas were equally unpopular with moderates and the release of detainees worried those in the Border country.

Moderates also agreed with ultras that the Irish government should be pressured over extradition and cooperation on security, a recent example being the declaration that 'Anti-terrorism should know no sovereign boundaries, and if hot pursuit or direct army-to-army communication is necessary – across the border – permission should be given, (BT 16.3.94). They too deplored what they saw as empty words and promises that efforts would be made to end the conflict, and they shared the ultra impression that the British Government had no will to win. It was accused of indifference and lack of concern to the extent that 'the Ulster people have been left virtually alone, and friendless, to face the full brunt of the terrorism' (PDN 23.7.76). The idea of there being 'an acceptable level of violence' in Northern Ireland was equally abhorred, as was the evidence that mainland violence is of greater concern to the government:

> As long as the shooting and violence is confined to that dear land across the Irish Sea, then nobody gets too excited any more ... But if a small firebomb or a five-pound lump of gelignite explodes in the centre of London, Birmingham, Sheffield, Cardiff or Glasgow, that is not acceptable. All available security forces are on the alert. Leave is cancelled (PDT 28.8.74).

Finally, like ultras, many moderates approved of British prime ministers and Secretaries-of-State who were perceived as effective on the security front.

There are, however, differences between ultras and moderates. In particular the *Belfast Telegraph* over much of the period took a sympathetic view of British efforts to contain the conflict. The paper early perceived the new crisis as differing from the sectarian rioting of the past; the implications were therefore different. This time 'the centre of gravity is ... moving from Stormont to Whitehall' (BT 15.8.69). This paper did not disapprove of this (BT 17.1.72) and it even defended the concept of 'an acceptable level of violence' by interpreting it as meaning merely that the military campaign would be a long haul (BT 16.12.71). Its reaction to Bloody Sunday was also very different from that of ultras:

> The first point to be made is that the march was illegal ... [but] a massive confrontation was fully predictable. The question is: Was it handled well or badly? ... on the evidence so far of civilian deaths on the streets, and the relatively minor injuries sustained by the troops, one is entitled to ask if this time the policy of minimum force was, in fact, abandoned ... unless it can be proved that all 13 of those who died were actively involved in shooting or bombing, the Army will have to answer charges that they over-reacted (BT 31.1.72).

The editor concluded that joint control of security might have been at fault, leaving no alternative but for Westminster to take over complete control of security. Hence the suspension of Stormont was inevitable:

> The last resort has been reached. Mr Heath presented a package which the Northern Ireland Government could not accept, and direct rule is the outcome. It has always been on the cards since August, 1969, when the Labour Government agreed to a request to put in troops. Thus began the conflict between Westminster and Stormont on the handling of security. Internment has not ended the violence, and eventually Westminster was bound to demand greater control over the situation, which Stormont has now rejected. The first point to be made is that direct rule is *not* a surrender to IRA violence. Anyone who thinks that way has no conception of British determination to resist one of the most evil forces which has ever been let loose in the western world. The fact is that the experiment of trying to direct the anti-terrorist campaign through Stormont and Westminster ... failed, partly because Stormont had lost the confidence of a section of the community. A fresh start had to be made, and only Westminster could make it, unencumbered by traditional mistrust ... The second major point ... Far from threatening the link, direct rule in many ways strengthens it. Ulster's founding fathers had no wish for a provincial parliament, open to attack from within ... These are sad days for Northern Ireland, and especially for Mr Faulkner. The Westminster takeover must be regarded as an admission of Stormont's failure to reconcile the communities. Perhaps its job was an impossible one, because of the conditions in which it was created. But recriminations are useless. It is time to make a new beginning, to rebuild the trust which has been eroded over the past few years, and pull together for the first time. Let's prove to a doubting world that Ulster can do it (BT 24.3.72).

Another difference is that, whereas ultras assigned the entire responsibility for security to Westminster and professed that they were prevented from taking a part in bringing peace, moderates were much more likely to assign a role to ordinary people in the search for peace, whether this involved merely being restrained, cooperating with the security forces, taking reasonable precautions, where appropriate joining the part-time forces or simply praying for peace. Local politicians have an even greater duty to play their part, which the Portadown papers in particular feel they are not doing, instead 'sulking in their tents while ... Ulster burns and her people are murdered and mutilated' (CT 24.11.76).

The *Belfast Telegraph*, however, was almost alone in its perception that a military solution is not possible (see, *inter alia*, BT 16.12.71, 8.12.82). This view lies behind the relatively temperate nature of its criticisms of British security policy. It also took a very moderate line on such thorny issues as internment, seeing it on this occasion as not only counter-productive but morally wrong:

> another watershed in the history of Northern Ireland ... ends a system that created intense bitterness, controversy and conflict. Continuing protests, riots and anti-Government propaganda arose directly from a measure which offended all concepts of freedom though many considered it was a necessary evil ... Internment had been tried and tested before, but the conditions of 1971 were vastly different ... It was introduced clumsily and at the start it was used heavily against one section of the community. The burning sense of injustice it created among the Roman Catholic population gave the IRA even more support ... Internment not only helped to create recruits, indirectly it helped to train them ... Some people take the view that the only way to deal with terrorists is to keep them behind bars indefinitely. This takes no account of the moral argument against internment, or of the real difficulties facing a Secretary of State who is conscious of the enormous propaganda value that attaches to internment (BT 5.12.75).

Some moderates did make suggestions for an improvement in security, including improved surveillance of known IRA strongholds, but the implication of most of these calls to catch IRA men was merely that such men should be arrested and imprisoned. Although generally hard-line on security, the *Impartial Reporter* summed up the dilemma: '[to] stamp out the revolutionaries by ruthless military force and shoot any one found with arms or explosives ... [is] not possible in view of the contradiction with British democracy' (IR 4.5.72), adding later that 'everyone must accept how difficult it is to defeat a modern guerilla movement, backed up by declared activists' (IR 3.3.88). There was, however, wide agreement on the question of the Border. Many agreed that something should be done to stop republican militants crossing it so easily.

The main cry from the Border counties of Fermanagh and Armagh, however, was for more troops: 'If necessary the whole British Army of the Rhine should be brought in ... more profitably employed than wasting foreign currency in Germany. They are no longer a tactically significant force' (IR 8.1.76). Other ideas savoured of this implicit perception that it was a war situation. It was variously suggested that there should be martial law, a curfew or at least a car curfew, identity cards and 'a form of internment' (PDT 25.5.84). The term 'war' is used outright too. As the term 'civil war' would imply that Protestants and Catholics in general are fighting there are only a few uses of this term to describe the conflict. More common is the perception that it is simply a war:

Surely there is good reason why an overall security 'Supremo' should be appointed, along the lines of Ulster born Gerald Templer, who brought peace to Malaya in the 1950s after an equally vicious war against Communist insurgents (CT 4.8.76).

Nevertheless, the absence of support for the kind of extreme measures associated with modern warfare suggests that most moderates perceived the conflict in civil war terms. The terms 'criminal' and 'terrorist crimes' were rarely used and these were generally confined to cases where civilians were murdered. In addition moderates tended to be more consistent than ultras, in that some approved in principle of talks with the IRA, and despite its change of direction, the *Belfast Telegraph* decided that 'Sir Patrick Mayhew was justified in carrying on an extended debate with the IRA top brass' (BT 30.11.93). They were not, however, optimistic about the results, and the following conditions have not changed:

In recent days, as the clamour for action on the part of the Government to placate the IRA still further in order to achieve an extension of the cease fire grew to large proportions, there were strong calls by influential sections of the British Press for the Government to have talks with Provisional Sinn Fein ... Peace is the cherished ideal of 98% of the population of the Province, but to concede large scale demands by the Provos, in exchange for dubious benefits of a short time cessation of violence, carries great risks. For real peace to break out there must be an absolute and unconditional repudiation of violence by the Provisionals and an acknowledgement that their campaign has been completely counter-productive (PDT 15.1.75).

As violence continued despite the 1975 talks moderates tended to move to the position that the talks should end.

Deaths from the IRA's role in the conflict did in fact decrease, and whereas ultras continued to criticise the 'lack' of a security policy, moderates frequently gave credit where they felt it was due.

Soldiers and policemen were praised for their 'devotion to duty, the willingness to sacrifice all, and the all-round heroism' (PDN 17.10.75). Improvements in security were often noted, but with the important qualification that 'no stone must be left unturned to reach the situation in Ulster where life and limb are no longer at continual risk' (IR 18.9.80).

General support for British security policy, however, was rare even among moderates and often can be inferred only from an absence of condemnation of the government. The *County Down Spectator*, the *Belfast Telegraph* and a few letter-writers did refrain from blaming the government for events such as the bombing of the Abercorn, the La Mon Hotel and the Droppin Well, in all of which civilians were included in the dead and wounded, and they did not echo moderates in calling for extreme measures. This reaction to the latter is typical:

> To some this means finding scapegoats, issuing bloodthirsty threats and asking for Northern Ireland to be transformed into what would appear to be an armed camp, under virtual martial law. Others, more realistically, accept that there are no radically new solutions to a terrorist campaign which can strike without warning, anywhere, at any time. Everything has been tried, at one time or another, and the most effective means are still in use, painstakingly and quietly getting results in terms of arrests. Dramatic calls for 'selective internment', or sealing the border, or capital punishment capture the headlines, but have been repeatedly rejected, with good reason. Clearly the level of vigilance must be stepped up ... But where the detection of terrorists is concerned, there is no substitute for community cooperation ... The reaction in Britain has been predictably angry, as it was after the London bombings. Force is no way to change British hearts and minds. Each time the killers strike, they simply do more damage to themselves, and their corrupted cause (BT 8.12.82).

Some moderates expressed pain and horror, in a way that ultras did not, at the scale of the conflict, seeing:

> despair ... betrayal, isolation ... anger ... thousands of people scarred in mind ... a whole generation ... raised on violence ... a breakdown in the fabric of Ulster society ... Homes deprived of fathers, mothers, brothers, sisters and even babies. Hatred and bitterness ... rampant on all sides (CT 7.1.76).

Despite the many features that ultras and moderates share in their attitudes towards British security policy and the conflict in general, one notable difference is that moderates, though equally opposed to republican violence, did not claim that it is supported by all or even many Catholics, and in most cases included both Catholics and Protestants as victims in the general suffering: 'Families ... on both sides of the religious divide have suffered so much' (IR 9.4.87). The ultra claim that the Border is the site of a campaign of Protestant genocide was rarely made by moderates, although the INLA murder of Pentecostalists in a prayer meeting at Darkley horrified the *Belfast Telegraph* into calling that an act of genocide (BT 21.11.83). The *Impartial Reporter* for a long time tended to use the word genocide in inverted commas but by 1987 it was talking about 'genocidal acts which continue in our midst' (IR 29.1.87), and on the bombing of the Remembrance Service at Enniskillen, it was stated that 'Protestants ... naturally feel they have borne the brunt of the barbaric violence in Northern Ireland', though this was accompanied by a plea for reconciliation (IR 19.11.87). This paper was to harden its approach further:

> Working-class Protestants without jobs and in poor housing conditions must find it ironic to hear themselves described as the privileged community ... Protestants point out that it is their community which is under constant attack. Evil loyalist paramilitaries have killed innocent Catholics and loyalists are as guilty as their Republican counterparts of evil sectarianism. But the sustained attack from terrorists has come from the IRA, who are trying to bomb, maim and kill Protestants into submission (IR 21.4.88).

Rather than attempt to deepen divisions, the Portadown papers have tended to portray both Protestants and Catholics as essentially calm, patient, law-abiding, peace-loving people who desire only normality and who suffer the current strife with steadfastness and courage.

MANY CONTINUITIES are observable over the three periods and modern claims thus have a history, often spanning the century: that the British offer words not action, and let political directives prevent the military from having a free hand; show a lack of will instead of the necessary 'firmness'; fail to understand the security problems or the true nature of the enemy; refuse to listen to Protestants, who do understand these things; talk to the enemy instead of imposing military defeat; take attacks on the 'mainland' more seriously than those in Ireland; and in many cases secretly or openly aspire to a united independent Ireland. At the same time there have always been Protestants who advocate extreme measures and the suspension of civil liberties, thus treating the conflict as a war while maintaining that it is not.

Although there are also many similarities between ultra and moderate perceptions of British security policy in the modern period, there are significant differences too. For ultras it is a continuation of the age-old conflict between good and evil, that is, between Protestants and their Catholic enemies, a conflict that can be ended only by complete victory for the righteous. Since British security policy has shrunk from all-out war on what essentially means the Catholic population, it is fiercely criticised and its legitimacy questioned. For moderates the strife is seen as one between a tragically divided community.

The contradiction between the ultra conception of the conflict as a war and the labelling of republican militants as criminals is paralleled by the seeming contradiction between the moderate conception of the conflict as a war and their refusal to countenance the kind of draconian solutions advocated by ultras. Ultras would have preferred the British Army to be under Stormont rather than Westminster control. Stormont had always succeeded in the past in putting down Catholic 'trouble-making' and many refuse to believe that the British government should be concerned with its own international image at the expense of the semi-independent status of Northern Ireland under its own government. Ultra claims that Northern Ireland is an integral part of the United Kingdom are therefore contradictory in the light of their resentment at British government initiatives such as the implementation of the Hunt Report, the insistence on Westminster control of the army and the original insistence on a peace-keeping rather than trouble-shooting role.

The ambivalent and hostile attitudes towards the British metropolis revealed by the newspaper data are typical of the settler attitudes noted in chapter 1. Memmi's observation that settlers both glory in the achievements of the 'mother country' and resent its interference appears peculiarly appropriate, as do the settler views of the metropolis as morally decadent and concerned only with its own interests. Settlers typically resent above all metropolitan interference in 'native policy'. This resentment is at its deepest when the metropolis seeks to hand over a degree of power to the 'natives'. Nevertheless settlers seek independence only as a last resort. The British government too has acted on the whole like metropolitan powers everywhere, in holding its own interests paramount, treating its troublesome 'settlers' with contempt when not dependent on their votes or support, and refusing to accept their understanding of the 'natives'.

The newspaper data on violence and security policy can also usefully be considered in the context of wider studies of violence in settler societies. Violence is held to be a normal feature of settler societies where the political incorporation of the 'natives' is resisted, and draconian security policies similar to those of Northern Ireland were evolved in, for example, Rhodesia, instead of a search for an acceptable political compromise. Similarly, ultra fury was aroused by the British Army's role of 'protecting Catholics', just as settler fury was aroused by British protection of the 'natives' in southern Africa, and ultras see the 'solution' to the current crisis solely in terms of the military defeat of the IRA and, presumably, a perpetuation of the 'emergency' legislation which has been in force since the foundation of Northern Ireland. To remain 'under siege' is preferable to sharing power with Catholics or entering a united Ireland. For self-styled moderate newspapers like the *Belfast Telegraph*, on the other hand, sharing power with Catholics within Northern Ireland is acceptable, but the 'peace – but not at any price' (BT 22.12.93) slogan shows that for some moderates too a state of siege is preferable to absorption into an all-Ireland state. However outrageous to unionists was the British resignation to 'an acceptable level of violence', it is clear that for many a continuing conflict is preferable to a united Ireland.

9 Settler Ideologies – Persistence or Change?

THE MAIN THEME of this book has been to show that significant strands of Protestant ideology in the twentieth century can be explained by Ulster's history as a settlement colony, and to explore the extent to which settler ideology has survived, changed or disappeared in modern Northern Ireland.

There have been changes in the structure of Ulster. The six counties have changed from being a part of Ulster, to the self-governing entity of Northern Ireland, to the present condition of 'direct rule colony', whose continuation in the United Kingdom is conditional upon a majority of its people so wishing. There have been demographic changes, with the fall in the Protestant birth-rate relative to that of Catholics. The Catholic population has thus, notwithstanding its greater rate of emigration, increased from about a third to over 40 per cent. The economy has declined and over half the employed population receive their wages directly or indirectly from the British government, while the large numbers on welfare now include significantly more Protestants than formerly. The dominance of the Unionist Party has been broken by the rise of other unionist parties such as the DUP and APNI as well as by smaller splinter parties. Moderates have a much higher profile now, though the NILP has never recaptured the voters it won during the 1940s.

Protestant ideology cannot be treated as if it fed off only internal factors. There are other important actors: Northern Catholics, the British state, the Irish state, and global forces such as the United States of America and the European Union. As well as changes in world power relations, the rapid transmission of information and the arrival of television in so many homes have played their part. The twenty-six counties have changed their status over the course of the century from being an integral part of the United Kingdom of Great Britain and Ireland, through the Irish Free State, to the Republic of Ireland. It is beyond my brief to deal with changes in Northern Catholics and the Irish state, but it is appropriate to review the changes important to Northern Ireland Protestants in the recent history of the major actor, the British metropolis.

The United Kingdom has undergone major changes throughout the course of this century. The world empire it once ruled is lost and hegemony has passed to one of its ex-colonies, the United States of America. Its ability to wage war successfully has been increasingly in doubt since the Boer War, and it has undergone debilitating wars since then. It has become a member of the European Union, subject to legislation made jointly with other members at Brussels. Manufacturing industry and merchant shipping have greatly declined, and British ownership of wealth production has often been replaced by that of transnational companies. While still a wealthy and powerful state, it is no longer in the first rank. At the same time it has steadily increased the franchise in both national and local voting and thus has become a parliamentary democracy, with a strong social welfare tradition among its people. Although the Liberal Party so hated by Ulster Protestants in the Home Rule crises has declined, the equally-detested Labour Party has replaced it; and the Conservative Party which supported the Ulster rebellion has not only formed part of the post-war consensus which engendered the welfare state, but has also produced prime ministers like Edward Heath, who prorogued Stormont, and Margaret Thatcher, who signed the Anglo–Irish Agreement. Religion is a matter of indifference to the majority of its people and few would fight under its banner or understand those who do so. The royal family, raised to a pinnacle of respectability by Victoria, forms the content of popular scandal. In other words, the state to which Irish Protestants protested their allegiance has changed. To be 'British' today does not carry the same connotations as it did at the beginning of the century, and the old certainties of moral superiority are greatly weakened.

Certainly there are continuities with the past. There are still those who yearn for lost power, sovereignty, empire even; and from the Northern Irish point of view, the British government still follows its perceived self-interest while failing to deal with the problems there. English arrogance is still perceptible long after there has ceased to be much to be arrogant about.

While they have recognised the existence of the changes in Britain, ultras are unwilling to accept any changes that threaten the gains made by themselves or their ancestors, whereas there are moderates willing to accept a degree of change. Although there have long been moderates in Ireland, they have become particularly visible in the modern period, perhaps reflecting the unloosening of the shackles of rigid conformism, first under O'Neill and subsequently under direct rule. Ultra perceptions, however, have been collected with ease from all three periods in this study, and these show great similarities with those of other settler societies. They also show great persistence, and comparison of 1912–21 data and that from 1968 to the present shows many telling similarities. A close examination of some self-styled moderates, however, also reveals continuities with the past. The Downing Street Declaration must not repeat the mistakes of Hillsborough in legitimating an Irish dimension: 'most people yearn for peace, but not at any price'

(BT 23.11.93). Sinn Féin is 'fundamentally undemocratic in nature' (BT 14.1.94) and any joint authority must be rejected, although the same paper claimed shortly afterwards that 'devolved institutions here could quickly form North–South links' (BT 14.3.94), a view little removed from that of some ultras. The reform of South Africa led the *Impartial Reporter* to 'despair that too many of our people still fail to live in harmony and prefer to exist in a time warp' (IR 28.4.94), perhaps a reference to the front-page news that the Craigavon Society had been formed as a new group within the UUP, headed by a local councillor well known for his ultra views, and aimed at ensuring that the leadership did not stray from the path of unionism. One editor told me in late 1994 that there had been so little change over the past thirty or more years that it was hard to write editorials now, even on events such as the Downing Street Declaration, touted outside Northern Ireland as a significant breakthrough in the search for peace.

So far as British policy concerning Catholics is concerned, ultras have evaluated British input in almost wholly negative terms. British governments of every hue, except for a short period under Margaret Thatcher, have demonstrated their inability to understand the Northern Ireland problem. On close examination this means inability to understand that Catholics are untrustworthy liars who secretly or openly hate the British and the Protestant faith and want only to reduce Northern Ireland to six counties within an all-Ireland Roman Catholic Gaelic republic. This British failure to understand the true nature of Irish Catholics has, in ultra eyes, serious implications for Protestant well-being: it has led to an inability to handle Catholics as they should be handled, notably in security policy; it has enabled Catholics to manipulate the British into believing that they are discriminated against, and thus obtain preferential treatment over Protestants; and most seriously it has led the British to consider sympathetically Catholic demands for a political voice and to regard the Irish Republic as a legitimate actor, hence putting Northern Ireland back into a dangerous all-Ireland context from which Protestants have assiduously sought to distance themselves from around 1912 onwards. The attempts to end the violent conflict by contacts with Sinn Féin were described disapprovingly by one paper: 'The wooing of Sinn Féin continues, with insufficient attention being paid to the impact on the Northern Ireland majority ... If the process goes on much longer, the danger is that there will be a growing alienation within the unionist community' (BT 25.2.94). In the zero-sum game described by Rose (1971), gains for Catholics can only be losses for Protestants.

Protestant alienation is primarily but not entirely an ultra phenomenon, but it is not a new one. It has been immanent in the situation at least from the late nineteenth century when unionists, threatened by a surge of Catholic nationalism, realised (despite some fighting talk) that in the last resort their only defence lay in the protection and goodwill of Great Britain. The British government, however, has proved that it is unable consistently to take the right line in dealing with Catholics. Those who claim to 'know' Catholics have always advocated coercion, not conciliation, but even Conservative governments have tended to oscillate between the two, and faith in the Conservative Party began to diminish when it agreed to the partition of Ireland, thus breaking its promise to block Home Rule for the whole island. Behind the British government lies British public opinion, formed by an ignorant and biased British press hostile to Irish Protestants.

The establishment of Northern Ireland nevertheless had certain compensations, in that the Northern government was allowed special legislation to deal with disaffected Catholics and was effectively left alone by Westminster, with British government intervention limited to the occasional provision of troops to quell unrest. For many Protestants being 'British' meant in practical terms little more than declaring allegiance to the British crown by volunteering for the British armed forces.

Alienation became most apparent when the British government broke the convention of non-interference and the fickle British public, Northern Ireland's war contributions long forgotten, began, largely thanks to television coverage, to evince distaste for loyalists. Direct rule was for many Protestants the final blow. Being British does not mean a willingness to be ruled by mainland Britain (and especially not by the English). Although this is most obviously a problem for ultras, moderates too dislike much about direct rule. They do not want a return to the Stormont system, but most desire some form of devolved government which would distance Northern Ireland from the kind of policies, often deemed inappropriate for local needs, imposed by the remote government in London. Moderates are perhaps more genuinely 'British' than ultras, in their adherence to the 'British' values of compromise, conciliation, the search for consensus and 'British standards of democracy'; but like ultras they prefer British rule to be confined largely to Great Britain.

There are real differences between ultras and moderates; yet it is hard to disagree with the comment that, whereas proportional representation was intended to bring out:

> the broad centre of Ulster political opinion ... What was not taken into account was that Unionist opinion at rank and file level was united on certain basic principles and ... once there were signs of those principles being eroded the scene was set for the showdown (NL 4.2.75).

For moderates, like ultras, remain committed to a British Northern Ireland.

THIS RAISES THE question of the relative proportions of ultras and moderates. It is agreed by many academic observers that ultras are more numerous than moderates, and that opinion polls are an unreliable guide since 'people express more moderate views than they really hold' (Whyte 1990:4–5). One estimate based on voting patterns is very pessimistic. In the 1974 election when the United Unionist Coalition took 58.1 per cent of the vote, the SDLP 22 per cent, the APNI 6.4 per cent and 'the once hopeful NILP collected a pathetic 1.6 per cent', one editor despaired of the situation:

> The moderate centre made little impact in the latest Northern Ireland election and in prevailing war-like conditions it is unlikely to improve its showing. Too many moderates talk about the necessity of achieving reconciliation, and are not prepared to translate their good intentions into votes. But then being realistic perhaps the moderates only represent six per cent of Northern Ireland's population at present (PDT 16.10.74).

In 1993 the DUP published its document, 'Breaking the Logjam', which advocated majority rule devolution, with a majority defined as 60 per cent. According to the *Belfast Telegraph*, 'The DUP may be seen as extremists in Britain, but if they stood on this manifesto, they would probably get solid endorsement at the polls' (BT 11.11.93).

Is this pessimism justified? Can the proportion of moderates even be counted? It cannot be assumed that all moderates have voted for the APNI, UPNI or NILP, nor that all ultras have voted for the DUP, United Ulster Unionist Council (UUUC) or Vanguard. Those who vote for the UUP can fall into either category. Its candidates include some dedicated to power-sharing, some to modified majority rule, some to full-blown majority rule and some to full integration with Britain. Putting aside all the pitfalls in analysing voting figures, it can be estimated that between 1973 and 1985 the proportion of moderate voters ranged from a low of 13.5 per cent in the Constitutional Convention election of 1975 to a high of 37 per cent in the 1973 district council elections, with North Down, the wealthiest part of Northern Ireland, consistently returning the highest number of moderate votes (Clayton 1993:xiii–xv). The most recent district council elections, in 1993, show that the APNI has retained but not improved its position, but the UUP has moved some way towards power-sharing in adopting the principle of 'proportionate sharing of responsibility'. It remains to be seen whether this is simply a phrase meaning polite majority rule. The election in 1995 of the hardliner David Trimble as leader of the UUP certainly suggests that a majority of the Ulster Unionist Council are ultras.

CONCLUSION

Ireland was Britain's first imperial possession, seized by force and partially settled through English government policy, most notably in the Plantation of Ulster. Northern Ireland is the remnant of the original colony, six counties held back from decolonisation and chosen by Ulster Protestants (the descendants of the original settlers, if not always by blood, then by position in society) so as to give them a substantial electoral majority. The great majority of Protestants are unionists, in the sense of wishing to maintain the formal union of Great Britain and Northern Ireland which forms the United Kingdom. To what extent though have settler ideologies declined, and how far have they persisted?

A large number of Protestants can be classified as moderates who wish to retain British citizenship while living at peace and sharing power with their Catholic neighbours in a reformed but still British Northern Ireland. The majority, however, consists of ultras who wish to retain local power in Protestant hands by a variety of means from constitutional to terrorist. This ultra group is the one which most displays elements of the settler ideology which has been observed in a range of settler societies throughout the world.

Britain is no longer an imperial power, but the dwindling of imperialist aims in the metropolis does not imply a parallel decline in the colonialist ideology of settlers. On the contrary: in areas faced with a combination of native inhabitants demanding power and a metropolis which has lost the imperial urge, the settler mentality is likely to come to the fore. This has been demonstrated in Rhodesia where moderate whites in favour of some degree of power-sharing with Africans were progressively squeezed out of settler politics, and those determined to maintain white hegemony took over imperial power from the metropolis in declaring independence unilaterally. In Algeria, when the French will to hold the territory finally faltered, ultras went as far as to attack the metropolis itself in their bid to maintain their privileged position in the colony. In Northern Ireland too it has been demonstrated that the settler mentality has displayed greater durability than the empire which spawned it.

There are obvious implications arising from this retention of a settler mentality in the light of such changes in the metropolis: the relationship between settlers and the metropolis also changes, and hence the way in which settlers view the metropolis shows a distinct shift. The existence of the Northern parliament at Stormont, effectively left alone by Westminster, did much to exclude the people of Northern Ireland from the process of change which saw Britain's metamorphosis from empire into nation-state (and welfare state) and eventually into European state. These changes were noted, commented on and sometimes mourned; but there was little Protestants could do to obstruct the process. Stormont came to serve for some as a reminder of what had seemed great about Britain, for others as a hindrance for social progress; either way, its presence marked off Northern Ireland as separate and 'different', both in the eyes of its inhabitants and of the mainland British. The replacement of the local parliament by a system of direct rule interspersed with futile attempts to restore devolved government on a basis of sharing power with Catholics has done little to diminish these feelings on both sides of the North Channel, and the Protestant alienation never far below the surface throughout this century has re-emerged. One important element of this alienation has been the worsening economic situation, which has led even some moderates to see the work of the Fair Employment Agency as irrelevant. Following a report that it had found Catholics holding only 27 per cent of jobs in Craigavon Borough Council and only 3.8 per cent of senior posts, in a borough where they constitute 39 per cent, the *Portadown Times* reported:

> perhaps the most telling speech was made by Councillor Tom French. He stressed that no attempt should be made to reverse discrimination by putting Protestants out of jobs to make way for Catholics. We agree entirely with Councillor French, that the main priority is to attract enough jobs to the province, so that allegations about discrimination become of secondary importance. Instead of appearing to concentrate its attention on achieving a balance between the two religions in a situation where employment is diminishing, the Government should be gearing its efforts to bringing more jobs to the province (PDT 7.10.88).

One important strand in this alienation, and the most important for ultras, has been the result of differing perceptions of 'the native question' on the part of Protestants on the one hand and the British metropolis on the other. To Catholics living in areas of high unemployment with daily encounters with British security forces there may appear to be little difference between local Protestants and the British, but as far as ultras in particular are concerned there is a wide gap, and this has been the case on a number of occasions.

On 31 August 1994 the IRA announced 'a complete cessation of military operations' and the DUP reaction was to warn of civil war. Over the next six weeks one Catholic was killed by loyalists and there were at least eight loyalist attacks on Catholics and nationalists. There were also riots in Protestant areas of Belfast. The Combined Loyalist Military Command announced a ceasefire on 13 October. How much has changed since the paramilitary ceasefires? It is still too early to judge, and a ceasefire is not the same as a peace treaty. The economic problems of the region are likely to continue without amelioration. The gap between the unemployment rates of Protestants and Catholics has changed little in twenty years. The gulf between Protestants and Catholics, particularly in working-class areas, has not been bridged, even if there is now more cooperation at local government level. Local democracy has not been restored at regional level and every attempt at installing a power-sharing administration has failed. The DUP rejected the Downing Street Declaration, which Paisley called 'an evil sell-out ... a dagger through the heart of Ulster' (report in PDT 21.1.94). Ultras prefer to call it the 'Anglo–Irish Joint Declaration' to remind its supporters of the hated Anglo–Irish Agreement, but one change in ultra thinking is demonstrated by Gregory Campbell's 'Platform' article in the *Londonderry Sentinel*. The DUP now prefers to believe, not that all Catholics are inimical to the Union, but only at least 70 per cent of them, and the term 'ethnic cleansing' has to some extent replaced 'genocide' as an explanation of population shifts within Northern Ireland (LS 27.1.94). Although James Molyneaux initially accepted the Declaration, the very rumour of cross-border institutions drove the UUP to restore relations with the DUP after splitting over the Declaration, and the publication of the Framework Document in February 1995 ended Ulster Unionist support for the Conservative government. The majority of Protestants, whether ultra or moderate, are no more satisfied with British performance in Northern Ireland than they ever have been since the Dublin Castle system of colonial rule. The British have, as often accused by Catholics as well as Protestants, continued to demonstrate their lack of ability to handle the problems in Ireland and their preference for the pursuit of their own interests over those of the people of Northern Ireland.

The behaviour of many Ulster Protestants, here called ultras, is inexplicable to many Britishers, who see them as dogmatic, old-fashioned, unwilling to compromise or listen to reason, immoderate, prejudiced, hypocritical, politically inept and, despite their protestations of loyalty to Britain, essentially un-British. Moderates, to their distress tarred with the same brush, wish that the British people would be more understanding and sympathetic, that 'past errors, by all concerned, would be consigned to the dustbin of history' (Brian Pendry IR 3.12.87), that Catholics would look only to the future, and that ultras would change their behaviour so that all people of good will, Protestant and Catholic, could work out a political settlement that would keep Northern Ireland British in a way with which everyone would be happy.

Unfortunately history will not go away because it is wished away. Without asserting that Ireland's colonial history is the only salient factor in the situation in Northern Ireland today, it cannot be ignored. To do so omits a vital element in understanding the situation, and without understanding it attempts at solution are useless.

Is there a solution? Moderates think there is, and so it seems have British governments, which have spent large amounts of money on containing republican guerrilla groups and on social security payments and subsidies, and a smaller amount of political energy in trying to get the local political parties to talk to each other, excluding until recently Sinn Féin – which has a significant number of Catholic voters – officially on the grounds that it supported violence. The British declaration that they have 'no selfish strategic or economic interest' in remaining in Northern Ireland against the wishes of a majority of its people may well be true for the majority in Britain; and no colonial situation has ever ended without the metropolitan government negotiating with those it previously branded untouchable. Nor has any settler society survived unscathed where the 'natives' have constituted a majority. Ultras in particular are well aware that, although a majority in the North, Protestants are a minority in the whole of Ireland, and however ambivalent the Irish government might now be about the six counties, given its constitution it could hardly refuse to incorporate them into the Republic if asked to do so by a British government or by an eventual nationalist majority in Northern Ireland. Whether either eventuality is realised is an open question but ultras are well aware that they exist as possibilities. This is a large part of the explanation for their intransigence and for the hatred of Catholics that some of them explicitly or implicitly evince, whether disguised as a hatred of their doctrine or rationalised in terms of Catholic violence and their ancient status as the enemy. A vote for Sinn Féin is certainly a vote to end the British status of Northern Ireland and a vote for the SDLP can justifiably be seen in the same way. Whatever integrationists might like to claim about Catholic support for the Union, and there is no doubt that there are Catholics who vote for unionist parties, the majority of Catholics vote for parties which aspire ultimately to merge the six counties into the Irish state. Ultra fears therefore have a real basis which prevents them from joining in the moderate campaign to work out a civil relationship with Catholics that will enable them to retain the advantages of the Union with devolved power-sharing administration in Northern Ireland. Ultras want none of this. Distrust and dislike of Britain turned the DUP away from its integrationist phase, and although a minority aspire to independence as a means of permanently keeping the Irish state at bay, the majority of ultras seek the return of Stormont, ideally with increased powers but in any case with majority rule. They point to ecumenism and O'Neillism as having opened a chink in Protestant armour through which the Catholic hordes poured, with the ready acquiescence of the British government and foolish moderates within Northern Ireland.

Two strands of ideology have been explored here, those of moderates and ultras. Dissidents are few and the lack of headway they have made to attract membership indicate that there is no secret ground-swell of Protestant support for a united Ireland. Moderates believe that a reformed Northern Ireland can win Catholic support. This position is tenable only if Northern Ireland can indeed be reformed in a way which will win Catholic support. This has not yet happened and seems unlikely while the majority of Protestants retain an ultra stance. Ultras believe that Protestants can survive culturally and politically only in a Protestant statelet with majority rule and minimal British interference except for military protection on demand, as was the case from 1921 to 1969. The Stormont system succeeded in minimising conflict and maximising Protestant gains, as any successful settler state must do. Whether modern ultras admit it or not, what they want is a settler-type state with permanent Protestant power to ensure their survival. They are aware that the foe is still 'numberless' and still the foe. It is unlikely that the Protestants of the North would 'disappear' in a united Ireland as they are so numerous that continued endogamy would be feasible as it has not been in the South. In this sense ultra fears are not consonant with reality. In other ways, however, and taking into consideration the colonial settlement origins of Protestants in Ireland, ultra ideology displays more of a 'fit' with existing reality than moderate.

On the other hand, any complete account of settler colonisation needs an examination of the 'natives' on similar lines to what I have here attempted for settlers. Although Catholics are not the perceived audience of most unionist newspapers, their attitudes and actions inspire much of the material surveyed here. After all, without 'natives' there are no settlers in the sense explored here. A similar survey of nationalist local papers, for example, would be of great interest.

Furthermore, the most powerful actor in the triangular relationship is the British state. The degree of direct involvement of the British state in the process of colonising Ireland contrasts with the commercial and 'adventurer' type of nineteeth-century British colonisation which has given rise to so much of the literature on settler societies. The Plantation of Ulster, for example, and the role of Dublin Castle in the nineteenth century suggest that colonisation in Ireland involved an attempt at British state-building – an attempt which failed. It is salient too that Ireland was its first, and nearest, colony; and the implications of the fact that Britain was the first capitalist, and later industrial, nation require examination. It has been argued that the prime motive for the colonisation of Ireland was strategic, with the economic motive less important. Today, however, Ireland seems to have lost any strategic significance, the 1939–45 war being the last occasion on which Britain had to watch its 'back door' (despite ultra claims that the Soviet Union was planning to use Northern Ireland to launch an attack on Britain). At the same time it has lost its economic significance and Northern Ireland has become a net burden on the British exchequer. So the question is, why does Britain not withdraw from Northern Ireland?

The habitual secrecy surrounding the decisions, policies, and in many cases, activities of the British state makes it difficult to fathom its motivation and aims. The role and status of the British secret services in Northern Ireland is a particularly murky area. Does the British state remain because of the 'settler' problem? Do the British see Northern Ireland as a useful training ground for the military, as republicans claim? Do the British not 'understand' Ireland, as is often claimed? Perhaps not; but they certainly 'understand' their own interests, and like all metropolitan powers, they put these interests first. More likely then is the fear that concession in Ireland raises the wider prospect of the further unravelling of the UK state. Certainly the Conservative Party is committed to the Union (which of course includes Scotland and Wales as well as Northern Ireland) but more of a mystery is the role of the Labour Party, which has formed the government at significant periods in this century, that is, after the 1939–45 war and at the start of the current crisis. The Secretary of State most popular with ultras was, after all, Roy Mason. These questions certainly need examining.

'Settler' ideology has shown considerable decline among moderates, yet their desire for reform within the region is unrealistic. On the other hand, although in all other settler societies moderates have been marginalised, in Northern Ireland they have the advantage of the support of the British state, which moreover appears to favour the solution preferred by moderates, that is, power-sharing with Catholics. This means, however, that moderates are reliant on British state power.

It seems unlikely that the British will 'solve' the problem. Given ultras' ancient and, to a large extent, well-founded fears of Catholic aspirations, Northern Ireland will not be reformed. For this to happen ultras would have to stop behaving like settlers, forget their legitimate concerns and sit down with their enemies. So far they have refused to do this. If, however, the British state conceives its interests in terms of withdrawal from Northern Ireland, it will withdraw; and that is precisely what ultras fear will happen. Yet this fear has not persuaded them to abandon their objections to the power-sharing that British governments have insisted on. The ideological fixity noted by Hartz and others in settler societies is thus observable among the majority of Northern Ireland Protestants, and 'settler' ideology shows considerable persistence in Ulster.

Finally, changes in Northern Ireland should not be played down, and nor should continuities in Great Britain – but whereas Ulster's political status, economy and demography have changed, important elements of settler ideology remain. Despite the narrow stretch of sea between Northern Ireland and the rest of the United Kingdom, the former is 'a place apart', where for some little has changed since the late, sixteenth century, and the most important task is to keep the enemy at bay – whether that 'enemy' is the Catholic population, the Republic of Ireland, or those 'passing friends', the fickle and alien British.

Bibliography

Place of publication is London except where stated otherwise.

Adamson, I (1974). *The Cruthin: The ancient kindred*. Newtownards: Nosmada Books.

Adamson, I (1982). *The Identity of Ulster: The land, the language and the people*. Belfast: the author.

Alatas, S H (1978). *The Myth of the Lazy Native: A study of Malays, Filipinos and Javanese from the sixteenth to the twentieth century and its function in the ideology of colonial capitalism*. Cass.

Anderson, J (1988). 'Ideological variations in Ulster during Ireland's first Home Rule crisis: an analysis of local newspapers', in C Williams and E Kofman, *Community Conflict, Partition and Nationalism*. Routledge, pp 133–66.

Aughey, A (1990). 'Recent interpretations of unionism', *Political Quarterly* 61(2):188–99.

Aughey, A and McIlheney, C (1984). 'Law before violence? The Protestant paramilitaries in Ulster politics', *Eire-Ireland* 19(2):55–74.

Austin, L (1977). 'Visual symbols, political ideology and culture', *Ethos* 5(3):306–25.

Austin, R L (1983). 'The colonial model, subcultural theory and intragroup violence', *Journal of Criminal Justice* 11(2):93–104.

Baker, D G (1983). *Race, Ethnicity and Power: A comparative study*. Routledge and Kegan Paul.

Bardon, J (1992). *A History of Ulster*. Belfast: The Blackstaff Press.

Barth, F (ed) (1969). *Ethnic Groups and Boundaries: The social organisation of culture difference*. Bergen-Oslo: Universitets Forlaget.

Barton, B (1989). *The Blitz: Belfast in the war years*. Belfast: The Blackstaff Press.

Bell, D (1986). *Acts of Union: Youth sub-culture and ethnic identity amongst Protestants in Northern Ireland*. Paper to the Sociological Association of Ireland, Annual Conference, April 1986.

Bell, R (1985). 'Culture: the voice of the UDA', *Belfast Review* 10:2–4.

Berreman, G D (1972). 'Race, caste and other invidious distinctions in social stratification', *Race* 13:385–414.

Betts, R F (1976). *The False Dawn: European imperialism in the nineteenth century.* Minneapolis: University of Minnesota Press.

Boal, F W and Douglas, J N H (eds) (1982). *Integration and Division: Geographical perspectives on the Northern Ireland problem.* Academic Press.

Boyce, D G (1970). 'British conservative opinion, the Ulster question and the partition of Ireland 1919–21', *Irish Historical Studies* 22:89–112.

Boyce, D G (1979). 'Normal policing: public order in Northern Ireland since partition', *Eire-Ireland* 14(4):35–52.

Boyce, D G (1990). *Nineteenth-Century Ireland: The search for stability.* Dublin: Gill and Macmillan.

Brewer, J (1992). 'Sectarianism and racism, and their parallels and differences', *Ethnic and Racial Studies* 15(3):352–64.

Bruce, S (1992). *The Red Hand: Protestant paramilitaries in Northern Ireland.* Oxford: Oxford University Press.

Butler, D (1991). 'Ulster unionism and British broadcasting journalism, 1924–89', in B Rolston (qv) pp 99–121.

Canavan, B (1988). 'Review of MacDonald's *Children of Wrath.*' *History Workshop: A Journal of Socialist and Feminist Historians* 26:207–8.

Canny, N (1973). 'The ideology of English colonialism: from Ireland to America', *William and Mary Quarterly 3rd series*, 30:575–98.

Cathcart, R (1984). *The Most Contrary Region: The BBC in Northern Ireland.* Belfast: The Blackstaff Press.

Christian, H (ed) (1980). *The Sociology of Journalism and the Press.* Sociological Review Monograph 29, University of Keele.

Clayton, P M (1993). *Settler Ideologies in Twentieth-Century Ulster: Persistence or decline?* PhD thesis, Queen's University Belfast.

Cormack, R J, Gallagher, A M and Osborne, R D (1993). *Fair Enough? Religion and population in the 1991 Population Census.* Belfast: Fair Employment Commission.

Crotty, R (1986). *Ireland in Crisis.* Dingle: Brandon.

Curtis, L (1984). *Ireland: The propaganda war.* Pluto Press.

Curtis, L P (1968). *Anglo-Saxons and Celts: A study of anti-Irish prejudice in Victorian England.* Bridgeport, Conn.: University of Bridgeport.

Curtis, L P (1971). *Apes and Angels: The Irishman in Victorian caricature.* Newton Abbot: David and Charles.

Denoon, D (1983). *Settler Capitalism: The dynamics of dependent development in the southern hemisphere.* Oxford: Clarendon Press.

Eldridge, C C (1978). *Victorian Imperialism.* Hodder and Stoughton.

Elliott, P (1976). *Reporting Northern Ireland: A study of news in Britain, Ulster and the Irish Republic.* Leicester University: Centre for Mass Communication Research.

Emmanuel, A (1972). 'White settler colonialism and the myth of investment imperialism', *New Left Review* 73 (May–June):35–57.

Faber, R (1966). *The Vision and the Need: Late Victorian imperialist aims*. Faber and Faber.

Fanon, F (1965). *Studies in a Dying Colonialism*. New York: Monthly Review Press.

Fanon, F (1967a). *Black Skin White Masks*. Granada.

Fanon, F (1967b). *Toward the African Revolution (Political Essays)*. New York: Grove Press.

Fanon, F (1967c). *The Wretched of the Earth*. Preface by J P Sartre. Harmondsworth: Penguin Books.

Farrell, M (1983). *Arming the Protestants: The formation of the Ulster Special Constabulary and the Royal Ulster Constabulary, 1920–1927*. Pluto Press.

Field, H J (1982). *Toward a Programme of Imperial Life: The British Empire at the turn of the century*. Oxford: Clio Press.

Fieldhouse, D K (1966). *The Colonial Empires: A comparative survey from the eighteenth century*. Weidenfeld and Nicolson.

Fieldhouse, D K (1981). *Colonialism 1870–1945: An introduction*. Weidenfeld and Nicolson.

Gailey, A (1987). *Ireland and the Death of Kindness: The experience of constructive unionism 1890–1905*. Cork: Cork University Press.

Gladwin, T N (1980). *Slaves of the White Myth: The psychology of neocolonialism* (with the collaboration of Ahmad Saidin). Atlantic Highlands, NJ: Humanities Press.

Glasgow University Media Group (1982). *Really Bad News*. Writers and Readers Publishing Cooperative Society Ltd.

Goldring, M (1991). *Belfast: From loyalty to rebellion*. Lawrence and Wishart.

Good, K (1976). 'Settler colonialism: economic development and class formation', *Journal of Modern African Studies* 14(4):597–620.

Guérin, D (1973). *Ci-gît le colonialism. Algérie, Inde, Indochine, Madagascar, Maroc, Palestine, Polynésie, Tunisie. Témoignage militant*. Paris, La Haye: Mouton.

Hancock, I (1984). *White Liberals, Moderates and Radicals in Rhodesia 1953–80*. Croom Helm.

Harkness, D (1983). *Northern Ireland since 1920*. Dublin: Helicon Ltd.

Hartz, L M (1964). *The Founding of New Societies: Studies in the history of the United States, Latin America, South Africa, Canada and Australia*. New York: Harcourt, Brace and World, Inc.

Hechter, M (1975). *Internal Colonialism: The Celtic fringe in British national development 1536–1966*. Routledge and Kegan Paul.

Hennessey, T (1993). 'Ulster Unionist territorial and national identities 1886–1893: province, island, kingdom and empire', *Irish Political Studies* 8:21–36.

Hickman, A S (1960). *Men who made Rhodesia*. Salisbury, Southern Rhodesia: The British South Africa Company.

Hole, H M (1928). *Old Rhodesian Days*. Macmillan and Co Ltd.

Hone, P F (1909). *Southern Rhodesia.* George Bell and Sons.

Hughes, A J (1963). *East Africa: The search for unity – Kenya, Tanganyika, Uganda and Zanzibar.* Harmondsworth: Penguin Books.

Huttenback, R A (1975). *The British Imperial Experience.* Westport, Conn.: Greenwood Press.

Huttenback, R A (1976). *Racism and Empire: White settlers and colored immigrants in the British self-governing colonies 1830–1910.* Ithaca and Cornell University Press.

Irish Information Partnership (1989). *Extracts from Agenda: Summary tables.* Information Service on Northern Ireland Conflict and Anglo–Irish Affairs.

Jackson, A (1989). 'Unionist history (i)', *The Irish Review* 7:58–66.

Janowitz, M (1967). *The Community Press in an Urban Setting* (2nd edition). Chicago: Free Press.

Katz, E and Lazarsfeld, P (1955). *Personal Influence.* Chicago: Free Press.

Kennedy, D (1988). *The Widening Gulf: Northern attitudes to the independent Irish state 1919–49.* Belfast: Blackstaff Press.

Kiernan, V G (1982). *European Empires from Conquest to Collapse 1815–1960.* Leicester: Leicester University Press.

Kuper, L (1972). 'Race, class and power: some comments on revolutionary change', *Comparative Studies in Society and History* 14:400–21.

Lanternari, V (1980). 'Ethnocentrism and ideology', *Ethnic and Racial Studies* 3(1):52–66.

Lebow, R N (1979). *White Britain and Black Ireland: The influence of stereotypes on colonial policy.* Philadelphia: Institute for the Study of Human Issues.

Lecky, W E H (1916). *A History of Ireland in the Eighteenth Century.* Longmans, Green and Co.

Lemon, A and Pollock, N (1980). *Studies in Overseas Settlement and Population.* Longman.

Levine, K (1985). 'A tree of identities, a tradition of dissent: John Hewitt at 78', *Fortnight* 213:16–17.

Lijphart, A (1975). 'The Northern Ireland problem: cases, theories and solutions', *British Journal of Political Science* 5:83–106.

Lustick, I (1985). *State-Building Failure in British Ireland and French Algeria.* Berkeley: University of California, Institute of International Studies.

Lüthy, H (1964). 'Colonisation and the making of mankind', in G H Nadel and P Curtis (qv) pp 29–37.

MacDonald, M (1986). *The Children of Wrath: Political violence in Northern Ireland.* Cambridge: Polity Press.

MacDonald, M (1991). 'Blurring the difference: the politics of identity in Northern Ireland', in Y Alexander and A O'Day, *The Irish Terrorism Experience* (Aldershot: Dartmouth) pp 81–96.

Mannoni, O J D (1964). *Prospero and Caliban: The psychology of colonialism*. New York and Washington: Frederick A Praegar.

Mansergh, N (1936). *The Government of Northern Ireland*. George Allen and Unwin Ltd.

Mason, D (1985). 'Nationalism and the process of group mobilisation: the case of "loyalism" in Northern Ireland reconsidered', *Ethnic and Racial Studies* 8(3):408–25.

Mason, P (1970). *Patterns of Dominance*. Oxford University Press.

Memmi, A (1974). *The Coloniser and the Colonised*. Introduction by J-P Sartre. Souvenir Press.

Memmi, A (1990). *The Coloniser and the Colonised*. New Introduction by L O'Dowd. Earthscan Publications.

Miller, D (1978). *Queen's Rebels: Ulster loyalism in historical perspective*. Dublin: Gill and Macmillan.

Miller, D. (1994) *Don't Mention the War: Northern Ireland, Propaganda and the Media*. Pluto Press.

Mirande, A (1978). 'Chicano sociology – a new paradigm for social science', *Pacific Sociological Review* 21(3):293–312.

Moloney, E (1991). 'Closing down the airwaves: the story of the broadcasting ban', in B Rolston (qv) pp 8–50.

Moxon-Browne, E (1991). 'National identity in Northern Ireland', in P Stringer and G Robinson, *Social Attitudes in Northern Ireland* (Belfast: Blackstaff) pp 23–9.

Nadel, G H and Curtis, P (1964). *Imperialism and Colonialism*. Collier-Macmillan.

O'Dowd, L G (1990). New Introduction to A Memmi (qv) pp 29–66.

Olivier, S P (1975). *Many Treks made Rhodesia*. Bulawayo: Books of Rhodesia, Rhodesiana Reprint Library – Silver Series.

Patterson, H (1982). 'Paisley and Protestant politics', *Marxism Today* 26(1):26–31.

Paulin, T (1983). 'At the Cape of Unhope', *Fortnight* 192:21–2.

Peck, A J A (1966). *Rhodesia Accuses*. Salisbury, Rhodesia: Three Sisters Books.

Porter, B (1975). *The Lion's Share: A short history of British imperialism 1850–1970*. Longman.

Ridley, H (1983). *Images of Imperial Rule*. Croom Helm.

Roberts, M H P (1986). *Northern Ireland and the Algerian analogy: A suitable case for Gaullism?* Belfast: Athol Books.

Robinson, K (1965). *The Dilemmas of Trusteeship: Aspects of British colonial policy between the wars*. Oxford University Press.

Robinson, P (1982). 'Plantation and colonisation: the historical background', in F W Boal and J N Douglas (qv) pp 19–47.

Rolston, B (ed) (1991). *The Media and Northern Ireland: Covering the troubles*. Macmillan.

Rolston, B (1993). 'The training ground: Ireland, conquest and decolonisation', *Race and Class* 34(4):13–24

Rose, R (1971). *Governing without Consensus: An Irish perspective.* Faber and Faber Ltd.

Ross, R (ed) (1982). *Racism and Colonialism.* The Hague: Martinus Nijhoff Publishers.

Schlesinger, P (1987). *Putting 'Reality' Together: BBC News.* Methuen.

Scott, J (1990). 'Documents in social research', *Social Studies Review,* September: 6–10.

Shorter Oxford English Dictionary (1959). Oxford: The Clarendon Press.

Stewart, A T Q (1967). *The Ulster Crisis.* Faber and Faber Ltd.

Sunar, D G (1978). 'Stereotypes of the powerless – a social psychological analysis', *Psychological Reports* 43(2):511–28.

Svirsky, L (ed) (1947). *Your Newspaper: Blueprint for a better press.* New York: The Macmillan Company.

Thornton, A P (1965). *Doctrines of Imperialism.* New York: John Wiley and Sons, Inc.

Thornton, A P (1978). *Imperialism in the Twentieth Century.* Macmillan.

Todd, J (1987). 'Two traditions in unionist political culture', *Irish Political Studies* 2:1–26.

Trew, K (1983). 'A sense of national identity: fact or artefact?', *Irish Journal of Psychology* 6(1):28–36.

Walker, B (1990). 'Ireland's historical position – "Colonial" or "European"?', *The Irish Review* 9:36–40.

Wallerstein, I (1974). *The Modern World System I: Capitalist agriculture and the origins of the European world-economy in the sixteenth century.* New York: Academic Press.

Wallerstein, I (1980). *The Modern World System II: Mercantilism and the consolidation of the European world-economy, 1600–1750.* New York: Academic Press.

Weitzer, R J (1985). *The Internal Security State: Political change and repression in Northern Ireland and Zimbabwe,* PhD thesis, University of California, Berkeley.

Weitzer, R J (1990). *Transforming Settler States: Communal conflict and internal security in Northern Ireland and Zimbabwe.* Berkeley: University of California Press.

Whyte, J H (1990). *Interpreting Northern Ireland.* Oxford: Clarendon Press.

Willing's Press Guide (1938–1971). *A Comprehensive Index and Handbook of the Press of the United Kingdom of Great Britain, Northern Ireland and Eire, together with the principal Dominions, Colonial and Foreign Publications.* Willing's Press Service Ltd.

Willing's Press Guide (1972–1986). *A Guide to the Press of the United Kingdom and to the principal publications of Europe, the Americas, Australasia, the Far East and the Middle East.* East Grinstead: Thomas Skinner Directories.

Winks, R W (ed) (1969). *The Age of Imperialism.* Englewood Cliffs, New Jersey: Prentice Hall.

Worsley, P (1967). *The Third World.* Weidenfeld and Nicholson.

Index